Exports of Manufactures from Developing Countries

William R. Cline

Economic growth in the developing countries is closely linked with growth of their exports, especially of manufactured goods. But can industrial countries accommodate growing imports of these products, or will they respond with protectionist measures, choking off the markets and inhibiting growth in the third world?

In this study William R. Cline analyzes the history of manufactured exports during the 1970s and early 1980s and considers their prospects for the rest of this decade. Using a specially developed data base, he traces the growth of those exports and examines changes in import penetration of industrial countries as well as in product composition and trading partners. To explore the probable trends in protection in industrial countries, he develops statistical tests that relate estimates of the presence of major nontariff barrier protection in the late 1970s to the economic and political characteristics of industrial sectors. Once these relationships are identified, he applies them to projections of future imports to predict the likely incidence of new protection through 1990. His central finding is that developing countries should be able to achieve substantial growth in manufactured exports without provoking serious new protection in industrial countries. The author warns, however, that macroeconomic forces such as unemployment and exchange-rate misalignment could cause increased protection even though microeconomic trends within industrial sectors would not be predicted to do so.

William R. Cline, a former senior fellow at the Brookings Institution, is now a senior fellow at the Institute for International Economics. He is the principal author of *World Inflation and the Developing Countries* (Brookings, 1981) and coeditor (with Sidney Weintraub) of *Economic Stabilization in Developing Countries* (Brookings, 1981).

WILLIAM R. CLINE

Exports of Manufactures from Developing Countries
Performance and Prospects for Market Access

THE BROOKINGS INSTITUTION
Washington, D.C.

Library of Congress Cataloging in Publication data:
Cline, William R.
Exports of manufactures from developing countries.
Includes bibliographical references and index.
1. Developing countries—Manufactures. 2. Developing
countries—Commerce. I. Title.
HD9738.D442C55 1984 382'.4567'091724 84-17059
ISBN 0-8157-1464-5
ISBN 0-8157-1463-7 (pbk.)

1 2 3 4 5 6 7 8 9

THE BROOKINGS INSTITUTION is an independent organization devoted to nonpartisan research, education, and publication in economics, government, foreign policy, and the social sciences generally. Its principal purposes are to aid in the development of sound public policies and to promote public understanding of issues of national importance.

The Institution was founded on December 8, 1927, to merge the activities of the Institute for Government Research, founded in 1916, the Institute of Economics, founded in 1922, and the Robert Brookings Graduate School of Economics and Government, founded in 1924.

The Board of Trustees is responsible for the general administration of the Institution, while the immediate direction of the policies, program, and staff is vested in the President, assisted by an advisory committee of the officers and staff. The by-laws of the Institution state: "It is the function of the Trustees to make possible the conduct of scientific research, and publication, under the most favorable conditions, and to safeguard the independence of the research staff in the pursuit of their studies and in the publication of the results of such studies. It is not a part of their function to determine, control, or influence the conduct of particular investigations or the conclusions reached."

The President bears final responsibility for the decision to publish a manuscript as a Brookings book. In reaching his judgment on the competence, accuracy, and objectivity of each study, the President is advised by the director of the appropriate research program and weighs the views of a panel of expert outside readers who report to him in confidence on the quality of the work. Publication of a work signifies that it is deemed a competent treatment worthy of public consideration but does not imply endorsement of conclusions or recommendations.

The Institution maintains its position of neutrality on issues of public policy in order to safeguard the intellectual freedom of the staff. Hence interpretations or conclusions in Brookings publications should be understood to be solely those of the authors and should not be attributed to the Institution, to its trustees, officers, or other staff members, or to the organizations that support its research.

Foreword

THE EXPERIENCE of the past three decades has shown that the economic growth of developing countries is closely tied to the growth of their exports, especially of manufactured products. In recent years, however, industrial countries, which are the largest outlet for these exports, have tended to close off markets to developing countries as these countries become proficient in producing manufactured goods. Even though the Tokyo Round of Trade Negotiations of 1979 liberalized both tariff and nontariff barriers to trade, protection by industrial countries has increased in several important instances, threatening to hinder economic growth in the third world.

The growing external debt of developing countries has further complicated the problem. From 1973 to 1983 the external debt of the third world countries outside OPEC rose from $130 billion to $664 billion, of which more than 60 percent was owed to Western banks and other private creditors. To restore their creditworthiness and meet their debt-servicing obligations, those countries will need to increase their exports of manufactures significantly. If they are unable to do so, the effect on the banking systems of industrial countries could be severe.

In this book William R. Cline examines the performance of manufactured exports from developing countries in the 1970s and the prospects for the continued access of those exports to markets in industrial countries in the 1980s. He presents a quantitative analysis of the forces leading to protection and applies those estimates to projections of manufactured exports to determine whether protectionism is likely to grow in the next few years. His analysis shows that developing countries should be able to expand their exports without causing a major increase in protection in industrial countries. Policymakers in both the developed and the developing countries, however, will need to take measures to improve the environment for open trade.

vii

William R. Cline, a senior fellow at Brookings when he prepared this study, is now a senior fellow at the Institute for International Economics. He is grateful to Lawrence B. Krause and Robert M. Stern for their comments on the full manuscript and to Bela Balassa, Colin Bradford, J. Michael Finger, Norman Hicks, Helen Hughes, Donald Keesing, Jean Waelbroeck, Larry Westphal, and Martin Wolf for their comments on various sections. Dana Lane edited the manuscript, William Hutton provided research assistance, and Antoinette G. Buena, Delores Burton, and Susan E. Nichols did the typing. Ward & Silvan prepared the index.

The U. S. Department of Commerce and Sydney Stein, Jr., provided financial support for the study. The views expressed are those of the author and should not be ascribed to the Department of Commerce or Sydney Stein, Jr., to those who commented on the manuscript, or to the trustees, officers, or other staff members of the Brookings Institution.

BRUCE K. MAC LAURY
President

September 1984
Washington, D.C.

Author's Preface

I COMPLETED the calculations for this study in late 1981. Since then, much has happened to the international economic environment. The worst global recession since the 1930s and extraordinarily high real interest rates have combined with the second oil shock to plunge many of the developing countries into severe recession and debt-servicing crises. The high exposure of Western banks in developing countries means that, even more than before, the success of export expansion in those countries will affect not only their own development but also the stability of the international financial system.

In a few instances, changing circumstances have modified the implications of the empirical analysis of this study. For example, the 1978 data base that was used to examine import penetration indicated that developing countries supplied little steel to industrial countries. But by 1983, after a new regime of quotas had limited U.S. imports of steel from Europe, developing countries had increased their share in U.S. steel imports to nearly one-half, precipitating new efforts by the U.S. steel industry to curtail these imports and creating a conflict between the objectives of the domestic industry and the U.S. foreign and economic policy goals of helping Argentina, Brazil, and Mexico recover from their debt crises. Similarly, Canada has now obtained export restraints on Japanese automobiles, an understandable development in light of similar protection by the United States in 1981 and by other major industrial countries even earlier. The estimated coverage of Canadian protection is understated as a result, and the statistical functions explaining Canadian protection may be distorted by the exclusion of automobiles from the list of protected sectors.

Nonetheless, because the analysis of this study takes a long-range view, focusing on potential trends in trade and protection through 1990,

ix

its findings remain relevant despite the dramatic international economic events of 1982–83 and the various changes in specific sectors. Indeed, in at least one sector (U.S. motorcycles) a projected occurrence of new protection has already taken place.

More broadly, the cyclical downswing in 1981–82 that increased the pressure for protection was already giving way in 1983–84 to a U.S.-led global recovery. Another source of protectionist pressure in the United States, overvaluation of the dollar, is likely to be reversed at some point. Foreign exchange markets should eventually take account of the massive U.S. external deficits, causing a decline in the dollar even if U.S. interest rates (the lure to foreign capital that props up the dollar) do not fall significantly relative to foreign rates. As the dust settles on the sharp cyclical swings of the early 1980s, the longer-term prospects analyzed here should emerge more clearly.

The central implication of my analysis is that developing countries should be able to achieve substantial rates of growth of manufactured exports through 1990 without provoking a wide range of new protection in industrial countries. Although extremely ambitious export growth, such as the 30 percent annual real growth rates that have occurred in South Korea in the past, would be likely to precipitate protection, brisk growth rates of 10 to 15 percent for manufactured exports should not do so. If accurate, this conclusion is important for growth prospects in developing countries and for the viability of their debt. It is compatible with the rates of growth of total exports required for debtor countries to reestablish their creditworthiness over the medium term (approximately 6 to 7 percent in real terms, from the depressed base of 1982).

If manufactured exports can grow at 10 to 15 percent annually in real terms, total export growth should be sufficient to enable developing countries to reestablish substantial growth in per capita income through the rest of the decade. For this favorable outcome to be achieved, however, policymakers in industrial countries must keep the trade regime relatively open and pursue macroeconomic policies consistent with sustained domestic growth, and their counterparts in the developing countries must pursue exchange rate and other policies that provide a sound basis for export expansion.

W.R.C.

Contents

Text Tables

Appendix Tables

Figures

Exports of Manufactures
from Developing Countries

CHAPTER ONE

Trends in the 1970s

IN recent years protectionism has increased in many important instances despite the general liberalization of tariff and nontariff barriers achieved in the Tokyo Round of Trade Negotiations concluded in 1979.[1] Europe and the United States have tightened quota regimes for textile imports. The United States negotiated voluntary export quotas or orderly market agreements on shoes from the Republic of China (hereafter Taiwan) and the Republic of Korea (hereafter South Korea or Korea) and color television sets from Japan, Taiwan, and Korea, although in 1981 it allowed these quotas to expire. The United States imposed a trigger-price antidumping mechanism and ultimately quotas on steel imports, and induced voluntary restraints on automobiles from Japan. Other industrial countries have taken similar protective measures (for example, against imports of footwear in Canada, and steel, chemicals, fertilizer, and television sets in the European Community).

In many cases the new protectionism is focused on imports from developing countries. A major shortcoming of the Tokyo Round was the failure to achieve agreement on a safeguards code (which would limit national protection to safeguarding industries jeopardized by imports), primarily because developing countries (and the United States) felt the legitimization of selective safeguards, as desired by Europeans, would worsen the problem of protection in industrial countries against imports of manufactures from developing countries. This tendency to protect is partly caused by the fact that the traditional, labor-intensive goods exported by developing countries have been characterized in industrial

1. See for example, Bahram Nowzad, *The Rise in Protectionism*, pamphlet series no. 24 (Washington, D.C.: International Monetary Fund, 1978); and William R. Cline, ed., *Trade Policy in the 1980s* (Washington, D.C.: Institute for International Economics, 1983), pp. 66–75.

1

countries by lagging employment growth arising from relatively slow demand growth and continuing increases in labor productivity. As a result, protective efforts such as safeguard actions tend to involve a disproportionately high share of goods from developing countries.[2]

Despite these trends, imports of manufactured goods from developing countries still represent a small aggregate share of the market in industrial countries. In 1978 this share was 15.20 percent of total manufactured imports and only 2.23 percent of domestic consumption of manufactured goods, even under the relatively wide definition of manufactures adopted in this study (appendix E) and based on trade and production data for the seven largest industrial countries (tables 1–3 and 1–9).[3] At somewhat more disaggregated levels, imports from developing countries appear not to have been responsible for declines in employment, with the partial exceptions of the footwear and apparel industries. As Krueger (and others) have shown, when the changes in demand for domestic employment are broken down into their components—changes in market demand for the product, changes in output per worker (productivity growth), and changes in import penetration—slow growth or decline of manufacturing employment in individual product sectors is primarily caused by the first two influences and only modestly by the influence of imports.[4] Nevertheless, the narrow product concentration and rapid growth of manufactured imports from developing countries have prompted considerable protectionist reaction.[5]

This study examines the performance of exports of manufactures from developing countries over the last decade and the prospects for

2. In seventeen cases from 1975 to 1979 in which the U.S. International Trade Commission found injury, imports from developing countries accounted for 46 percent of total imports, compared with a developing-country share of 20.6 percent in U.S. manufactured imports generally. Charles Pearson, "Adjusting to Imports of Manufactures from Developing Countries," in Joint Economic Committee, *Special Study on Economic Change*, vol. 9: *The International Economy: U.S. Role in a World Market*, 96 Cong. 2 sess. (Government Printing Office, 1980), p. 446.

3. For the average ratio of imports to consumption, the figures in table 1–9 are weighted by gross national product in dollar values, from *1980 World Bank Atlas* (Washington, D. C.: World Bank, 1980).

4. Anne O. Krueger, "LDC Manufacturing Production and Implications for OECD Comparative Advantage," paper prepared for the Conference on Prospects and Policy for Industrial Structure Change in the United States and Other OECD Countries (University of Minnesota, 1979).

5. Organization for Economic Cooperation and Development, *The Impact of the Newly Industrializing Countries on Production and Trade in Manufactures*, Report by the Secretary-General (Paris: OECD, 1979).

their continued access to markets in industrial countries in the 1980s. Chapter 2 presents a quantitative analysis of the forces leading to protection, and chapter 3 applies these estimates to projections of manufactured exports from developing countries to determine whether the incidence of protection is likely to increase substantially over the next decade in response to dynamic export growth in the developing countries. This first chapter sets the stage for the analysis by reviewing the past performance of these exports and examining some common hypotheses about the changing nature and extent of this trade.

The data base used for the study is described in appendix A. The developing countries in the analysis comprise Latin America and the Caribbean, all countries in Africa except South Africa, in Asia except Japan, and in Oceania except Australia and New Zealand. While the data analyzed here present a profile of trends in exports of developing countries' manufactures to industrial countries, one should keep in mind that manufactured exports from developing countries to each other (approximately 35 percent of their total manufactured exports)[6] are not included in the analysis.

The data analyzed in the study refer to imports of manufactures from developing countries by the seven major industrial countries: the United States, Canada, West Germany, France, Italy, the United Kingdom, and Japan. In this chapter the size and growth of these imports in the 1970s, their growth relative to income growth in each industrial country market, and the individual shares of principal developing countries in these imports are examined. The growth of the imports is then analyzed more closely in terms of sectoral detail and in real as opposed to nominal terms through the construction of detailed price indexes (appendix A). Trends in import penetration by developing countries are then reviewed by relating these imports to apparent consumption in industrial countries. The product composition of these imports is scrutinized next, with a division into traditional and nontraditional product groups. The evolution

6. United Nations Conference on Trade and Development, *Trade and Development Report, 1981* (Geneva: UNCTAD, 1981), p. 49. The figure for 1979 refers to a narrower concept of manufactures than is used in this study; it excludes processed foods, beverages, tobacco, and nonferrous metals. The corresponding figure for the broader definition of manufactures used here would be considerably smaller, however, considering that for all products the share of exports of nonoil developing countries sold to developing countries (even including those in the oil-producing export countries) amounted to only 3.5 percent in 1979. General Agreement on Tariffs and Trade, *International Trade 1980/ 81* (Geneva: GATT, 1981), table A3.

of this composition is considered by individual industrial country, by individual major developing-country supplier, and by leading product lines. An analysis of trade ties seeks to discover whether traditional patterns of principal developing and industrial country trading partners have shifted. The hypothesis of "stages of comparative advantage" is explored by determining whether low-income countries have replaced middle-income countries as the main suppliers of traditional goods. Finally, the question whether developing countries have tended to replace Japan as a source of supply to other industrialized countries is investigated.

Magnitude, Growth, Market Destination, and Suppliers

From 1969 to 1978 exports of manufactures from developing countries to the seven largest industrial countries grew from $13.9 billion to $65.8 billion (excluding refined petroleum).[7] If these numbers are deflated by the UN index of unit values for manufactured exports from all sources, those from developing countries grew from $13.9 billion to $26.7 billion at 1969 prices (table 1-1), for an annual average growth rate of 7.6 percent in real terms.

These aggregates indicate an important role for manufactures in the exports of developing countries. In 1978 the developing countries' exports of approximately $200 billion to the seven major industrial countries had the following composition: 52 percent in oil, 33 percent in manufactures (as defined in this study), and 15 percent in raw materials other than oil. The definition of manufactures used in this study is broad; it includes products such as processed foods, sugar, and copper that are conventionally omitted in official international studies.[8] Neverthe-

7. In 1980 the seven countries examined here accounted for 82.8 percent of total imports from developing countries into the twenty industrial countries of the OECD (excluding Luxembourg). Calculated from International Monetary Fund, *Direction of Trade Statistics Yearbook, 1981* (IMF, 1981), pp. 8, 15, 19.

8. GATT gives a figure of $41.5 billion for imports of manufactures from developing countries into industrial countries in 1978. GATT, *International Trade, 1978/79*, table G. The GATT definition of manufactures is narrower: SITC categories 5 through 8, excluding category 68 (nonferrous metals). This study uses the ISIC listing of manufacturing industries, categories 3111–3909, excluding petroleum refineries (3530) and those portions of food categories 3116, 3119, and 3121 corresponding primarily to raw coffee, cocoa, and tea. Inclusion of nonferrous metals makes the figure here approximately $4.7 billion higher than the GATT figure. The rest of the divergence is accounted for primarily by inclusion within the ISIC manufacturing categories of several food products with SITC classifications below categories 5 through 8. See appendixes A and E.

Table 1-1. *Imports of Manufactures from Developing Countries into Seven Industrial Countries, 1969 and 1978*[a]
Billions of dollars

| Importing country | 1969 | | 1978 | | 1978/1969 (col. 3 divided by col. 1) |
	Amount (1)	Percent of total (2)	Amount (3)	Percent of total (4)	(5)
United States	4.85	35.0	29.92	45.5	6.17
Canada	0.36	2.6	1.78	2.7	4.94
West Germany	1.87	13.5	8.49	12.9	4.54
France	1.33	9.6	4.82	7.3	3.62
Italy	0.93	7.8	3.40	4.9	3.65
United Kingdom	2.45	17.7	6.92	10.5	2.82
Japan	2.09	15.1	10.65	16.2	5.10
All seven	13.86	100.0	65.80	100.0	4.75
All seven, 1969 prices	13.86	100.0	26.73	100.0	1.93

Sources: UN trade tapes. Deflator: United Nations, *Monthly Bulletin of Statistics*, vol. 34 (March 1980), p. xxii; vol. 26 (March 1972), p. xiv.
a. International standard industrial classification (ISIC) numbers 3111 through 3909, excluding 3530 (petroleum refineries).

less, even the traditional classifications, when adjusted for the more obvious items that may be reclassified as manufactured, indicate that manufactures exceed raw materials in importance for the exports (excluding oil) of developing countries (appendix E). Thus future opportunities for the exports of manufactures will matter vitally to the overall export and growth prospects of developing countries.

Not only are manufactures important in the exports of developing countries, especially those without oil, but also the growth performance of these exports has been impressive. Even under the comprehensive definition applied in this study, which includes copper and processed foods, that growth was a robust 7.6 percent annually in 1969–78. And if the narrow, more conventional definition of the General Agreement on Tariffs and Trade (GATT) is used (standard international trade classification, SITC, sections 5–8, excluding copper, or subsection 68), the performance was even more impressive. Exports of manufactures from developing countries thus defined grew 15.6 percent annually in real terms from 1965 through 1973 and 12.4 percent from 1973 through 1980, although they slowed to an annual growth of only 4.1 percent in 1980–82.[9] Faster growth under the narrower definition is explained by the slow

9. World Bank, *World Development Report, 1983* (World Bank, 1983), p. 10.

Table 1-2. *Growth of Imports of Manufactures from Developing Countries Relative to Growth of Gross National Product in Seven Industrial Countries, Annual Average, 1969–78*

	Real growth rate (percent)		
Importing country	GNP (1)	Manufactured imports from developing countries (2)	Apparent income elasticity (col. 2 divided by col. 1)
United States	3.1	10.8	3.5
Canada	4.3	7.6	1.8
West Germany	3.1	7.0	2.3
France	3.7	4.4	1.2
Italy	4.1	3.8	0.9
United Kingdom	2.4	1.5	0.6
Japan	5.8	8.4	1.4

Source: International Monetary Fund, *International Financial Statistics*, vol. 31 (May 1978), and vol. 34 (February 1981); and table 1-1. Real values for 1978 obtained using UN deflator (see table 1-1).

growth of products it omits: several of the processed foods, beverages and tobacco, and especially copper, as shown by the sectoral growth rates calculated in appendix B.

In short, manufactured exports from developing countries are both important to their total exports and, at least through the 1970s, were rapidly growing. Table 1-1 shows that, among the industrial country markets, imports into the United States grew the fastest. The dollar value of U.S. imports of manufactures (broadly defined) from developing countries rose sixfold from 1969 to 1978 while the corresponding expansion was less than fivefold for all seven industrial countries. By 1978 the United States accounted for 45.5 percent of these imports into the seven industrial countries, compared with only 35.0 percent in 1969. The United States is by far the largest market for these goods; Japan, in second place, accounted for only 16.2 percent in 1978.

Table 1-1 also shows substantial dispersion among industrial countries in the growth of their manufactured imports from developing countries. The fastest import growth occurred in the United States and Japan; the slowest, in the United Kingdom, Italy, and France. Table 1-2 shows that these divergences cannot be explained fully by differing growth rates of gross national product in the respective markets. In the United States and the Federal Republic of Germany (hereafter West Germany or Germany), these imports grew faster relative to GNP growth than in the other countries. In contrast, the sharp difference between real growth of these imports into the United Kingdom (1.5 percent) and Japan (8.4 percent) was due almost wholly to the large difference between the growth rates of the two economies. The apparent elasticity of manufactured imports from developing countries with respect to income (percent change in the former relative to percent change in the latter) was substantially higher in the United States (3.5) and Germany (2.3) than in the other countries (averaging approximately 1.4).[10]

Although there is no inherent reason to expect consumer tastes to differ among these countries, past studies have found a higher income elasticity of manufactured import demand for the United States than for other industrial countries,[11] and the results in table 1-2 are consistent with that finding as applied to developing-country supply. At the same time, the active involvement of U.S. multinational corporations in promoting the growth of developing countries' exports of products such as made-to-order apparel, electronic components, and automobile engines as part of strategies to develop international sources of supply may partly explain the more rapid growth in the U.S. market. It is also possible that a higher apparent income elasticity in the United States and Germany reflected more open markets than in other countries, but the direct evidence on protection presented in chapter 2 fails to confirm this explanation.

The growth of manufactured imports from developing countries was sufficiently rapid to enable those countries to raise their share of total imports of manufactures into the seven industrial countries from 13.9

10. Note that in this interpretation the term *apparent income elasticity* is not a pure income elasticity, but the outcome of shifts in both supply and demand. There is little reason to expect the pure income elasticity of demand for these goods to be twice as high in the United States as in Japan. It is more likely that influences such as those mentioned in the text caused the supply curve of developing-country exports of manufactures to shift outward more rapidly in the U.S. market, or the demand curve to shift outward faster for reasons other than income growth.

Note also that the apparent income elasticities here are comparable to those estimated by Balassa, except that his estimates for Europe are much higher (5.7) than those here, and his result for Japan is lower (0.8). Lower elasticities for the European Community (1.46) are found by Carl Hamilton and Mordechai Kreinin. Bela Balassa, "Structural Change in Trade in Manufactured Goods between Industrial and Developing Countries," World Bank Staff Working Paper 396 (1980), p. 5; Hamilton and Kreinin, "The Structural Pattern of LDCs' Trade in Manufactures with Individual and Groups of DCs," *Weltwirtschaftliches Archiv*, vol. 116 (1980), p. 270.

11. H. S. Houthakker and Stephen P. Magee, "Income and Price Elasticities in World Trade," *Review of Economics and Statistics*, vol. 51 (May 1969), p. 122.

Table 1-3. *Percent of Imports of Manufactures from Developing Countries into Seven Industrial Countries, 1969 and 1978*[a]

Importing country	1969	1978
United States	17.5	24.1
Canada	3.1	5.0
West Germany	10.4	9.9
France	10.0	8.2
Italy	11.0	9.3
United Kingdom	16.5	11.3
Japan	32.7	33.4
All seven	13.9	15.2

Source: Author's calculations.
a. ISIC numbers 3111–3909, excluding 3530 (petroleum refineries).

percent in 1969 to 15.2 percent in 1978 (table 1-3). This increase in the trade market share of developing countries by approximately one-tenth over a decade is considerably more modest than the onslaught of manufactured imports from developing countries feared in recent years. Once again, however, there are differences among markets. The share of developing countries in manufactured imports into the United States rose from 17.5 to 24.1 percent, a one-third increase. There was also a substantial rise in their trade market share in Japan. In Europe, however, the import share actually fell slightly over the period, especially in the United Kingdom (from 16.5 to 11.3 percent).[12]

In the case of the United States, exchange-rate changes were a possible influence in raising the developing countries' share in import supply. The dollar weakened relative to the yen and European currencies in the 1970s, and developing countries often pegged their exchange rates to the dollar. These changes could have helped make developing-country products more competitive with those from industrial countries in the U.S. market, although without extensive analysis it is impossible to measure this influence. Similarly, the relative lowering of dollar-related exchange rates of developing countries could have helped raise their share in Japan's import market. It is unclear, however, why their market share stagnated in Europe while it rose in the United States and Japan.

One possible explanation for the divergence between the trends in Europe and those in the United States and Japan is that four East Asian

12. It is possible that trade diversion caused by the entry of the United Kingdom into the European Community contributed to this decline.

Table 1-4. *Shares of Selected Developing Countries in Imports of Manufactures into Seven Industrial Countries, 1969 and 1978*[a]
Percent

Developing country	1969	1978	Developing country	1969	1978
Hong Kong	1.33	1.55	India	0.75	0.63
Singapore	0.00	0.40	Indonesia	0.13	0.23
South Korea	0.42	1.89	Israel	0.27	0.36
Taiwan	0.59	2.02	Malaysia	0.39	0.52
Argentina	0.62	0.47	Pakistan	0.29	0.12
Brazil	0.71	1.02	Other	7.31	5.00
Colombia	0.09	0.08	All	13.88	15.24
Mexico	0.98	0.95			

Source: Author's calculations.
a. Excluding 3530 (petroleum refineries). See table 1-3 for the list of industrial countries.

countries accounted for most of the rising market shares. Because of geographical and other ties these countries exported more heavily to Japan and the United States than to Europe.

Whatever the reasons, there was a widening of the already significant gap between the share of developing countries in manufactured imports in the United States and Japan, on the one hand, and their share in major European countries, on the other hand. In 1969 their share was nearly twice as high in the United States and Japan as in Europe, and by 1978 the gap had widened to a ratio of nearly three to one (table 1-3).

Among the developing countries, South Korea, Hong Kong, Taiwan, and Singapore showed the most dramatic growth in shares in the market of industrial countries for manufactured imports. Together, they accounted for 2.3 percent of manufactured imports from all sources into the seven industrial countries in 1969, and this share had soared to 5.9 percent by 1978 (table 1-4). Correspondingly, the share of these four countries in all imports of manufactures from developing countries into the major industrial countries rose from 16.9 percent in 1969 to 38.5 percent in 1978. The 1970s were clearly the decade of massive market expansion by the four East Asian export-oriented economies, and by its end these four alone accounted for nearly two-fifths of developing-country exports of manufactures to industrial countries. If these four countries are excluded, the share of developing countries actually declined from 1969 (11.5 percent) to 1978 (9.4 percent).

Argentina, India, and Pakistan are the only individual countries shown in the table that experienced substantial erosion in their shares in the markets of industrial countries for manufactured imports. Brazil, Colombia, Indonesia, Israel, and Malaysia increased their trade markets, but by far smaller proportions than the four East Asian export economies.

Real Growth in Major Sectors

Aggregate data do not reveal the high rates of growth found in a number of important product sectors. For sectoral analysis it is necessary to construct detailed price indexes that permit the calculation of real growth rates. Appendix B presents an analysis of import price indexes, based on detailed unit values for imports from developing countries (five-digit SITC categories).

On the basis of the analysis in appendix B, sectoral growth in real terms showed a sharp divergence between low growth in processed foodstuffs and nonferrous metals and extremely high growth for a relatively large number of other manufactured products. Table 1-5 reports real growth rates for the four-digit international standard industrial classification (ISIC) sectors accounting for imports of $1 billion or more in 1978. The salient sectors with high growth include apparel, footwear, chemicals, plastics, and radio and television. By contrast, nonferrous metals and processed foods held down the overall growth rate because of their low growth and their relatively heavy weight in total value. Besides the high-growth sectors shown in table 1-5, sectors with real growth in excess of 20 percent annually and with imports exceeding $500 million in 1978 included furniture, rubber, other metals, other machinery, motor vehicles, aircraft, clocks and watches, and sporting goods (appendix table B-2).

From 1969–70 to 1978 the high real growth of footwear (23 percent annual average) and radio and television (30 percent, though the estimate is apparently overstated by a downward-biased price index) undoubtedly played a role in the emergence of protection in the late 1970s. Growth was high—even for apparel (15 percent)—despite protection under the Long-Term Arrangement in Cotton Textile Products (1962–73) and the Multi-fiber Arrangement (MFA), beginning in 1974. However, a considerable portion of this growth was achieved only at the cost of upgrading quality as a means of adjusting to quantity limits; and, as demonstrated in chapter 3, apparel exports grew much more slowly after 1977 when the MFA became more restrictive (especially in Europe).

Table 1-5. *Real Growth Rates for Product Sectors Exceeding $1 Billion of Imports from Developing Countries into Seven Industrial Countries, 1978*[a]

ISIC number	Product sector	Imports from developing countries, 1978 (billions of dollars)	Average annual growth rate, 1969–70 to 1978 (percent)
3111	Meat	2.116	−2.2
3113	Preserved fruits and vegetables	1.791	8.5
3114	Canned fish	3.590	10.8
3115	Agricultural oils	2.380	4.1
3118	Sugar	1.561	−4.0
3119	Confectionery (excluding cocoa)	1.182	6.4
3121	Food not elsewhere classified (excluding coffee)	1.723	5.2
3211	Textile spinning	5.089	0.2
3220	Apparel	9.220	15.1
3240	Footwear	1.287	22.7
3311	Sawmills	1.967	6.5
3511	Industrial chemicals	1.645	13.3
3560	Plastics not elsewhere classified	1.532	15.2
3710	Iron and steel	1.503	14.7
3720	Nonferrous metals	4.664	0.5
3832	Radio, television, and communication equipment	5.240	29.9
3901	Jewelry	1.919	9.6
3909	Manufactures not elsewhere classified	1.145	4.6

Source: Table B-2 in appendix B.
a. See table 1-3 for the list of industrial countries.

Market Penetration

Even high growth rates of manufactured imports from developing countries do not necessarily imply difficulties of adjustment within industrial countries if the imports remain small relative to domestic consumption and production. Most studies of developing-country exports conclude that their overall penetration into industrial country markets is quite small in the aggregate, but that in some individual product sectors this penetration is relatively high and may involve difficulties in domestic adjustment.

Table 1-6. *Frequency Distribution of Import-Penetration Ratios,*
United States, 1970–78
Number of four-digit ISIC categories

Penetration ratio (percent)[a]	Imports from developing countries			Imports from all countries		
	1970	*1976*	*1978*	*1970*	*1976*	*1978*
Less than 5	71	66	65	51	42	35
5–10	7	7	7	14	16	17
10–15	1	3	5	5	8	14
15–20	1	3	3	5	4	4
20–30	0	1	0	3	6	5
More than 30	0	0	0	2	4	5
Total	80	80	80	80	80	80

Source: Author's calculations.
a. Imports from designated country group relative to apparent U.S. domestic consumption.

The data base developed for this study makes it possible to examine import penetration at the level of eighty four-digit ISIC categories of manufactured products.[13] Import penetration is measured as the ratio of imports (from developing countries) to apparent consumption (domestic production plus total imports minus total exports). For the years 1970 and 1976, further analysis of import penetration is given in appendix A.

Table 1-6 shows that the frequency of four-digit ISIC categories with high penetration ratios for imports into the United States from developing countries rose substantially from 1970 to 1978. In 1970 only two sectors showed developing-country penetration above 10 percent; by 1978 this had risen to eight sectors. Table 1-7 reports the U.S. ratios for ten high-penetration categories. Of these, the most significant increases in developing-country penetration over the period 1970–78 occurred in wearing apparel, footwear, watches and clocks, and jewelry. The table shows that the increases in these sectors between 1976 and 1978 were relatively sharp. The increases in apparel (9.5 percent to 12.4 percent) and footwear (9.7 percent to 14 percent) were of special significance because they occurred despite major nontariff barriers in these sectors. By contrast,

13. Comparison of data on imports and apparent consumption required reclassification of five-digit SITC data from UN trade data tapes into four-digit ISIC categories. The method of conversion is presented in appendix A. For domestic production data, United Nations data on gross output are used. Where necessary, the disaggregation of three-digit ISIC production data to the four-digit level is based on United Nations, Department of International Economic and Social Affairs, *The 1973 World Programme of Industrial Statistics: Summary of Data from Selected Countries* (UN, 1979).

Table 1-7. *Product Sectors with High Penetration Ratios for U.S.*
Imports from Developing Countries, 1970, 1976, and 1978
Percent

ISIC number	Product sector	Import-penetration ratios					
		Developing countries			All countries		
		1970	*1976*	*1978*	*1970*	*1976*	*1978*
3114	Canned fish	12.7	17.4	16.3	35.3	41.9	38.7
3118	Sugar	17.4	13.7	9.8	19.2	16.9	13.2
3215	Cordage, rope, and twine	9.1	21.7	16.9	19.4	26.1	20.5
3220	Apparel (except footwear)	3.4	9.5	12.4	6.4	11.9	15.3
3231	Tanneries and leather finishing	8.1	18.2	9.1	23.5	30.3	14.4
3233	Leather products (except footwear)	5.4	18.0	11.1	15.0	23.8	14.2
3240	Footwear	0.8	9.7	14.0	10.4	21.3	29.3
3832	Radio, television, and communication equipment	1.5	6.1	6.8	7.5	15.2	16.1
3853	Watches and clocks	0.6	11.8	13.8	16.7	26.9	35.3
3901	Jewelry and related articles	5.0	11.9	18.2	22.6	32.2	49.4

Source: Author's calculations.

import penetration in processed foods remained relatively constant, though high.

Table 1-8 provides evidence on the portion of the U.S. import market in manufactures that is relatively high or relatively low in market penetration. As shown in the table, only 11 percent of U.S. manufactured imports are in products with import penetration from developing countries in excess of 10 percent. However, fully two-thirds are in sectors with total import-penetration ratios (from all sources) above 10 percent. Chapters 2 and 3 and appendix D examine in detail the implications of present and future import penetration for the likelihood of protection.

Table 1-9 reports estimates of the average and median sectoral penetration ratios for developing countries in the manufacturing markets of seven industrial countries.[14] The table shows a clear upward trend from 1970 to 1976 and a significant continued increase in at least the United States and West Germany from 1976 to 1978. Despite these

---

14. The average ratio merely equals total imports divided by total apparent consumption, for all manufacturing sectors combined.

Table 1-8. *Percentage of Total Value of U.S. Manufactured Imports, by Selected Product Groupings, 1978*[a]

Products with import penetration (percent)		Percent of U.S. manufactured imports[b]
From all countries	From developing countries	
Less than 10	Less than 2.5	18.0
Less than 10	2.5–10.0	6.2
More than 10	Less than 2.5	41.8
More than 10	2.5–10.0	19.1
More than 10	More than 10.0	11.3

Source: Author's calculations.
a. Total manufactured imports (including refined oil) for 1978 were $128.1 billion.
b. Categories sum to less than 100 percent because of the exclusion of petroleum refineries (7.5 percent of manufactured imports).

Table 1-9. *Imports of Manufactures from Developing Countries Relative to Domestic Apparent Consumption, Seven Industrial Countries, 1970, 1976, and 1978*[a]
Percent

Importing country	Average[b]			Median		
	1970	1976	1978	1970	1976	1978
United States	1.05	1.94	2.28	0.38	0.85	1.25
Canada	0.95	1.38	1.41	0.25	0.77	0.73
West Germany	2.15	1.90	2.46	0.39	0.65	0.94
France	0.95	1.53	1.71	0.16	0.38	0.49
Italy	2.19	2.32	2.30	0.24	0.49	0.90
United Kingdom	1.52	2.33	1.95	0.56	0.98	1.11
Japan	1.90	2.55	2.50	0.23	0.74	0.72

Source: Author's calculations.
a. Comprises four-digit ISIC product sectors.
b. Weighted by sectoral apparent consumption.

increases, the average and median levels of import penetration from developing countries remained quite low in 1978 (with average penetration of approximately 2 percent and the median approximately 0.9 percent).

The 1978 levels of import penetration from developing countries are reported in table 1-10, for twenty-six high-penetration sectors (out of eighty sectors) for the seven major industrial countries. The table includes sectors in which at least one country had a penetration ratio of at least 7 percent. Certain other sensitive sectors are included as well (steel and radio, television, and communication equipment).

The penetration ratios in sensitive sectors that have experienced protectionist pressure are of special interest. For wearing apparel (3220) market penetration by developing countries is high in all countries, ranging from 7.2 percent (Italy) to 15.2 percent (United Kingdom). For textiles (spinning and weaving, 3211) penetration is relatively high in Italy, the United Kingdom, and West Germany, but low (only 3.6 percent) in the United States, probably because of competitive gains from capital-intensive modernization in U.S. textile mills.

The footwear sector (3240) is also sensitive in terms of protectionist pressures. In the United States penetration by developing countries is relatively high (14 percent), and the level is nearly 10 percent in Canada. In the other countries, however, the ratio is relatively low.[15] In Europe low penetration may reflect the presence of Italy, a competitive footwear supplier with the advantage of duty-free entry into European Community markets.

The systematically low penetration estimates for steel (3710) show that, at least in the late 1970s, this troubled sector did not owe its difficulties to imports from developing countries. The same may be said for the sensitive sector of radio, television, and communication equipment (3832), although the U.S. ratio is moderately high (6.8 percent). Market penetration in leather manufactures (3233) is high in the United States and Canada, moderately high in West Germany and the United Kingdom, but low in Japan and Italy, where this labor-intensive sector appears to remain relatively more competitive (or, in the case of Japan, subject to protection).

Among the prominent sectors associated with protectionist pressures, then, only apparel (3220) shows an unambiguous pattern of high market penetration by developing countries. Penetration is high in some markets but low in others for other sensitive products: textiles, cordage, manufactures of leather, footwear, and radio, television, and communication equipment. And for steel, the source of import competition has not come primarily from the developing countries, but from Japan and to some extent from Europe (although by 1983 large increases in steel imports

15. The figure for Italy is an approximation based on the ratio of imports (from developing countries) to production rather than to consumption. Classification problems apparently bias the estimate of consumption, which is unreasonably small (only a small fraction of production and exports and less than one-tenth the consumption of footwear in the United Kingdom).

Table 1-10. *Penetration Rates for Imports from Developing Countries into Seven Industrial Countries,*
High-Penetration Sectors, 1978
Percent

ISIC number	Product sector	United States	Canada	West Germany	France	Italy	United Kingdom	Japan
3113	Preserved fruits and vegetables	2.7	6.2	12.7	8.9	7.5	11.1	6.6
3114	Canned fish	16.3	9.4	3.3	7.9	9.7	1.3	13.2
3115	Agricultural oils	3.2	6.0	16.7	17.1	14.1	13.2	3.6
3116	Grain mill products	0.2	0.4	2.9	2.8	11.5	2.2	2.3
3118	Sugar	9.8	8.9	0.8	10.9	3.0	15.0	6.7
3119	Confectionery	7.6	3.8	2.3	10.3	2.4	8.6	1.3
3140	Tobacco	3.9	0.3	3.4	2.3	1.3	10.4	0.8
3211	Spinning and weaving	3.6	5.4	7.8		14.7	8.6	7.5
3212	Made-up textiles (except apparel)	0.9	1.9	3.0		1.0	3.3	2.1
3214	Carpets and rugs	2.1	1.3	24.4	4.4[a]	2.0	6.9	1.9
3215	Cordage, rope, and twine	16.9	20.0	2.1		0.3	1.2	0.8
3220	Apparel (except footwear)	12.4	10.9	13.9		7.2	15.2	7.8

Code		(1)	(2)	(3)	(4)	(5)	(6)	(7)
3231	Tanneries and leather finishing	9.1	9.6	7.8	5.2[b]	29.6	18.6	5.5
3232	Fur dressing	n.a.	3.7	9.7		2.5	2.8	3.4
3233	Leather products (except footwear)	11.1	10.3	8.8		1.2	6.9	1.9
3240	Footwear	14.0	9.8	2.4		0.5[c]	4.9	5.8
3311	Sawmills	2.4	1.7	2.0[d]	3.1[d]	5.1	10.5	1.7
3319	Wood and cork products not elsewhere classified	4.6	1.8			6.2	0.9	0.6
3540	Miscellaneous petroleum and coal products	6.1	1.4	2.1	1.0	7.6	2.2	13.2
3710	Iron and steel	1.2	0.5	0.4	0.6	0.4	0.4	0.3
3720	Nonferrous metals	4.0	1.4	6.1	5.6	14.4	5.8	5.6
3832	Radio, television, and communication equipment	6.8	3.2	2.6	1.7	2.5	2.8	1.0
3853	Watches and clocks	13.8	15.1	13.2	n.a.	3.9	11.2	3.1
3901	Jewelry	18.2	12.2	n.a.	n.a.	n.a.	n.a.	31.9
3903	Sporting goods	11.8	19.5	10.9	n.a.	8.8	7.0	2.5
3909	Manufactures not elsewhere classified	4.9	3.7	n.a.	n.a.	9.2	5.8	2.0

Source: Author's calculations.

n.a. Not available.

a. 3211–20.

b. 3231–40.

c. Imports/production.

d. 3311–20.

from developing countries had occurred, especially in the U.S. market, where imports from Europe faced quotas).

Product Composition

An important question is whether the product structure of manufactured imports from developing countries has changed substantially as the magnitude of these imports has grown. Changing structure could imply greater dynamism of the process of export growth and less eventual difficulty with protection to the extent that developing countries diversify their exports rather than continue to concentrate on some traditional products that have encountered protection in industrial country markets, such as apparel and footwear.

Table 1-11 presents the product composition in 1969–70 and 1976–78 of manufactured imports from developing countries in the seven major industrial countries. The data are divided into traditional and nontraditional products. Broadly, the traditional goods tend to be in the first half of the ISIC listing of industries, and the nontraditional products in the second half. The traditional products are divided into three groups: processed foods, tobacco, and beverages; textiles, apparel, and footwear; and nonferrous metals, which contain the important traditional export, copper. There is also a residual category (wood, pottery, and jewelry). All these products have been areas of traditional export concentration for developing countries.

The remaining products are considered nontraditional. They are divided, according to categories suggested by Sanjaya Lall, into "process" products with relatively standard technology and "engineering" products in which technology tends to be tailor-made in response to individual markets.[16] A residual category, for nontraditional products that are difficult to classify as process or engineering, is also included.

It is worth noting that the categories used in table 1-11 produce factor ratios consistent with what would be expected for the respective groupings. The nontraditional products have higher capital–labor ratios (in-

16. Sanjaya Lall, "The International Allocation of Research Activity by U.S. Multinationals," *Oxford Bulletin of Economics and Statistics*, vol. 41 (November 1979), p. 325. Lall hypothesizes that multinational corporations' research and development tend to be conducted in parent countries for process industries, and in host countries for engineering industries.

Table 1-11. *Composition of Imports of Manufactures*
from Developing Countries into Seven Industrial Countries,
Traditional and Nontraditional Goods, 1969–70 and 1976–78
Percent

Period and importing country	Traditional goods[a]					Nontraditional goods[b]			
	I	II	III	IV	All	I	II	III	All
1969–70									
United States	34.5	24.3	5.4	9.7	73.9	12.7	9.5	3.9	26.1
Canada	32.6	41.6	5.2	4.2	83.6	10.6	3.4	2.2	16.3
West Germany	36.1	27.4	2.8	24.5	90.8	5.0	2.8	1.6	9.4
France	43.9	19.8	2.7	22.9	89.6	5.0	1.4	4.0	10.4
Italy	29.5	28.6	1.4	32.7	92.2	3.7	1.9	2.3	7.9
United Kingdom	38.7	24.1	4.4	21.1	88.3	6.6	3.8	1.4	11.7
Japan	30.6	28.5	2.8	25.4	87.3	5.3	2.6	4.9	12.7
All seven	35.2	25.8	3.9	18.8	83.6	8.1	5.2	3.2	16.4
1976–78									
United States	19.6	28.6	4.4	5.8	58.5	13.7	21.8	6.1	41.6
Canada	17.8	43.2	5.2	1.4	67.5	11.5	15.6	5.4	32.5
West Germany	24.0	42.5	3.7	8.1	78.2	7.2	11.2	3.5	21.8
France	39.6	25.7	4.8	10.2	80.3	9.2	6.5	4.1	19.8
Italy	26.3	35.5	4.2	13.2	79.3	8.4	7.9	4.4	20.6
United Kingdom	31.3	30.1	5.3	7.8	74.5	8.6	14.3	2.5	25.4
Japan	35.9	31.4	3.9	10.0	81.2	7.6	7.7	3.6	18.9
All seven	25.8	31.7	4.4	7.7	69.5	10.6	15.2	4.6	30.4

Source: Author's calculations. Figures are rounded.
a. I = food, beverages, tobacco; II = textiles, apparel, footwear; III = wood products, pottery, jewelry; IV = nonferrous metals.
b. I = process industries: paper, printing, drugs, soaps, chemicals, plastics, rubber, sporting goods, miscellaneous; II = engineering industries: machinery, transportation equipment, other equipment, instruments, radio, television, electrical products; III = primary and fabricated metals (excluding primary nonferrous), nonmetallic minerals.

cluding human capital) and higher skill intensity than the traditional goods, and among the traditional sectors the most labor-intensive (lowest capital–labor ratios and skill intensities) are in the nonfood manufactures.[17]

At the aggregate level, the composition of manufactured imports from developing countries shows a relatively large rise in the share of

17. Based on U.S. data, the ratio of physical capital to labor is $13,707 (1972) per worker for traditional goods versus $17,750 for nontraditional goods, and the ratios of human capital to labor are $8,140 per worker and $10,889 per worker, respectively. Calculated from Bureau of Labor Statistics capital stock data bank (real 1972 physical capital, standard industrial classification [SIC] categories); U.S. Census of Manufactures, 1972, for SIC labor data; U.S. Department of Commerce correspondence between SIC and ISIC; and UN, *The 1973 World Programme of Industrial Statistics*. Human capital is obtained by capitalizing, at a 10 percent interest rate, the difference between the annual wage bill and the hypothetical wage bill if all workers were paid only the average wage for unskilled workers in the sector (operatives).

nontraditional products, from only 16 percent in 1969–70 to 30 percent in 1976–78. By far the largest cause of this shift is the sharp drop in the share of traditional exports of nonferrous metals. This decline reflects the sharp erosion of the price of copper, which was cheaper in nominal terms in 1976–78 than in 1969–70, and far cheaper in real terms.[18]

Among other traditional goods, the share of food products has declined sharply. The share of textiles, apparel, and footwear rose substantially, 26 to 32 percent of the total for all manufactures. This trend reflects rapid growth in these exports in the early 1970s, before the tightening of the Multi-fiber Arrangement and the introduction of footwear protection in 1977 and after (see chapter 2).

Among nontraditional products, there has also been significant compositional change. The greatest change has been a rise in the share of engineering goods, from only 5.2 percent of imports in 1969–70 to 15.2 percent in 1976–78. In this category the dominant products are radio, television, and communication equipment, and to a lesser extent transportation equipment.

In short, there does seem to have been substantial compositional change away from foodstuffs and nonferrous metals and toward textiles, apparel, footwear, and engineering goods such as communication equipment and radio and television.

The trends in product composition differ across the seven industrial markets. In the United Kingdom the share of nontraditional products rose sharply, with the largest surge being in engineering goods. In the other markets the rise of nontraditional goods was relatively modest. Once again, the U.S. market stands out as the most dynamic, this time in terms of the shift from traditional to nontraditional products. As with the increased growth of manufactured imports from developing countries into the United States, the U.S. multinational corporations probably played an important role in the compositional shift—for example, through the use of foreign assembly export platforms in electronic products.

The divergence in compositional trends was considerably sharper among the supplying developing countries than among the industrial country markets. Among the individual developing countries shown in table 1-12 are three distinct groups. The largest contains seven countries

18. In the London market the average price of copper in 1976–78 was 63 U.S. cents; in 1969–70 it was 65 cents. IMF, *International Financial Statistics*, vol. 34 (February 1981), p. 50, and vol. 29 (May 1976), p. 39.

Table 1-12. *Composition of Exports of Manufactures from Thirteen Developing Countries to Seven Industrial Countries, Traditional and Nontraditional Goods, 1969–70 and 1976–78*[a]
Percent

Developing country	1969–70				1976–78			
	Traditional goods			Nontra-ditional goods	Traditional goods			Nontra-ditional goods
	I[b]	*II*[c]	*All*		*I*[b]	*II*[c]	*All*	
Hong Kong	2.0	51.4	54.6	45.4	2.4	55.4	59.2	40.8
Singapore	29.6	18.2	65.6	34.4	5.1	14.5	28.3	71.5
South Korea	10.8	43.3	71.4	28.6	11.1	44.8	62.2	37.8
Taiwan	23.9	27.5	65.4	34.6	13.1	29.3	51.2	48.8
Argentina	83.6	8.7	92.6	7.4	63.0	23.1	86.3	13.8
Brazil	57.7	23.9	89.4	10.6	49.7	18.0	72.5	27.5
Colombia	33.3	44.4	93.3	6.7	4.0	79.1	86.2	13.7
Mexico	33.7	23.5	68.3	31.6	20.6	14.2	45.9	54.1
India	29.3	53.3	84.2	15.8	25.8	53.5	86.6	13.4
Indonesia	70.8	1.4	91.2	8.8	50.2	3.7	92.2	7.8
Israel	13.3	64.1	80.7	19.3	11.1	60.7	73.4	26.6
Malaysia	16.1	1.9	98.2	1.8	22.6	6.8	71.6	28.4
Pakistan	14.0	8.2	96.1	4.0	18.1	72.4	90.7	9.4

Source: Author's calculations. Figures are rounded.
a. See table 1-11 for the list of the industrial countries.
b. Food, beverages, and tobacco.
c. Textiles, apparel, and footwear.

that experienced major increases in the share of nontraditional goods in their exports to the industrial countries (ranging from 12 to 27 percentage points): Brazil, Mexico, Korea, Taiwan, Singapore, Israel, and Malaysia. In a second group the rise of nontraditional goods was modest (Argentina, Colombia, and Pakistan), and in a third group the share of nontraditional goods actually fell (Hong Kong, India, and Indonesia).

Although it is beyond the scope of this study to analyze the reasons for the divergence, some explanations may be hypothesized. In Brazil exchange-rate and export-subsidy policies favored development of new manufactured exports over traditional foodstuffs; in Mexico assembly plants reexporting processed components to the United States were important. The decline of traditional goods in Malaysia reflected a sharp decline in the share of nonferrous metals. In India and Hong Kong a rise in the share of textiles, apparel, and footwear accounted for much of the rise in traditional exports (and decline in the nontraditional share). More generally, however, the individual country trends resemble the aggregate pattern: for ten out of the thirteen industrial countries the share of nontraditional exports rose, and for many it rose sharply.

So that the leading trends in product composition may be identified more clearly, it is possible to single out the product sectors that were responsible for the largest changes in trade values attributable to changes in market shares of developing-country supply in industrial country imports. Applying the change in this market share between 1969–70 and 1976–78 to the actual total imports of industrial countries from all sources in 1978 (for each product category) yields an estimate of the value of imports from developing countries that may be attributed to the increase (or decrease) in their share of industrial country markets.[19]

Nine product sectors showed increases in developing-country exports of $400 million or more attributable to increased shares in industrial countries' import markets over the period, and five product sectors showed decreases of $400 million or more (table 1-13). The largest and most striking increase was in apparel, where the developing countries' share rose from one-third to one-half of the import market in industrial countries. An increase in comparable trade value, and one pointing toward greater dynamism in the shift toward nontraditional goods, came from radio, television, and communication equipment. Of the other products showing a large rise in value attributable to a rising market share, footwear and watches and clocks had the sharpest increases in market shares, which rose to nearly one-third of industrial country imports by 1978. The export gains attributable to more modest increases in market shares in iron and steel, plastics, motor vehicles, and fabricated metal products are notable because developing countries have not had comparative advantage in these products traditionally and their rising market shares suggest dynamic changes in comparative advantage. In the case of motor vehicles, automobile parts exported from Brazil and Mexico dominate the figures.

The large loss of exports of nonferrous metals indicates that, in addition to the stagnating price of copper, a significant loss of market share contributed to the diminished importance of nonferrous metals in developing countries' exports. The loss of market share in textile

19. Specifically, with s_0, s_1 as the shares of developing countries in total imports of the product into seven industrial countries in 1969–70 and 1976–78, respectively, and M as the value of these imports in 1978, the increment in imports from developing countries attributable to increased market share is $M = (s_1 - s_0)M_{78}$.

Table 1-13. *Product Sectors with Major Changes in Developing Countries' Exports of Manufactures Attributable to Changes in Trade Shares, 1969–70 and 1978*[a]

ISIC number	Product sector	Share of developing countries in imports of seven industrial countries (percent)[b]		Developing countries' exports attributable to change in market share, 1978 (millions of dollars)
		1969–70	*1978*	
3111	Meat	17.9	12.4	−928
3114	Canned fish	32.8	42.9	843
3118	Sugar	76.1	60.5	−400
3132	Wine	21.8	2.4	−430
3211	Textile spinning	35.7	30.5	−866
3220	Apparel	33.5	52.1	3,284
3240	Footwear	8.1	29.7	935
3560	Plastics not elsewhere classified	8.6	15.3	672
3710	Iron and steel	2.9	5.9	762
3720	Nonferrous metals	34.3	26.3	−1,422
3819	Fabricated metal products not elsewhere classified	5.1	11.2	436
3832	Radio, television, and communication equipment	8.9	23.1	3,221
3843	Motor vehicles	0.2	1.2	535
3853	Watches and clocks	2.4	31.1	654

Source: Author's calculations.
a. Sectors with attributed changes exceeding $400 million. Excludes petroleum refineries.
b. See table 1-11 for the list of industrial countries.

spinning and weaving is especially significant. It reflects the facts that industrial countries actually have a trade balance surplus in textiles and that the joint treatment of textiles with apparel for purposes of protection under the MFA results more from allied political interests of textile and clothing producers in industrial countries than from the consequences of underlying trade pressures, which differ markedly between the two sectors.

Trading Partners

Just as the product composition of developing countries' exports has shifted away from traditional goods (with the important exceptions of

Table 1-14. *Percentage of Manufactured Exports to Two Largest Trading Partners, from Thirteen Developing Countries, 1969 and 1978*[a]

Developing country	1969			1978		
	First	Second	Total	First	Second	Total
All thirteen	35.0 (U.S.)	17.7 (U.K.)	52.7	45.5 (U.S.)	16.2 (Japan)	61.7
Hong Kong	56.0 (U.S.)	22.1 (U.K.)	78.1	53.8 (U.S.)	16.3 (FRG)	70.2
Singapore	40.8 (U.K.)	31.3 (U.S.)	72.1	51.2 (U.S.)	12.9 (FRG)	64.1
South Korea	67.3 (U.S.)	24.5 (Japan)	91.8	49.5 (U.S.)	29.4 (Japan)	78.9
Taiwan	63.0 (U.S.)	17.2 (Japan)	80.2	64.3 (U.S.)	17.8 (Japan)	82.1
Argentina	26.6 (U.K.)	23.3 (U.S.)	49.9	28.2 (U.S.)	23.5 (FRG)	51.7
Brazil	46.8 (U.S.)	16.3 (FRG)	63.1	50.6 (U.S.)	13.6 (FRG)	64.2
Colombia	56.5 (U.S.)	25.3 (FRG)	81.8	52.2 (U.S.)	31.4 (FRG)	83.6
Mexico	61.6 (U.S.)	17.0 (Japan)	78.6	81.6 (U.S.)	7.4 (Japan)	89.0
India	38.5 (U.S.)	29.1 (U.K.)	67.6	35.5 (U.S.)	19.7 (U.K.)	55.2
Indonesia	37.4 (U.S.)	33.5 (FRG)	70.9	30.4 (Japan)	29.1 (U.S.)	59.5
Israel	45.8 (U.S.)	20.0 (U.K.)	65.8	45.4 (U.S.)	15.9 (FRG)	61.3
Malaysia	42.5 (U.S.)	23.8 (Japan)	66.3	48.2 (U.S.)	13.1 (Japan)	61.3
Pakistan	31.7 (U.K.)	24.4 (U.S.)	56.1	28.0 (Japan)	20.2 (FRG)	48.2

Source: Author's calculations.
a. Exports to seven major industrial country markets only (table 1-11). Excludes petroleum refineries.

apparel and footwear), it might be expected that the destination of these exports would have shifted away from their traditional trading partners. The weakening of former colonial ties, the continued emergence of global marketing by multinational corporations, and the development of new export product lines all suggest that trading partner patterns would diversify over time. The rise in the cost of oil might be a factor working in the opposite direction, as higher transport prices induce greater concentration of exports in geographically close markets.

The actual trends in trading partners show only one pattern tending to confirm this expectation: a weakening of the commercial links between the United Kingdom and Commonwealth countries. In contrast, an even more dominant pattern emerges: a rise in the dominance of the United States as trading partner, not only for countries shifting away from the United Kingdom but also for traditional U.S. trading partners in Latin America.

Table 1-14 shows the replacement of the United Kingdom by Japan as the second largest market for developing-country exports, following the United States. From 1969 to 1978 the United Kingdom lost its position as the first- or second-ranked importer of manufactures from Argentina, Hong Kong, Singapore, Israel, and Pakistan. Its rank as second in trade with India remained, but its share of India's manufactured exports fell substantially. Slow economic growth in the United Kingdom may have accounted for some of the loss, but the elasticity of imports into the United Kingdom was also low (table 1-2). It is tempting to conclude that the pronounced diversification of Commonwealth developing countries away from the U.K. market was related not only to slow growth in that market but also to erosion of the relatively privileged access of Commonwealth countries to the U.K. market as a consequence of the entry of the United Kingdom into the European Community.

The other salient pattern in table 1-14 is the increase in U.S. dominance of the industrial country market for manufactured imports from developing countries, which rose from a share of slightly over one-third to slightly under one-half. Perhaps most striking, the U.S. share rose for major Latin American suppliers (except Colombia), contradicting the expectation of natural diversification in trading partners. This increase was exceptionally high for Mexico, which sent 82 percent of its manufactured exports (among major industrial country markets) to the United States in 1978, the highest degree of dependence on a single market among all the countries examined. Except in Latin America no pronounced pattern of rising reliance on the U.S. market emerged, however, and the U.S. market share fell substantially for Korea (representing an expected diversification away from heavy reliance on the U.S. market in the earlier stages of the exporting of Korean manufactures).

Japan and West Germany were the countries that tended to displace the United Kingdom (and in some cases, the United States) as the first- or second-ranked market for individual countries' manufactured exports, as a consequence of the high growth rates of their imports of these products (table 1-2).

The hypothesis of diversification among trading partners is not confirmed by the data in table 1-14 in another sense: for all developing countries, the concentration of these countries' exports of manufactures in the top two markets rose from 1969 (52.7 percent) to 1978 (61.7 percent), indicating increased trading-partner concentration instead of diversification. However, for eight of the thirteen individual countries listed, concentration in the top two markets declined, indicating that any aggregate trend toward concentration is somewhat misleading and not representative of several of the leading developing-country exporters. For this reason, it is more meaningful to conclude that the trend in concentration of market is ambiguous but certainly not a strong generalized trend toward decreased concentration, as might have been expected from the supposition of market diversification.

Substitution among Developing-Country Suppliers

One fashionable and intriguing hypothesis about manufactured exports from developing countries is that a process of stages of comparative advantage is taking place, whereby some of the developing countries will gradually replace the middle-income "newly industrialized" countries (NICs) as suppliers of traditional labor-intensive manufactures, while the NICs move upward on the ladder of product sophistication toward exports with greater technological and skilled-labor content. Following the hypothesis, the East Asian group of four export economies (Korea, Hong Kong, Taiwan, and Singapore), and perhaps some Latin American countries, would be expected to graduate from such traditional exports as foodstuffs, textiles, apparel, and footwear and move into such nontraditional exports as automobile parts and electronic equipment. At the same time, a second tier of lower-income countries would replace the first tier of NICs as major suppliers of the traditional manufactured exports.

The data in table 1-15 do not generally support the hypothesis of successive stages of comparative advantage among developing countries, though there is some support for the hypothesis that the NICs have increased their market share at the expense of industrial country exporters in nontraditional goods. The table shows the shares of four groupings of developing countries in their manufactured exports of major products to industrial countries. The first two groupings represent the first tier of NICs (Latin America and East Asia). The third group contains primarily major lower-income countries, and the fourth group, all other developing countries, contains primarily low-income countries (including all those in Africa).

Only two of nine traditional product sectors, processed meat and apparel, show evidence of a shift in export market shares away from the Latin American and East Asian countries to other developing countries. In the apparel sector, the share of the four East Asian countries in industrial country imports from developing countries fell from 82.2 percent in 1969 to 72.8 percent in 1978, while the combined shares of primarily lower-income countries ("other major" and "all others" in the table) rose from 15.6 percent to 23.1 percent.

In the sector of spinning and weaving, the East Asian group of four increased its share over the period from 9.9 to 25 percent, while the share of the lower-income countries fell from 66.7 to 60.8 percent, just the opposite of the prediction of shifting stages in comparative advantage (if textiles are indeed considered a traditional good, perhaps an open issue in view of the more capital-intensive techniques being used in industrial countries and their strong competitive position in this sector). The shift was largely caused by the fall of the share of India and Pakistan, from 25.0 percent in 1969 to 10.5 percent in 1978. Nor do other sectors confirm the hypothesis. Latin American countries retain a high share of traditional food products, although these goods might be expected to shift to lower-income suppliers. In the case of footwear, the major Latin American countries and the East Asian group increased their already high share, while the share of the lower-income groups fell significantly.

The hypothesis of stages of comparative advantage predicts that middle-income countries will lose market shares to low-income developing countries in traditional manufactured exports. In nontraditional exports, however, the hypothesis has little to say about the market shares of these two groupings of developing countries relative to each other. Rather, the hypothesis predicts that the market share of the middle-income countries will rise relative to that of industrial country exporters. In the section of table 1-15 concerning nontraditional products, the figures in parentheses show each group's share in the imports of the major industrial countries from all sources. A rise in these shares means that a greater proportion of imports into the industrial countries is coming from developing countries and a smaller share from industrial countries (and Eastern European countries) than before.

The figures in parentheses tend to confirm the hypothesis of stages of comparative advantage. For four of the five nontraditional products, significant increases occurred in the shares of the two groupings of NICs in total import supply of the major industrial countries, indicating that these middle-income countries have partially replaced industrial countries as suppliers to this import market.

This conclusion does not mean necessarily that increased imports from NICs have caused an absolute decline in imports from the industrial countries. Instead, a rise in the import share of the NICs may reflect primarily a high NIC participation in a rising import-penetration ratio

Table 1-15. Shares of Selected Groups of Countries in Developing Countries' Supply of Major Categories of Exports of Manufactures to Seven Industrial Countries, 1969 and 1978

Percent

ISIC number	Product sector	1969				1978			
		Latin America[a]	East Asia[b]	Other major developing countries[c]	All other developing countries	Latin America[a]	East Asia[b]	Other major developing countries[c]	All other developing countries
Food									
3111	Meat	50.3	1.7	4.3	43.7	39.0	5.5	4.6	50.9
3113	Fruits and vegetables	13.2	28.8	11.8	46.2	22.5	24.5	7.8	45.2
3114	Fish products	21.7	11.6	12.7	54.0	14.6	31.1	15.4	38.9
					Traditional products				
Textiles, apparel, footwear, jewelry									
3211	Spinning and weaving	23.4	9.9	26.5	40.2	14.2	25.0	13.0	47.8
3220	Apparel	2.2	82.2	4.6	11.0	4.1	72.8	7.0	16.1
3240	Footwear	11.1	64.5	13.8	10.6	21.6	68.5	3.1	6.9
3901	Jewelry	6.3	7.3	34.7	51.7	7.4	12.9	60.4	19.3
Other									
3311	Sawmill production	15.0	34.6	15.6	34.8	10.4	43.4	19.6	26.6
3720	Nonferrous metals	3.7	2.6	10.7	85.3	7.4	1.4	22.5	68.8

Nontraditional products[d]

Process									
3511	Basic industrial chemicals	35.4 (1.9)	2.0 (0.1)	5.2 (0.3)	55.4 (3.0)	23.2 (1.8)	8.6 (0.7)	8.7 (0.7)	59.5 (4.6)
3560	Plastic products not elsewhere classified	10.5 (0.8)	78.3 (6.3)	4.3 (0.3)	6.9 (0.6)	14.2 (2.2)	76.5 (11.7)	4.0 (0.6)	5.3 (0.8)
3909	Manufactures not elsewhere classified	7.6 (2.9)	78.8 (29.8)	3.9 (1.5)	9.7 (3.7)	9.4 (3.0)	69.2 (22.1)	3.4 (1.1)	18.1 (5.8)
Engineering									
3832	Radio, television, and communication equipment	17.3 (1.4)	76.5 (6.2)	1.1 (0.1)	5.2 (0.4)	13.2 (3.0)	66.8 (15.4)	12.6 (2.9)	7.3 (1.7)
Other									
3710	Iron and steel	16.9 (0.4)	4.6 (0.1)	31.7 (0.8)	46.8 (1.2)	34.0 (2.0)	40.8 (2.4)	5.8 (0.3)	19.3 (1.1)

Source: Author's calculations.
a. Argentina, Brazil, Colombia, and Mexico.
b. South Korea, Hong Kong, Taiwan, and Singapore.
c. India, Indonesia, Israel, Malaysia, Pakistan.
d. The numbers in parentheses are shares in the total import supply.

for the importing country. The analysis of chapter 3 suggests that changes in import-penetration ratios for NICs and for industrial country suppliers are usually positively rather than negatively correlated. Thus the evidence in table 1-15 probably indicates that import penetration by NICs is rising faster than that by industrial country suppliers, so that NICs are "replacing" industrial country suppliers only partially and only at the margin.

In sum, except for the important case of apparel, there is little support for (and some major contradiction to) the first prediction of the hypothesis of stages of comparative advantage: that low-income countries replace middle-income countries in the supply of traditional manufactured products. The prediction could well be valid in the future, but it is not evident in the data for 1969–78. The hypothesis receives more support for its second prediction: that middle-income countries will partially replace industrial countries in supplying nontraditional manufactured exports.

Substitution of Japanese Supply

A related hypothesis holds that the developing countries have begun to replace Japan as a supplier of products to industrial country markets. This hypothesis is part of the approach of stages of comparative advantage: comparative advantage in goods of moderate sophistication and labor-intensity passes from Japan to the NICs, while comparative advantage in goods of low sophistication and high labor-intensity passes from the NICs to the lower tier of developing countries.

Empirical evidence supports the hypothesis that developing countries have begun to replace Japan as the supplier of several important manufactured goods. Table 1-16 shows that in the major sectors identified as having experienced large shifts in developing-country exports of manufactures attributable to changes in market share (table 1-13), there was a negative correlation between the changes in the shares of Japan and those of the developing countries in the imports of manufactures into Western industrial countries. In apparel, radio, television, and communication equipment, footwear, fish products, and iron and steel, sizable market share losses for Japan coincided with market share gains for developing countries. Because those gains were larger than Japan's losses, especially in apparel and footwear, the developing countries were replacing supply from other industrial countries as well as Japan. The other sectors in the table show no particular pattern. The one

Table 1-16. *Changes in Shares of Japan and Developing Countries in Import Markets of Industrial Countries, Selected Products, 1969 and 1978*
Percent

SITC number	Product sector	Japan[a] 1969	Japan[a] 1978	Change	Change for developing countries, 1969–78[b]
01	Meat products	0.0	0.0	0.0	−5.5
03	Fish	14.4	6.3	−8.1	10.1
65	Textile spinning and weaving	9.4	4.8	−4.6	−5.2
67	Iron and steel	17.2	14.2	−3.0	3.0
68	Nonferrous metals	1.1	1.9	0.8	−8.0
84	Apparel	11.3	2.3	−8.0	18.6
85	Footwear	10.8	1.5	−9.3	21.6
732	Motor vehicles	5.5	20.0	14.5	1.0
724	Radio, television, and communication equipment	43.9	31.3	−12.6	14.2
864	Watches and clocks	5.6	25.6	20.0	28.7

Source: Organization for Economic Cooperation and Development, *Statistics of Foreign Trade, series B* (Paris: OECD, 1978); UN, *Commodity Trade Statistics, 1969,* selected countries; UN trade data tapes; and table 1-6. Standard industrial trade classification categories are from UN, *Classification of Commodities by Industrial Origin; Relationship of the Standard International Trade Classification to the International Standard Industrial Classification,* series M, no. 43, 2d ed. (UN, 1966). These groups correspond approximately to the ISIC categories listed in table 1-9.
    a. Japan's share in the imports of Canada, France, West Germany, Italy, the United Kingdom, and the United States.
    b. Change in the developing countries' share in the imports of Japan and the other countries listed in note a.

significant surprise is the sector of textile spinning, where Japan's loss of market share would not be unexpected, but the loss of market share by developing countries is unexpected.

As in the case of general substitution of industrial country suppliers by the NICs, the replacement of Japanese supply by that from developing countries (table 1-16) does not necessarily imply absolute declines in the Japanese exports in question. The analysis in chapter 3 shows a positive correlation of changes in import penetration by developing countries and by Japan. The "replacement" indicated in table 1-16 is once again probably largely at the margin, deriving from the developing countries' large marginal share in the increased import penetration (rather than from reduction of Japanese supply).

Conclusion

The broad picture of trends in developing countries' exports of manufactures is one of dynamism, though with lower growth than commonly reported when other, narrower definitions excluding processed foods and nonferrous metals (and including exports to other developing countries) are used. By far the most dynamic market for these products has been the United States, whose share has risen to nearly one-half among the seven major industrial countries.

Real growth rates of imports from developing countries (based on analysis using specially calculated price indexes of imports) have been low for processed foods and nonferrous metals, but high for a large number of other manufactured products, notably apparel, footwear, radio and television, plastics, iron and steel, chemicals, furniture, rubber, motor vehicles (parts), clocks and watches, and sporting goods. For several of these and other sectors, real growth in the 1970s averaged more than 20 percent annually.

Import penetration into industrial country markets has remained low at an aggregate level. For some individual product sectors, however, penetration by developing-country supply has reached relatively high levels in a short time. For example, from 1970 to 1978 this penetration grew from 3 to 12 percent of the U.S. market in apparel, and from 1 to 14 percent in footwear. For all seven industrial countries, however, protectionist pressures in sensitive industries cannot be uniformly related to high market penetration by developing countries except in apparel. In other sensitive products, such as footwear, radio, television, and textiles, penetration by developing-country supply remains low in some industrial countries, and for the sensitive steel industry it remained uniformly low as of 1978.

The product composition of imports from developing countries has changed substantially in the direction of nontraditional goods. A major exception is the broad class of textiles, apparel, and footwear, traditional goods that nonetheless accounted for a larger share of these exports at the end of the decade of the 1970s than at the beginning. In value terms the major shifts in the composition of this trade include a surge in exports of apparel, radio, television, and communication equipment, and parts for motor vehicles.

Two popular hypotheses are not supported well by the data. There is no pronounced diversification away from traditional markets (except by the Commonwealth countries away from the United Kingdom), and there is no clear pattern of substitution of supply of unsophisticated, labor-intensive, traditional exports away from an upper-income tier of developing countries to a lower tier (with the limited exception of

n R. Cline

Exports of
Manufactures
from
Developing
Countries

apparel). A third common hypothesis is confirmed, however; in product sectors providing the most important export gains to developing countries through increased market shares, a pronounced pattern has emerged of market share loss by Japan in association with the market share gains by developing countries.

CHAPTER TWO

Determinants of Protection in Industrial Countries

ALTHOUGH several developing countries achieved impressive growth of manufactured exports to industrial country markets in the 1970s, it is unclear whether this performance can be repeated in the 1980s. Over the next decade economic growth in the advanced countries seems likely to be considerably slower than the postwar average (although not necessarily slower than in the troubled 1970s), raising doubts about market expansion. Moreover, the "new protectionism" of recent years creates the possibility of a spreading web of restrictions that could hinder the growth of manufactured exports from developing countries. Just at the time when the prevailing ideology and development strategy in many developing countries have shifted from import substitution behind protective barriers to a more efficient, outward-looking strategy emphasizing manufactured exports, protection might constrict the markets for those exports. In short, the old limitations on developing-country exports of manufactures from the side of supply (inappropriate domestic policy) might be replaced in the 1980s by new limitations on the side of demand (increasing protection and slow growth in industrial country markets).

The analysis of this chapter provides one basis for examining the future prospects for protection in industrial countries. Statistical analysis explains the existing patterns of nontariff barrier (NTB) protection. (As will be shown, tariffs are now so low that they are of secondary importance.) The subsequent application of the estimated statistical protection functions to projections of market growth and growth in manufactured exports from developing countries provides forecasts of the likelihood and extent of future protection (chapter 3).

Earlier studies of protection tended to examine tariffs, although some

34

studies considered NTBs as well. Appendix C reviews the literature on empirical estimates of protective response to imports. Broadly, the underlying explanatory variables used in this study are similar to those frequently used in past studies, although the specific statistical technique used (logit analysis) has rarely been applied for this purpose and the data sets and model specifications applied here are unique.

Major protection today usually takes the form of nontariff barriers. In the late 1970s tariff protection of manufactured imports into industrial countries averaged approximately 8 percent *ad valorem,*[1] and after the Tokyo Round of negotiations (1973–79) tariff protection was even lower. Data on post–Tokyo Round tariffs are examined below. These tariffs are low, averaging approximately 5 percent. With some exceptions, the problem of protection today is not a problem of high tariffs.

As tariff protection has receded, however, significant NTBs have developed in a number of important product sectors. These barriers include direct quotas on imports, but their increasingly common form is the "voluntary export quota" imposed by the supplying country on its own exports in response to the threat of direct quotas in the importing country. In recent years direct import quotas, voluntary export quotas, and other forms of NTBs have restricted imports in important product sectors such as apparel, textiles, footwear, shipbuilding, automobiles, steel, and television receivers.

Protection is shifting more and more from tariffs at modest rates applied to most products, to a dichotomy in which one broad group of products has practically free entry while another set of sensitive products has relatively severe protection provided by quotas and other NTBs. At present the data are not available to quantify the tariff equivalent of most of the nontariff barriers, but in most cases their protective effect appears to be high.

Estimation of a statistical model explaining the causes of NTBs is an important step for trade policy analysis. Aside from the few studies described in appendix C, estimates of this type do not exist; yet successful estimates would help clarify the forces that lead to protection. Moreover, statistical estimates of this type applied to future projections of the variables identified as causing protection permit forecasts of the likelihood of new protection in industrial sectors. Such forecasts have

1. For dutiable manufactured imports only, the corresponding figure was 11 percent. William R. Cline and others, *Trade Negotiations in the Tokyo Round: A Quantitative Assessment* (Brookings Institution, 1978), p. 10.

implications for policymakers in the North—to alert them to areas that may require special adjustment—as well as for planners in the South, in setting realistic export targets.

A Model of the Decision to Protect

The first step toward a satisfactory predictive model of protection is to consider the forces leading to protection.[2] In today's world, where "bound" tariffs exist on most products at relatively low rates, a decision to provide special protection to an industry typically involves adoption of some form of "voluntary" export restraint, orderly marketing agreement, or other form of quantitative restriction on trade. Such a decision may be seen as the consequence of the confrontation between pressures from industry and labor, on the one hand, and the disposition of the legislature and executive branch toward conferring protection, on the other. In economic terms, there is a market for protection. The firms and labor provide the demand side of this market while governing authorities provide its supply side.

Figure 2-1 formulates the market for protection in a supply-demand format. The horizontal axis shows the probability that the government will issue a decision to protect, with the probability varying from zero to 100 percent. Although in any given case the decision must be either to protect or not to do so, a probability (such as 40 percent) may be interpreted as meaning that in a series of cases the decision to protect will be taken with a particular frequency (for example, in four out of ten cases). The vertical axis shows the average price per unit (percentage point) of probability of protection.

To the industry and labor groups seeking protection, there are costs to the process of mobilizing political pressure for protection. If the lobbying costs for the industry and labor amount to, for example, $5 million, and the industry expects to receive a probability of 50 percent of achieving protection in return, the average price per probability unit (figure 2-1) is $100,000 ($5 million/50) per percentage point. At the same time, the value of additional protection at any given level is presumably

2. The conceptual framework of this section draws upon and seeks to extend the literature on the political economy of protection as set forth in appendix C, as does the specification of variables set forth in this chapter for the empirical implementation of the model.

Figure 2-1. *Supply and Demand for Protection*

Price per probability unit of protection

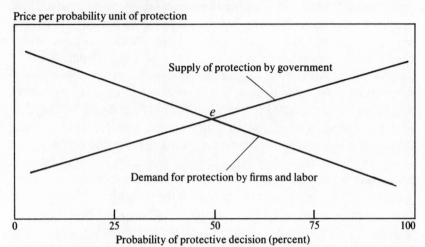

Supply of protection by government

e

Demand for protection by firms and labor

0   25   50   75   100
Probability of protective decision (percent)

diminishing. Thus the industry is prepared to pay less in additional lobbying costs to raise the probability of a favorable protective decision from 80 percent to 81 percent than it was prepared to pay to raise the probability from 50 percent to 51 percent. Together, these considerations imply a downward sloping demand curve for the probability of protection, but in a form that gives rising total payments as the total probability of protection increases (figure 2-1).[3]

For government officials, the supply of protection is determined by its perceived costs. The higher the cost of protection to society, the lower the government's willingness to grant it. In the first instance, the enlightened government evaluates the cost of protection as the loss of efficiency to the economy caused by the misallocation of resources for protection at home of goods more efficiently produced abroad. These costs of protection include ''deadweight loss'' from static misallocation of resources, loss of consumer benefits through higher prices (net of transfers to producers) as import supply is curtailed (both static effects), losses of economies of scale as possibilities for specialization through

3. In terms of normal supply-demand analysis, the demand curve is elastic over the relevant range so that total revenue rises with total quantity. It is conceivable, however, that at very high probability of protection the curve turns inelastic. Thus an industry already confident of protection might merely reduce its lobbying efforts if a new administration entered that was much more disposed toward protection than its predecessor.

trade are lost, macroeconomic losses as the trade-off between unemployment and inflation is worsened by higher import prices, and the loss of stimulus for technological change caused by decreased competitive pressure from imports (dynamic effects). In addition to these social costs, the government must consider the cost of transfer from society at large to the industry petitioning for protection. These transfers can often far exceed the net cost to society as a whole. And because legislators and the executive board must consider their opportunity cost in the form of a loss of support from group B if they arrange a benefit for group A at the expense of group B, they must take transfer costs into account.

All these considerations imply that the government will insist on a higher and higher total payment exacted from the industry and labor groups seeking protection (in terms of their political effort) as the government increases the total probability of granting protection. In addition, the incremental payment (political effort) it insists on is probably greater when the expected level of protection (probability of protection) is already high. For example, vulnerability of the administration to the charge of catering to special interest groups rises as it increases the frequency with which it grants protection. Thus the average price charged by the government per unit of probability of protection is at least constant and probably rising as total probability increases, and the supply curve of protection probability is most likely a rising curve, as shown in figure 2-1.[4]

The equilibrium probability of protection results from the intersection of the supply and demand curves (point *e*). To the left of this point, the value of the likelihood of extra protection to the interest group in question exceeds the cost perceived by the government of a unit increase in protection probability, and the two sides both benefit from a transaction that raises the likelihood of protection (the government because of political rewards and the industry because of financial benefits). Such a bargain will not be struck to the right of point *e*, because in this range the government insists on incremental political rewards greater than the industry is prepared to mobilize in view of the additional lobbying costs.

Figure 2-1 must be interpreted as heuristic rather than exact. In

---

4. If the model were formulated with the level of protection, rather than its probability of adoption at a fixed level, on the horizontal axis, a rising supply curve would be expected from the standard result of welfare analysis of tariff (and therefore tariff-equivalent) protection showing that the cost to society of protection rises geometrically with the level of protection.

particular, only special formulations would make it possible to use the same vertical "price" axis for both supply and demand. Unlike normal supply and demand for a product in which the price paid by the consumer equals the price received by the producer (so that a single price axis applies to both supply and demand), the transactions here are indirect. The industry pays lobbyists rather than the government itself, and the government does not necessarily measure the costs of protection at their full value—because the losers from protection (consumers) are not well organized. For these reasons, at the actual equilibrium probability of protection, e, the price of protection as seen by the government might not be identical to that paid for lobbying by the petitioning industry. However, for purposes of parametric analysis the supply-demand diagram remains useful because it illustrates that, other things being equal, a shift toward greater probability of protection occurs if there is an increase in the supply or demand for protection, causing a shift in the supply or demand curve to the right because of the factors discussed below.[5] Correspondingly, a decrease in either the supply or demand for protection, causing a leftward shift in the supply or demand curve, reduces the equilibrium level of protection. Finally, this broad approach could also be reformulated to treat the amount of protection as variable, rather than treating all protection as equal and examining only whether it is likely to be adopted.

The determinants of the demand for protection may include the elements shown in equation 2-1 (in light of the literature on protection, appendix C). The demand for protection is positively related to the level of import penetration (the ratio of imports to total consumption in a given

5. Moreover, even with divergence between the price to suppliers of protection and that to demanders, the problem can still be formulated in terms of supply-demand equilibrium, although it is more complicated. Diagrammatically, a third dimension must be added. Probability of protection is placed on the horizontal axis, price paid by demanders of protection on the vertical axis, and price perceived by the suppliers of protection on the depth axis. As long as a specific relation can be stated between price paid by demanders and price perceived by suppliers, a unique supply-demand equilibrium occurs where three planes intersect: one showing the protection demand curve (projected perpendicular to the demand price–protection probability surface); one showing the protection supply curve (projected perpendicular to the supply price–protection probability surface); and one showing the relation between supply price and demand price (projected perpendicular to the supply price–demand price surface). There are three equations and three unknowns, and thus there is a unique solution: for example, (1) $P_s = a_s + b_s P_r$; (2) $P_d = a + b P_r$; and (3) $P_s = c + d P_d$ in a linear form, where P_s = price perceived by suppliers of protection, P_d = price paid by demanders of protection, and P_r = probability of protection.

product) because the higher the import penetration, the broader the scope of the competition that will be cut back by imposition of protection and the greater protection benefits to producers. In the equation demand for protection D is positively related to import penetration:

(2-1) $D = f_1$ [import penetration (+), comparative advantage (−), concentration (+), export dependence (−)].

However, the demand for protection is lower if the industry's inherent comparative advantage is stronger (the second element in the demand equation) because the industry is more likely to avoid further loss to imports (or to recapture previous loss and expand exports). A third element in the demand equation, industry concentration, reflects the ease of coordinating industry efforts—and of forcing all members to bear a fair share of the cost—for lobbying purposes. With a low degree of industry concentration, many small firms will attempt to be "free riders" in enjoying the benefits of protection without contributing to the lobbying efforts needed to obtain it, and the industry will not raise as much funding for lobbying efforts as would a comparable industry with higher concentration among fewer firms. Furthermore, demand for protection will be lower if the industry has a high dependence on exports because exporters will fear foreign retaliation. In sum, the higher the import-penetration ratio (the ratio of imports to apparent consumption), the lower the industry's inherent comparative advantage, the greater its concentration, and the lower its export dependence, the more the industry will be prepared to pay (in proportionate terms) for a given probability of protection, and the higher the demand curve for protection will be.

On the side of supply, the basic determinants are as follows:

(2-2) $S = f_2$ [political importance (+), public sympathy (+), adjustment cost (+)].

In equation 2-2 the willingness of government to supply protection, S, increases with the political importance of the industry. Other things being equal, an industry that has wide voter support and strong representation in the legislature will be more able to obtain a protectionist response from the government. The "national security" argument for protection is a variant on the consideration of political importance of the industry. Protection supply may also be positively related to public sympathy for the industry. A sector widely perceived as being composed of "needy" or "deserving" workers and firms (lower-paid workers with fewer skills of use in alternative work) may have more success in obtaining protection than an industry perceived as "privileged" by virtue of high wages and ease of transition to other employment. Finally, with the enlightened government the supply of protection is influenced by the cost of adjustment required in the absence of protection. Social costs of adjustment to increased imports cause reduced domestic output, and the higher these costs, the greater the argument for at least delaying the full burden of adjustment by temporary protection.

In a reduced form of the model, the resulting equilibrium probability of protection P showing the interactions of the supply and demand curves has the relationships:

(2-3) $P = f_3$ [import penetration (+), comparative advantage (−),
concentration (+), export dependence (−),
political importance (+), public sympathy (+),
adjustment cost (+)],

where the signs following the influences indicate the direction of their impact on the probability of protection.

This model of protection focuses on cross-section or intersectoral differences in protection. In principle the model also could be used to analyze the general level of protection over time. However, overall measures of average protection are not available. Factors such as the level of unemployment, the presence of exchange-rate overvaluation, concern about inflation, and the presence of continuing multilateral trade negotiations also influence the path of protection over time. The difficulty of projecting such variables into the future is another reason for the approach taken here, which limits attention to intersectoral differences in protection. Before the specific variables used in implementing the model of protection described above are considered, the particular statistical technique to be used must be determined.

A Logit Analysis of Protection

Under today's trade conditions statistical analyses of protection cannot be limited to tariff protection. Instead, quantitative analysis must address the presence of serious nontariff barriers. This fact complicates quantitative analysis. When tariffs are the main form of protection, statistical tests may use the tariff rate as the dependent variable and may apply traditional techniques such as multiple regression analysis. So that NTBs may be accounted for, however, techniques that capture a discontinuous dependent variable must be applied: in this case, the binary alternative of presence or absence of the NTB.

Ideally, detailed price comparisons could be made to determine the tariff equivalent of NTBs. If the domestic price of a product protected by an NTB were 50 percent higher than the international price of an identical product, for example, one could say that the tariff equivalent of the NTB (as well as the tariff, if any) was 50 percent. The product could then be compared directly with products protected only by tariffs, in a statistical analysis using either the tariff or the tariff equivalent of NTB and tariff protection as the dependent variable. Without such price comparisons, NTBs must be represented in a discrete form, of which the simplest is a binary alternative with a value of unity for the presence of an NTB and zero in the absence of an NTB.

Discriminant analysis and logit analysis are two statistical methods for analyzing discrete phenomena. Both methods make it possible to estimate statistical functions that can be used to classify data into discrete, mutually exclusive categories (such as products with an NTB in place as opposed to other products). Discriminant analysis permits division of data into two or more separate groups, while logit analysis may be used for division into only two separate groups.

The option of using more than two classifications can make discriminant analysis an appealing technique in certain circumstances.[6] However, the underlying rationale of the technique is that the separate populations are inherently different, that they lie at polar extremes. Thus, in statistical classification of skull fossils, discriminant analysis may be used to distinguish between two clearly separate populations of different evolutionary periods. The technique takes it for granted that the difference between two (or more) discrete sets is intrinsic, and it sets out to describe as completely as possible the characteristic features of the intrinsically separate groups.

6. For a recent example that uses several classifications, see Stanley W. Black, "The Impact of Changes in the World Economy on Stabilization Policies in the 1970s," in William R. Cline and Sidney Weintraub, eds., *Economic Stabilization in Developing Countries* (Brookings Institution, 1981), pp. 43–81. An earlier application to only two classifications is given in Charles R. Frank, Jr., and William R. Cline, "Measurement of Debt Servicing Capacity: An Application of Discriminant Analysis," *Journal of International Economics*, vol. 1 (August 1971), pp. 327–44.

For most economic phenomena, however, the underlying populations of separate groups are not really polar extremes. Instead, the same forces operate on the members of both populations, but at different levels; they cause the members of one population to pass beyond a threshold where a discrete event happens but are not yet strong enough to cause the same event to occur for members of the other population. Logit analysis is conceptually more appropriate for this kind of discrete process than discriminant analysis. Logit analysis estimates the probability that a discrete event will occur. As the underlying forces leading to that event intensify, the logit function predicts a higher and higher probability of the event until the probability exceeds 50 percent (or some other cutoff point). Thus logit analysis has been used to explain the discrete decision of households to buy a major consumer durable. The method assumes that both the Joneses and the Smiths would buy an automobile under similar conditions but that only the Smiths have enough income to push them beyond the buying threshold. In contrast, discriminant analysis would assign the Joneses to a group not buying automobiles because of their low income while the Smiths are inherently in an auto-buying group.

Nontariff barrier protection occurs in response to continuous (rather than dichotomous) underlying economic forces. Apparel and footwear do not differ in a polar way from other product sectors, in contrast to the polar differences between skulls of Cro-Magnon and Neanderthal man, for example. Instead, one could expect that, given the same underlying forces (such as high import penetration and slow growth), other currently protected products would also succumb to protection. For this reason, it appears that logit analysis is preferable to discriminant analysis for examining the forces leading to serious protection by NTBs.

The logit model used in this study to analyze protection is the following:

$$(2\text{-}4) \qquad z = a + \sum_{i=1}^{11} b_i X_i$$

$$(2\text{-}5) \qquad p = \frac{1}{(1 + e^{-z})},$$

where z is the logit exponent, a is a constant, the eleven variables X_i are independent variables affecting protection, p is the probability that an NTB will occur, and e is the base of the natural logarithm. The dependent variable used in estimating equation 1 is unity if the sector has a serious NTB and zero otherwise.[7] The equation is estimated by using data for each of the four-digit categories of the international standard industrial classification (ISIC) for the country in question.

The equation estimated to explain protection draws upon cross-section rather than time series data. Thus the estimates are based on differences among eighty industrial sectors (four-digit ISIC, excluding petroleum refineries) at a single point in time. In principle it might be possible to analyze time series functions as well. For each sector a function might be estimated with annual data over several years, so that the function would capture the changing forces over time rather than the differences in protectionist forces among industries at a single point in time. In practice, however, most of the explanatory variables are available only for a single benchmark period of time, the late 1970s. The annual data required for time series analysis are not available. Furthermore, time series analysis would make no sense for the majority of sectors in which there is no NTB protection. There would be no protection to explain. Functions could be estimated only for the limited number of sectors that had passed through a series of years without protection and then had entered another period with protection. While in principle this problem could be circumvented by using pooled time series and cross-section data and considering all sectors jointly over several years of annual data, the annual data that would be required are not available. Instead, the analysis here is based on cross-section data for a single time period, broadly defined as the late 1970s, although the exact date varies for the individual variables.

The independent variables used to explain protection (the various X_i in equation 2-4) follow the general supply-demand model of protection set forth earlier in this chapter. The first several variables refer to demand for protection.

1. IMPORT PENETRATION ($X1$). The ratio of total imports to domestic apparent consumption, or the import-penetration ratio, is the first independent variable. The coefficient on this variable is expected to be positive; a higher penetration ratio is expected to increase the likelihood

7. Maximum likelihood estimation is used to calculate the coefficients a and b_i in equation 2-1. By iterative procedures, the coefficients are adjusted until they maximize the likelihood that the observed values of independent variables would be correctly associated with the observed values of the dependent variable. Eric Hanushek and John Jackson, *Statistical Methods for Social Scientists,* Quantitative Studies in Social Relations Series (Academic Press, 1977).

of protection by a serious nontariff barrier. Domestic firms are likely to consider imports more a threat as imports gain a larger share of the market. The returns to expenditure on lobbying are higher if the base of imports to be cut back by protection is larger, making the demand for protection rise with the import-penetration ratio.

There is, to be sure, a certain ambiguity about this variable. If it is generally accepted that a product should be supplied by imports (for example, tropical products), the import-penetration ratio would be high and protection would be low. Technically, the ambiguity may be viewed as a problem of simultaneity: in one relationship, high penetration might be a force causing high protection, but in another simultaneous relationship, the existing low protection may be causing high import penetration. In practice, the potential ambiguity of the penetration variable seems unlikely to be a major problem. In only a few sectors do natural resources, a possible source of acknowledged import superiority, dominate (and processed foods, where the role of natural resources tends to be greatest, are omitted from some of the final tests conducted below). Also, the analysis is at a sufficiently broad level of aggregation that the few, narrow product lines in which imports have established unchallenged dominance (for example, black-and-white television sets) are not observations by themselves but are part of broader groupings.

2. EXPORT–OUTPUT RATIO $(X2)$. The second explanatory variable associated primarily with the demand for protection is the ratio of exports to domestic production in the sector in question. In many manufactured products there is two-way trade. The import-penetration ratio may be high, but with a high ratio of exports to production, domestic firms are not particularly threatened by imports. Indeed, relying on exports, they are sensitive to the possibility that protection at home might trigger protection abroad and spoil their export markets. Sometimes two-way trade may represent imports in one subbranch of the product (for example, more simple and standardized product lines of a product) and exports in another subbranch (for example, product lines of the same good requiring greater technological sophistication). In this case the trade association is likely to be unable to marshal uniform support among its members for protectionist lobbying; the firms specializing in the export lines will dilute, if not block, the efforts of the firms specializing in import-competing product lines. The coefficient on this variable should be negative: higher exports relative to output should make the likelihood of protectionist pressure (and outcome) lower.

3. INDUSTRIAL CONCENTRATION ($X3$). Another influence that may affect the demand for protection is the concentration of domestic production. As Richard Caves has pointed out, industrial structure may affect protection in opposing ways.[8] Higher concentration facilitates cooperation among the producers in organizing and financing lobbying efforts for protection because it reduces the free-rider problem. That is, in an industry in which three or four firms account for the bulk of output, they can finance a protection campaign with little concern that a large portion of the benefits will be enjoyed by nonparticipating firms. But an industry composed of many small firms will find that firms accounting for a considerable portion of output may seek to enjoy protection benefits as free-riders, without contributing their fair share to a protection effort.

From the standpoint of the free-rider problem, concentration facilitates protection. But as Caves notes, high concentration also means that the industry is less likely to have a broad geographic base for legislative support of its protection goals. Other things being equal, the industry is likely to secure more votes for its plan if it is widely based throughout the country, but this dispersion may also mean that industrial concentration is low. The coefficient on the variable for industrial concentration is expected to be positive if the influence of concentration in overcoming the free-rider problem is dominant (more concentration, more protection), but the coefficient will be negative if the influence of geographical dispersion is dominant.

4. COMPARATIVE ADVANTAGE. The final broad influence on demand for protection is that of comparative advantage. Several alternative variable specifications may capture this influence.

–*Value added per worker* ($X4$). The first indicator of comparative advantage is value added per worker. In the traditional, Ricardian sense, comparative advantage is high in those sectors with high factor productivity. In addition, in the Heckscher-Ohlin tradition, whereby countries with abundant capital and skilled labor but scarce unskilled labor should have comparative advantage in products that are intensive in the use of capital and skilled labor, value added per worker acts as a proxy for the physical and human capital intensity of production. Other things being equal, value added per worker will be higher if there is more physical capital per worker and if the worker in question has more human capital in the form of specialized skills and education.

8. Richard E. Caves, "Economic Models of Political Choice: Canada's Tariff Structure," *Canadian Journal of Economics,* vol. 9 (May 1976), pp. 278–300.

In his early study of manufactured exports of developing countries, Hal Lary showed that these exports tend to be labor intensive as measured (inversely) by value added per worker.[9] The manufactured products successfully exported by developing countries tended to have low value added per worker, indicating high labor intensity. By extension, value added per worker may also help explain protection. Those industries with low value added per worker are intensive in the use of unskilled labor and therefore likely to be at a comparative disadvantage in trade with the developing countries where unskilled labor is relatively abundant and cheap. The domestic firms in such industries are likely to be under more pressure from imports and to exert more lobbying pressure for protection than are firms in industries with high value added per worker, high physical- and human-capital intensity, and more favorable comparative advantage. The coefficient on this variable is expected to be negative: higher value added per worker means lower likelihood of protection.

—*Physical capital per worker* ($X5$). A direct measure of factor intensity of production is the ratio of physical capital (plant, equipment) to employment in the industry. Following the Heckscher-Ohlin theory, whereby a country has comparative advantage in producing and exporting those products that use relatively large amounts of the factor of production that it possesses in abundance, industrial countries tend to have comparative advantage in capital-intensive goods. Import competition from developing countries would be expected to be the most severe in products with low capital–labor ratios. The expected coefficient is negative: higher capital per worker means less likelihood of protection.

—*Human capital per worker* ($X6$). Modern trade theory has emphasized that human capital must be taken into account in determining comparative advantage. Industrial countries are abundant in educated and skilled workers, while developing countries typically have a relative scarcity of skilled labor. The capital equivalent of education and skills, or human capital, may be measured by using the difference between the average wage and the wage for unskilled labor. This difference in annual wage may be seen as the annual return to the capital value of education and skills. Once a measure of human capital is available, the theoretical expectation is that the coefficient on the variable is negative: higher human capital per worker means less likelihood of protection.

9. Hal B. Lary, *Imports of Manufactures from Less Developed Countries* (Columbia University Press for the National Bureau of Economic Research, 1968).

—*Total capital per worker* ($X7$). An alternative to including separately the ratios of physical and human capital to labor is to treat them jointly as a single variable, total capital per worker. This combined variable assumes that human and physical capital are perfect substitutes, which need not be the case—especially if capital market imperfections (for example, lack of availability of education loans) keep the rate of return to human capital different from that to physical capital. As with the two individual variables, the coefficient on the joint variable is expected to be negative: higher total capital per worker is expected to be associated with lower likelihood of protection.

—*Skill ratio* ($X8$). An alternative to the human capital–labor ratio is to measure the intensity of skilled labor by the ratio of unskilled to total labor in a sector. The higher the ratio of unskilled to total labor, the lower is the intensity with which skilled labor is used as an input into production. For the same reasons discussed above with respect to the variable human capital–labor ratio, the ratio of unskilled to total labor would be expected to have a positive coefficient. The higher the fraction of unskilled labor, the greater is the likelihood of protection.

All these indicators of inherent comparative advantage ($X4$–$X8$) tend to be substitutes for each other to some extent. They may be expected to be closely related, or collinear. Thus, in a final empirical estimate only one of them may typically dominate in capturing the influence of comparative advantage; collinearity may cause the others to be statistically insignificant. Nevertheless, in the initial tests it is useful to include all five alternative specifications of the influence of comparative advantage to identify the ones that dominate in the absence of theoretical superiority of one over the other.

As for the supply side of the market for protection, the variables examined here represent several broad influences.

5. POLITICAL IMPORTANCE. Potentially the most important factor affecting the supply of protection is the political importance of the industry. The variable chosen to represent this influence is the industry's share of the total labor force in manufacturing ($X9$). The larger a sector's employment, the more numerous are the voters directly affected by the health of the sector, the greater is its political clout, and the more willing policymakers are to provide protection, other things being equal. The political influence of labor and firms in a product sector is likely to be greater if the number of workers in the industry is greater. The outstanding example in the United States and other industrial countries is the

sector of apparel and textiles. This sector typically accounts for approximately 11 percent of manufacturing labor in the industrial countries, and the political voice of so large an industry is huge. The coefficient on the variable is expected to be positive: a sector with a higher share of manufacturing labor is more likely to be protected, other things being equal.

One possible ambiguity concerning the labor size variable warrants special mention. As noted in appendix C, it has sometimes been argued that the size of the industry should be a negative influence on protection. The rationale behind this possible relationship is that larger industries are harder to organize and suffer more from the free-rider problem. The problem of organizing large industries may have been relevant in the nineteenth century (the period analyzed by J. J. Pincus, appendix C), when travel and communication were difficult, but it is no longer important. Indeed, because of certain fixed costs of organization (maintenance of an administrative office for a lobbying effort, for example), it is more likely that there are economies of scale to organization, which tend to offset the possible free-rider problem caused by the greater numbers of firms in larger industries. Thus, contrary to some previous studies, the analysis here envisions little if any reason for a negative relation between industry size and protection. To the extent that any such relation exists on the demand side, it should be substantially overshadowed by the influence running in the opposite direction on the supply side, from large industry size and labor force to large political weight and greater likelihood of success in petitioning for protection.

6. PUBLIC SYMPATHY. The degree of public sympathy for the industry is an influence on the supply of protection. Perhaps the best variable to capture this influence is the sector's wage rate ($X10$). Legislatures may be sensitive to the greater incidence of poverty among workers in low-wage industries, considering them to be more vulnerable to adjustment difficulties in the face of job displacement. Some studies have found that the wage rate performs well as a variable in explaining tariff protection.[10]

To some extent the wage variable blends the supply-side influence of public sympathy with the demand-side influence of comparative advantage. Industrial countries facing competition from developing countries are likely to find the competition keenest in industries that rely heavily

10. Gerald K. Helleiner, "The Political Economy of Canada's Tariff Structure: An Alternative Model," *Canadian Journal of Economics*, vol. 10 (May 1977), pp. 318–26.

on unskilled labor and are likely to have a comparative advantage in labor-intensive products, following the Heckscher-Ohlin theory of trade noted earlier. From the standpoint of both demand and supply, the coefficient expected for the variable is negative: higher relative wages mean less likelihood of protection.[11]

7. ADJUSTMENT COST. A final set of influences in the supply of protection is the cost of adjustment. The more severe the cost of adjustment to imports, the lower will be the net benefits of a simple free-trade policy, causing authorities to be more receptive to at least temporary protection. Two variables are used to capture the influence of adjustment cost.

—*Change in import penetration* ($X11$). The change in the import-penetration ratio may help explain protection, in addition to the level of import penetration ($X1$). A large rise in the import-penetration ratio over a given time period may be taken as an indication that adjustment costs are relatively high because the amount and speed of required adjustment are relatively high.[12] The coefficient on this variable would be expected to be positive: a larger rise in penetration causes higher likelihood of protection.

—*Growth rate* ($X12$). The final explanatory variable is the rate of real production growth in recent years in the industry, which also reflects the supply of protection from the standpoint of adjustment cost. A rapidly growing industry is less likely to experience adjustment problems from imports. Employment is likely to be growing in a growing industry (or, if technological change is rapid, at least not falling). Policymakers are more likely to adhere to free-trade principles if the industry in question is growing rapidly and shows no signs of acute need for protection to alleviate unemployment or chronic business losses. The growth rate may also influence demand for protection: slow or negative growth may generate greater pressure for protection as workers face job

11. Here again, however, there is room for ambiguity. Some would argue that protectionist pressures in steel and automobiles, for example, are the result of excessive wages through which the employees have helped price their goods out of the international market. If this "excess wage" influence dominates the "labor intensity" influence, the coefficient on the relative wage rate would be positive, and higher wages would be associated with higher likelihood of protection.

12. It is also possible that change in the penetration ratio influences the demand for protection. Protectionist pressure from domestic labor and producers may be greater in an industry that has experienced a surge in the import-penetration ratio from 5 to 20 percent in the preceding five years, for example, than from another industry that has had a 20 percent import-penetration ratio for many years.

losses (especially if technological change is rapid) and attempt to boost domestic jobs by reducing imports. The coefficient on this variable is expected to be negative: a higher growth rate means protection is less likely to be present.

This list completes the explanatory variables used in the protection analysis of this study. As noted above, the analysis examines cross-section variation in protection among industries, so that important time series influences on overall protection (the overall level of unemployment, inflation, and the exchange rate) are not incorporated. In addition, even some intersectoral considerations may be omitted, such as the effect of national security considerations on the supply of protection. However, the variables considered here should include the dominant influences on the public decision of whether to confer protection.

Protection Data

The logit analysis of protection developed in this study examines only nontariff barriers because tariffs have fallen low enough not to be in most cases a major obstacle to trade.[13] Nevertheless, before an examination of the data on nontariff barriers, it is useful to consider the general structure of tariff protection.

Table 2-1 presents data on tariffs in industrial countries after comple-

13. Note, however, that a recent study by Morici and Megna reaches the unconventional conclusion that the additional protection provided by NTBs is less important than the protection from tariffs alone. Peter Morici and Laura L. Megna, *U.S. Economic Policies Affecting Industrial Trade* (Washington, D.C.: National Planning Association, 1983). Nonetheless, the methods used by the authors would appear to understate the impact of NTB protection. Thus they estimate the effect of voluntary quotas on Japanese automobiles at a tariff-equivalent of 3.3 percent on non-Canadian automobiles imported into the U.S. market, far below a recent estimate by Robert Crandall that in 1981–82 these quotas raised the consumer price of Japanese automobiles by $920 to $960 a car. Stuart Auerbach, "Report Says Auto Limits Boosted Japan's Profits," *Washington Post*, June 27, 1984. The downward bias of the authors' estimates for the impact of footwear quotas is discussed in William R. Cline, *Footwear Imports and the Consumer* (Washington, D.C.: International Economic Analysis, Inc., 1984), p. 41. And the authors simply dismiss measures in the U.S. steel sector as having any protective content beyond justifiable countervailing duties against subsidies and dumping, an interpretation not widely shared by other trade experts. See, for example, Ingo Walter, "Structural Adjustment and Trade Policy in the International Steel Industry," in William R. Cline, ed., *Trade Policy in the 1980s* (Washington, D.C.: Institute for International Economics, 1983), pp. 483–525.

Table 2-1. *Tariffs on Manufactured Imports*[a]
Percent

Tariff	United States	Canada	European Community	Japan
Average, all imports	4.6	7.3	5.2	6.8[b]
Average, imports from developing countries	6.8	11.0	4.9	7.3[b]
Frequency by category				
Less than 5 percent	72.5	25.0	45.0	43.8
5–10 percent	16.3	48.8	46.3	35.0
10–15 percent	7.5	15.0	8.8	11.3
10–20 percent	2.5	6.3	0.0	1.3
Over 20 percent	1.3	5.0	0.0	8.8
Frequency by import value				
Less than 5 percent	84.3	17.3	45.5	36.8
5–10 percent	7.2	70.2	48.1	49.8
10–15 percent	3.5	5.9	6.4	7.1
15–20 percent	0.2	3.9	0.0	1.2
Over 20 percent	4.8	2.8	0.0	5.0
Frequency by value of imports from developing countries				
Less than 5 percent	69.1	28.4	49.5	25.1
5–10 percent	10.5	33.2	38.1	56.5
10–15 percent	5.7	8.3	12.4	13.1
15–20 percent	0.3	7.2	0.0	1.9
Over 20 percent	14.4	22.9	0.0	3.4

Source: Calculated from data provided by Office of the U.S. Trade Representative.
a. International standard industrial classification (ISIC) 3111–3909 excluding petroleum refineries, 3530. The tariff rates are for post–Tokyo Round duties after full implementation of negotiated reductions. The rates include zero tariff on nondutiable items.
b. Excludes tobacco, 3140.

tion of Tokyo Round tariff cuts.[14] These cuts are generally to be made in equal annual reductions from 1980 through 1987,[15] although Japan accelerated its completion of tariff cuts to March 1983.[16] The data in

14. The data in the table were calculated from tariff data tapes provided by the Office of the U.S. Trade Representative. Those tapes contained average tariffs (post–Tokyo Round) at the level of four digits of the standard industrial classification (SIC), with approximately 450 categories. A special correspondence provided by the U.S. Department of Commerce was applied to convert these SIC tariffs to average tariffs at the level of the 81 four-digit categories of the ISIC.

15. GATT, *The Tokyo Round of Multilateral Trade Negotiations: Supplementary Report* (Geneva: GATT, 1980), p. 4.

16. Gary R. Saxonhouse, "The Micro- and Macroeconomics of Foreign Sales to Japan," in Cline, ed., *Trade Policy in the 1980s*, pp. 259–95.

table 2-1 refer to tariff averages at the four-digit ISIC level. They exclude petroleum refineries (3530) and include zero tariffs on nondutiable imports. The data refer to import-weighted average tariffs and are therefore subject to the well-known qualification that they may be downward biased for failure to give adequate weight to sectors in which volume of imports has been repressed by high tariffs. However, given the generally moderate range of tariffs even at the most detailed level, the aggregation bias is probably not substantial.[17]

Table 2-1 shows that, after the Tokyo Round, tariff protection is low. In the United States and the European Community, the new tariffs average about 5 percent, and in Canada and Japan the average is about 7 percent. Tariffs are somewhat higher for imports from developing countries, especially in the United States and Canada: that is, imports from developing countries tend to be in product sectors with higher tariffs. The European Community is an exception, showing slightly lower tariffs on imports from developing countries than from all sources. For all four importing areas, however, the average tariffs facing developing countries are also low by any historical standard.

The frequencies of tariffs by tariff bracket, shown in the table, indicate a greater dispersion of tariffs in the United States and Canada than in the European Community and Japan. Thus the United States has a much higher frequency of import value entering under low tariffs (under 5 percent) and high tariffs (over 20 percent) than the European Community, which has the vast bulk of its tariffs concentrated in the range of zero to 10 percent. However, a single sector accounts for most of the high-tariff range in the U.S. data: textiles and apparel. At the four-digit level, apparel is the only sector with an average tariff over 20 percent (22.4 percent). In the sectors of textiles (3211–19) and apparel (3220), the more important form of protection against developing countries is the regime of quotas under the Multi-fiber Arrangement, although tariffs remain significant for protection against industrial country suppliers (who have remained exempt from the MFA).

Because the frequency of high tariffs is low even for imports from developing countries and because in the most important cases high-tariff

17. Unweighted tariff averages are perhaps even less reliable because they give equal weight to tariff line entries that may be of vastly different economic significance. The alternative of weighting by domestic consumption is infeasible because consumption data are not available at the level of detailed national tariff entries, typically numbering in the thousands.

imports are also restricted by major NTBs, this study limits quantitative analysis of protection to NTBs.

The NTBs examined here are narrowly defined. They do not include such bothersome and elusive barriers as govenment subsidies, discrimination in government procurement, distorted customs valuation, and discriminatory application of technical or health standards. Instead, the analysis concentrates on quantitative restrictions. One important type is the direct quota imposed by the importing country. The other important type is the voluntary export restraint self-imposed by the exporting country to avoid direct quota protection by the importing country.

The period of reference for the NTBs is broadly the middle 1970s to 1981. In some cases NTBs that existed during some part of the period were removed later. However, the analysis includes those cases because the tests examine cross-sectional data at a broad benchmark period of the late 1970s, rather than make a time series analysis of individual products.

Table 2-2 presents the main NTBs identified for the analysis of this study. In terms of the logit analysis, the dependent variable for protection takes the value 1.0 for each of the sectors listed in the table; for all other sectors the variable is zero.

Several patterns are evident in the protection listed in the table. One is that protection tends to cluster in a limited number of product sectors that are identical across countries. All the major industrial countries except Japan apply a broad range of NTBs against textiles (ISIC 3211–19) and apparel (3220) under the MFA. All except France and Germany have protected footwear (3240). All except Germany and Japan have experienced some protection of radio and television products. Protection is also clustered in the sectors of iron and steel (3710): the United States, France, Germany, Italy, and the United Kingdom; and automobiles (3843): the United States, France, Germany, Italy, and the United Kingdom.

The table also shows that Japan is exceptional in the structure of protection. Japan's nontariff barriers are limited almost wholly to processed foods and tobacco. Although it is possible that administrative guidance or other indirect NTBs affect Japanese imports of the remaining array of manufactured goods, these goods are generally not controlled by direct or voluntary quotas.

The table also indicates that protection is frequently directed toward

Japan (especially in Italy) or toward Korea and Taiwan. The analysis of this study considers that a significant NTB is present even if it affects only one major supplier such as Japan, because not only is the trade from the supplier in question frequently large but also the presence of such a barrier discourages other suppliers from investing in the export activity.

Use of the information on NTB protection in table 2-2 and of the data base on trade and domestic consumption developed in this study makes possible an examination of the fraction of the market for manufactured goods that is affected by major nontariff barriers in each industrial country considered. Table 2-3 shows the percentage of the market for manufactures affected by NTBs. The figures are derived by summing either imports or consumption in sectors affected by NTBs and taking the sum as a percentage of total imports or consumption, respectively. The first column includes imports from all sources. The second column repeats the procedure but incorporates only imports from developing countries. Sectors such as automobiles are included as protected in the second column even though the NTB is against Japan and not against developing countries. Thus, the second column gives the percentage of developing-country exports to the country in question in a sector jeopardized either directly because of nontariff barriers applied to developing countries or indirectly because of protection against other suppliers and the potential extension of that protection to any aggressive new suppliers.

As a check on the import-based figures, the third column of the table states the coverage of NTB protection by indicating the fraction of total apparent consumption of manufactured goods represented by sectors affected by major nontariff barriers. This measure equals the sum of domestic consumption in sectors affected by NTBs divided by total manufactured consumption. The measure is analogous to a weighted tariff average using consumption weights rather than import weights.[18] Consumption weighting is a necessary check on trade weighting because truly restrictive nontariff barriers could choke off imports entirely and

18. In fact, the figures that result from the calculation are the same as those that would result from a consumption-weighted tariff average if the tariff were zero for all sectors without an NTB and 100 percent for all sectors with an NTB. Of course, these figures are not meant to show tariff equivalents, and it is unlikely that the tariff equivalents of the NTBs are all, or even mostly, as high as 100 percent. Instead, table 2-3 represents breadth of NTB coverage, not height of the tariff equivalent of NTBs.

Table 2-2. *Major Nontariff Barriers in Seven Industrial Countries*

Country and ISIC number	Product sector	Nontariff barrier
United States		
3111	Meat	Global quotas and voluntary restraints by some countries on frozen and fresh meat of cattle, goats, and sheep
3112	Dairy	Import quotas by country, primarily affecting cheese, butter, and powdered milk
3118	Sugar	Country quotas until 1973. In 1977–79 variable import fees to offset difference between U.S. and foreign prices
3119	Confectionery	Country quotas on chocolate and candy containing cocoa
3211–15, 3219	Textiles	Country quotas under the Multi-fiber Arrangement (MFA)
3220	Apparel	Country quotas under the MFA
3240	Footwear	Orderly marketing agreements negotiated with Korea and Taiwan, 1977–81
3710	Iron and steel	Trigger-price mechanism for steel imports since 1977; voluntary export restraints existed from 1967 through 1974
3832	Radio, television, and communication equipment	Orderly marketing agreements limiting imports of color televisions from Japan, Korea, and Taiwan
3841	Shipbuilding	Merchant Marine Act of 1920 prohibits use of foreign-built vessels in coastal trade
3843	Motor vehicles	Voluntary export quota on automobiles adopted by Japan in 1981 for three years: 1.68 million units in first year, plus 16.5 percent of market growth in second
Canada[b]		
3211–14	Textiles	Country quotas under the MFA
3220	Apparel	Country quotas under the MFA
3240	Footwear	Global quota (32.5 million pairs) established in 1977
3832	Radio, television, and communication equipment	Voluntary export restriction by Japan on thermionic valves and tubes and transistors
West Germany[c]		
3211–15, 3219	Textiles	European Community country quotas under the MFA
3220	Apparel	European Community country quotas under the MFA

Table 2-2 *(continued)*

Country and ISIC number	Product sector	Nontariff barrier
West Germany (continued)[c]		
3610	Pottery, china, and earthenware	Bilateral quota (Japan) on tableware
3710	Iron and steel	European Community minimum price mechanism for steel; voluntary export restraints for several countries (since 1979)
3843	Motor vehicles	European Community voluntary export restraint by Japan, 1981
France		
3114	Canned fish	Quotas on tuna and sardines
3211–15, 3219	Textiles	European Community country quotas under the MFA
3220	Apparel	European Community country quotas under the MFA
3511	Industrial chemicals (except fertilizers)	Global quota on synthetic organic dyestuffs
3610	Pottery, china, and earthenware	Bilateral quotas on tableware
3691	Structural clay products	Bilateral quotas on tiles
3710	Iron and steel	Bilateral quotas (iron); discretionary licensing (ferroalloys); European Community minimum price system for steel; European Community voluntary export restraints for several countries (since 1979)
3832	Radio, television, and communication equipment	Bilateral quotas and discretionary licensing, radio-telephonic receivers, television receivers, and transistors; prohibition on radios from Taiwan; quota on radios from Korea
3843	Motor vehicles	Export restraint on agreement limiting automobiles from Japan to 3 percent of market
3909	Miscellaneous manufactures	Quotas on umbrellas and toys from Korea; import license on umbrellas from Taiwan
Italy		
3114	Canned fish	Bilateral quotas (Japan) on tuna and sardines
3211–15, 3219	Textiles	Country quotas under the MFA
3240	Footwear	Bilateral quota (Japan)
3529	Chemical products not elsewhere classified	Bilateral quota (Japan) on film
3551	Tires and tubes	Bilateral quotas (Japan)

Table 2-2 *(continued)*

Country and ISIC number	Product sector	Nontariff barrier
Italy (continued)		
3551	Tires and tubes	Bilateral quotas (Japan)
3610	Pottery, china and earthenware	Bilateral quotas (Japan) on tableware
3691	Structural clay products	Bilateral quotas (Japan) on tiles
3710	Iron and steel	European Community minimum price mechanism for steel; European Community voluntary export restraints for several countries (since 1979)
3811	Cutlery, tools, and hardware	Bilateral quotas (Japan) on knives, spoons, and forks
3821	Engines	Bilateral quotas (Japan) on internal combustion piston engines
3832	Radio, television, and communication equipment	Bilateral quotas (Japan) on radio-telephonic and television transmitters and receivers and tubes and valves
3843	Motor vehicles	Bilateral quotas limiting Japanese automobiles to 2,200 units a year
3844	Motorcycles and bicycles	Bilateral quotas (Japan) on motorcycles
United Kingdom		
3211–15, 3219	Textiles	Country quotas under the MFA
3220	Apparel	Country quotas under the MFA
3240	Footwear	Quantitative restrictions on imports from Korea and Taiwan
3710	Iron and steel	European Community minimum price mechanism for steel; European Community voluntary export restraints from several countries (since 1979)

leave the import weights of the restricted sectors disproportionately small, causing import weighting to understate the extent of coverage of NTB protection.

The figures in table 2-3 indicate that the coverage of major NTBs is extensive. In most countries between 25 and 40 percent of the domestic markets for manufactures appear to be affected by such NTBs. The data also suggest the surprising result that the United States currently has the highest coverage (but not necessarily the highest intensity) of NTB protection in manufactures among the seven major industrial countries.

Table 2-2 *(continued)*

Country and ISIC number	Product sector	Nontariff barrier
United Kingdom (continued)		
3832	Radio, television, and communication equipment	State trading in transistorized radio and television receivers; import quotas on black-and-white televisions (Taiwan, Korea)
3843	Motor vehicles	Industry-to-industry agreement to limit Japanese imports to 10 percent of market
Japan		
3111	Meat	Quotas on beef; discretionary licensing
3112	Dairy	State trading on butter; discretionary licensing for milk and cheese
3113	Preserved fruits and vegetables	Discretionary licensing on jams, canned fruits, and juices
3114	Canned fish	Discretionary licensing; voluntary export restraint (Korea) on tuna
3116	Grain mill products	Discretionary licensing of cereal flours and worked cereal grains
3140	Tobacco	State trading
3231	Tanneries and leather finishing	Discretionary licensing
3240	Footwear	Discretionary licensing

Sources: General Agreement on Tariffs and Trade (GATT), working group documents 4900 (1979) and 5090 (1981); Bahram Nowzad, *The Rise in Protectionism* (International Monetary Fund, 1978); Vincent Cable and Ivonia Rebelo, "Britain's Pattern of Specialization in Manufactured Goods with Developing Countries and Trade Protection," Staff Working Paper 425 (World Bank, 1980); European Parliament, *Report on the European Automobile Industry*, December 15, 1980, Document 1-673/80; *Japan Times Weekly*, May 9, 1981; European Community Mission to the United States; Kiyoshi Kawahito, "Japanese Steel in the American Market: Conflict and Causes," *World Economy*, vol. 4 (September 1981), pp. 229–50.

a. International standard industrial classification.

b. Subsequent to the calculations made for this study, Canada obtained limitations on imports of automobiles from Japan.

c. Excludes many restrictions on Eastern European products.

Except for Canada, the estimates show no marked difference when weighting by imports from developing countries as opposed to all sources. Developing countries do not appear to be especially discriminated against, and the burden of NTB protection on their products such as apparel and footwear appears to be broadly comparable to the burden of NTB protection on products produced primarily in industrial countries (especially Japan), such as steel and automobiles.

These data warrant cautious interpretation. They are broadly rather than narrowly stated because they include all imports in a category affected by NTBs even if the actual protection is applied to only one or

Table 2-3. *Proportion of Market for Manufactured Imports Affected by Major Nontariff Barriers, Seven Industrial Countries*[a]
Percent

	Weighting by		
Country	Imports from all sources	Imports from developing countries	Consumption
United States	45.1	43.0	34.1
Canada	10.9	35.3	9.6
West Germany	27.5	30.8	19.5
France	36.5	25.0	27.2
Italy	32.4	29.4	33.7
United Kingdom	25.7	23.8	22.1
Japan	22.1	27.5	7.4

Sources: Table 2-2 and project data bank.
a. Excluding petroleum refineries, 3530. Nontariff barriers are for the period of the late 1970s to 1981. Trade and consumption data are for 1978.

a few supplier countries. This approach is justified by the fact that once a large supplier is restricted in a product market, a cloud of uncertainty is cast over the product, discouraging rapid expansion by other suppliers who must face the prospect of a similar restriction if their supply grows too large.

The difference in protection coverage between the United States and other industrial countries may be overstated by the fact that U.S. nontariff barriers tend to be overt while those in some other countries are sometimes covert. For example, the agreements limiting Japanese automobiles in the markets of France and the United Kingdom have only recently come to light. The estimates in table 2-3 are best interpreted as measures of the coverage of "acknowledged" nontariff barrier protection; insofar as countries like France and Japan tend to have a disproportionately high incidence of disguised protection through administrative guidance or other techniques as is often alleged, the coverage of protection is understated for those countries.[19]

19. Balassa and Balassa have questioned the estimates in table 2-3, and in particular the implication of the table that NTB coverage is higher in the United States than in the European Community and Japan. Bela Balassa and Carol Balassa, "Industrial Protection in the Developed Countries," *The World Economy*, vol. 7, (June 1984), pp. 179–96. Ironically, their own estimates find the same result. When their estimate of increased protection in 1981 is added to their base in 1980, by their own data the coverage of import restrictions in 1981 was 32.7 percent of the market for U.S.

Another consideration suggesting that the U.S. nontariff barriers are overstated relative to those of other countries is that imports of manufactures from developing countries have grown much more rapidly in the U.S. market than in other industrial countries (chapter 1). To be sure, factors other than relative NTBs may have accounted for import trends: macroeconomic policy and microeconomic performance, and strategies of multinational corporations. Also NTBs on footwear and television sets began near the end of the decade after rapid import growth had already occurred, and import growth in textiles and apparel was more rapid before the 1977 tightening of the MFA. Nevertheless, without precise measures of the tariff equivalents of nontariff barriers, actual import trends do provide an alternative measure for revealed protection.

---

manufactures, 26.0 percent in the European Community, and 15.7 percent in Japan (their table 4, share of total consumption basis.) Their text discussion of the difference between the two studies inappropriately focuses on 1980 rather than 1981 (the appropriate year for comparison with the estimates here), thereby missing the large increment in U.S. protection caused by the introduction of automobile quotas.

The authors omit steel from U.S. protection before 1982 despite the presence of the trigger-price mechanism. They also argue that the estimates here (table 2-3) fail to take into account Community protection, under the Common Agricultural Policy (CAP), of milk products, pig meat, beef, veal, and processed fruits and vegetables (by communication with the authors). However, the GATT data base (table 2-2) generally omits reference to Community protection in these sectors. The main effect of the CAP is to protect raw materials rather than processed foods, although some ambiguity between the two can arise in a comprehensive definition of manufactures. In any event, exclusion of food, beverage, and tobacco products (ISIC 3111–40) yields little change in the results here. On this basis, the shares of manufactures protected are (in percent): United States, 32.4; Canada, 11.8; Germany, 23.6; France, 33.2; Italy, 39.9; United Kingdom, 28.3; and Japan, 0.4 (using consumption weights).

The Balassas also seem overzealous in including automobiles in the sectors protected by Japan (on grounds of inspection standards). It strains credulity to treat the Japanese auto market as equally protected (by minor harassment, if any, through inspections) as those of the United States and Europe (where explicit voluntary quota limits exist), despite the obvious revealed comparative advantage of Japan in automobiles.

Finally, the Balassas attempt to measure severity of protection (inversely) by import penetration, and conclude that because of its low ratio of imports to consumption (in sectors identified as protected, including automobiles) Japan is more highly protected than the United States and the European Community. Yet this approach fails to recognize that because of its low endowment of natural resources Japan's natural comparative advantage is in manufactures, and low import penetration there is to be expected. This point has been cogently argued by the Council of Economic Advisers and empirically supported by Saxonhouse. Council of Economic Advisers, *Economic Report of the President* (Government Printing Office, 1983), pp. 51–76; and Saxonhouse, "Micro- and Macroeconomics of Foreign Sales to Japan."

The U.S. market coverage in table 2-3 is heavily influenced by automobiles (10.4 percent, consumption basis) and iron and steel (5.7 percent). Yet NTB protection in these two sectors appears to be considerably less restrictive than the protection of the same sectors in Europe. The 1981 U.S. restrictions on Japanese automobiles were designed to reduce imports by approximately one-fourteenth, which still left a market share for Japan of more than 20 percent; by contrast, in Italy, France, and the United Kingdom, Japanese automobiles were restricted to much smaller market shares (table 2-2). Similarly, in steel the U.S. trigger-price mechanism was not protective enough to prevent continued surges in imports, and by January 1982 the steel industry proceeded to file antidumping suits against European suppliers even though the actions meant that the U.S. government would suspend the trigger-price mechanism.[20] In Europe, by contrast, import quotas supporting sectoral adjustment programs for steel were presumably more restrictive in their impact.

When consumption-based weighting is used, the estimates in table 2-3 show the United States at approximately the same degree of NTB coverage as France and Italy. Ironically, the import-weighting basis means that, between two countries with identical sectors covered by nontariff barriers, the proportion of market covered will appear higher for the country with more liberal NTBs—because that country will import relatively more in these categories and therefore they will attain a higher weight in total imports.

In short, for several reasons it would be wrong to conclude from table 2-3 that the United States is substantially more protective than the other industrial countries, although the estimates do suggest (contrary to the common view) that the U.S. market is no more open than markets of other major countries. In general, despite their limitations, the estimates of table 2-3 demonstrate that nontariff barrier protection of manufactures is substantial and that, among the seven major industrial countries, protection is relatively comparable.

The eventual adoption of voluntary quotas on European steel exported to the U.S. market, in the fall of 1982, did place the U.S. market on a more restricted basis than before. Even then, however, quotas emerged because the Europeans preferred them to the countervailing duties that otherwise would have been imposed to offset subsidies. Intra-European differences in the extent of subsidies meant that the bulk of countervailing

20. Jane Seaberry, "Steel Firms to File Import Complaints," *Washington Post,* January 9, 1982.

penalties would fall on the less efficient, more heavily subsidized European countries, and voluntary quotas permitted an allocation of trade limitation that was more acceptable to those countries.[21]

The Effect of Protection on Trade

The question whether existing nontariff barrier protection actually affects exports of manufactures from developing countries warrants consideration before analyzing the determinants of protection or projecting prospective future protection. If protection could be circumvented (because of loose enforcement, for example), little cause for concern about protection, present or future, would exist. However, the available evidence indicates that protection has a clear effect on imports of manufactures from developing countries, substantially cutting back their growth rates.

Table 2-4 summarizes the reductions in import growth caused by the imposition of nontariff barriers in eleven instances. The growth of imports almost always fell sharply after the barrier was imposed. The evidence in the table indicates that these barriers must be taken seriously as strong prospective influences on growth of trade in the products involved.

After the United States imposed orderly marketing agreements limiting footwear imports from Korea and Taiwan in 1977, the growth rate of these imports in real terms fell from an annual average of 30.4 percent to an annual decline of 1.5 percent. The figures on steel imports in the United States reflect subperiods of varying protection. In the early 1970s when quotas were in place, steel imports were actually declining. After removal of quotas in the mid-1970s, imports grew at a brisk rate of 8.3 percent a year. But after the trigger-price mechanism was implemented in late 1977, they slowed down to only 2.6 percent annual growth.

For apparel, the table shows a sharp deceleration in real value growth after the tightening of the MFA in 1977. Notably, even after the tightening, real value continued to grow at a surprisingly strong 6 percent for imports from the Far East into the European Community. This performance reflects upgrading of products to more sophisticated goods.

21. C. Fred Bergsten and William R. Cline, "Trade Policy in the 1980s," *Policy Analyses in International Economics*, no. 3 (Washington, D.C.: Institute for International Economics, 1982).

Table 2-4. *Effect of Nontariff Barriers on Growth of Imports, Selected Products*

Importing country or area and product	Supplier	Period	Presence of NTB	Annual growth rate of real imports (percent)
United States				
Footwear	Korea, Taiwan	1971–77	No	30.4
		1978–81	Yes	−1.5
Television receivers	Japan	1971–77	No	6.8
		1978–80	Yes	−7.4
	Korea, Taiwan	1971–78	No	26.2
		1979–81	Yes	−1.2
Textiles	All	1971–74	Yes	−6.2
		1971–77	Yes	−4.8
		1978–81	Yes	−1.6
Apparel	All	1971–74	Yes	2.9
		1971–77	Yes	8.1
		1978–81	Tighter	−1.8
Steel	All	1971–73	Yes	−3.3
		1974ª–77	No	8.3
		1978–81	Yes	2.6
European Community				
Textiles	Hong Kong,	1971–77	Yes	10.0
	Korea, Taiwan	1978–80	Tighter	2.9
Apparel	Hong Kong,	1971–77	Yes	16.9
	Korea, Taiwan	1978–80	Tighter	6.0
Canada				
Footwear	All	1971–77	No	7.1
		1977–81	Yes	−0.7
United Kingdom				
Footwear	Taiwan	1971–77	No	45.0
		1977–80	Yes	8.7
	Korea	1973–79	No	57.5
		1979–80	Yes	−19.1

Source: Calculated from table F-2, appendix F.
a. 1973 base for growth.

If physical volumes are considered instead, the decline is more vivid. Thus, Martin Wolf has calculated that the physical volume of European Community imports of MFA products (including both textiles and apparel) from countries covered by agreements (excluding those with preferential treatment) grew by only 0.9 percent annually in 1976–81.[22]

22. Martin Wolf, "Managed Trade in Practice: Implications of the Textile Arrangements," in Cline, ed., *Trade Policy in the 1980s*, p. 467.

Even when product upgrading is allowed for, however, growth of apparel imports has clearly been hurt by the tightening of the MFA. Growth in the real value of imports of apparel fell from 8.1 percent annually in 1971–77 in the United States to − 1.8 percent in 1978–81 (all sources); in the European Community the decline was from 16.9 percent to 6 percent (from Hong Kong, Korea, and Taiwan).

Table 2-4 shows a similar drop in growth rates for imports of textiles into the European Community from the Far East. In the United States, however, textile imports have been declining in real terms for a full decade, reflecting not only early protection but also the process of capital-intensive modernization and increasing competitiveness of U.S. production.

The analysis that follows derives quantitative models to predict the presence or absence of nontariff barriers by sector. Ideally, such models could also gauge the predicted severity of these barriers and their resulting impact on growth rates of imports of the products in question. Such a model would permit the projection of future growth of exports of manufactures from developing countries with and without predicted protection. In the absence of data permitting differentiation of nontariff barriers by severity and of methods for converting such information into changes in import growth rates expected from new protection, the analysis that follows uses a more simple binary prediction of the presence or absence of NTBs. It does so under the assumption, justified by the evidence just examined, that the presence of a significant NTB causes a substantial slowdown in the growth rate of imports of the product in question and that new protection when it arises is indeed a cause for concern.

The Level of Aggregation

The basic level of aggregation used below for quantitative analysis of the determinants of protection is the four-digit level of the ISIC. At this level manufacturing industries (including processed foods, beverages, and tobacco) are divided into eighty sectors (excluding oil refineries).

The practical reasons for the choice of the four-digit ISIC as the level of aggregation are that, first, standardized international data are available only on the basis of the ISIC as used by the United Nations and, second, the four-digit level is the most detailed for which internationally comparable data are available. Without a major research project devoted to further development of a new data base on protection and industry characteristics, there is little alternative to analysis using the four-digit ISIC.[23]

An important question is whether the four-digit level of the ISIC corresponds to the appropriate aggregation for analysis of the political economy of protection. A review of the sectors suggests that this level of aggregation is usually appropriate. Each sector tends to represent a politically meaningful grouping. For example, the category 3240 contains precisely the nonrubber footwear sector that has been the object of protection in several countries. Sector 3710, iron and steel basic industries, corresponds well to the politically meaningful grouping of steel interests, so important in U.S. and European protection. Sector 3843, manufacture of motor vehicles, is heavily dominated by automobiles, making it appropriate for the political grouping involved in automobile protection, although for the United States the analysis below uses data for the slightly narrower sector of automobiles per se.

Textiles and apparel constitute an important exception to the general appropriateness of the four-digit ISIC for analysis. There are six separate categories for textiles (3211–15 and 3219) and a sector for apparel (3220) in the four-digit ISIC; yet for purposes of public policy this sector has long acted as a unified whole. These various sectors have obtained protection primarily because of a firm political coalition between the textile industry as a whole and the apparel industry. Spokesmen for both industries consider their products to be in a single, broadly defined "textile" sector for purposes of lobbying. Thus, in response to questioning from a congressional committee about the need of the textile sector for protection in light of its favorable trade balance, in contrast to the trade deficit for apparel, the president of the American Textile Manufacturers Institute declared: "This is a total industry. We would have no textile industry if we had no apparel industry. We would have no apparel industry if we had no textile industry."[24] The same political coalition

23. The World Bank has undertaken a major research effort along these lines, but at the time of the preparation of this study the results of the project were not publicly available.
24. "Statement of Robert S. Small," in *Exemption of Certain Products from Tariff Reductions Negotiated in the Multilateral Trade Negotiations (MTN)*, Hearing before the Subcommittee on Trade of the House Committee on Ways and Means, 95 Cong. 2 sess. (GPO, 1978), p. 53.

between textiles and apparel appears to exist in the United Kingdom.[25] In view of the cohesion of the entire textile-apparel industry for purposes of protection seeking, the statistical tests in the analysis below treat all these sectors (3211–20) as a single sector.

Despite the general appropriateness of the four-digit ISIC for analysis as adjusted by consolidation of textiles and apparel, any level of aggregation chosen tends to overstate the coverage of protection in some cases and miss instances of protection in others. The approach adopted here designates a four-digit sector as protected if its most important products are affected by NTBs. For a small protected industry, such as that of clothespins, protection will escape notice in the method used here because this subsector will be too small to qualify the parent sector (wood products) as protected. In the other direction, a four-digit sector classified as protected may include a considerable set of unprotected activities, overstating the scope of protection.

Potentially the most serious instance of overstatement of protection is in television sets. The four-digit ISIC category containing television sets is 3882, "manufacture of radio, television, and communication equipment and apparatus." This sector includes products from twenty-one five-digit SITC (standard international trade classification) categories, and only one of these (72410) represents television receivers per se (and even this category includes unprotected black-and-white television sets as well as protected color televisions). On the basis of data from the office of the U.S. Trade Representative[26] and the United Nations data base used in this study, in 1976 U.S. imports of color television sets accounted for 14 percent of the total imports allocated to ISIC sector 3832. In this instance, then, the coverage of protection measured is excessive. It does not necessarily follow that the use of the full sector as a data observation of the presence of NTBs seriously biases the protection functions estimated, however. In particular, narrower specification limited to television sets would mean a higher import-penetration ratio and a lower magnitude for size of labor force. The prediction of an NTB could still be consistent with even the redefined and narrowed sectoral data considering the expected influences of import

25. Vincent Cable and Ivonia Rebelo, "Britain's Pattern of Specialization in Manufactured Goods with Developing Countries and Trade Protection," World Bank Staff Working Paper 425 (World Bank, 1980), p. 52.
26. See table 2-5.

Table 2-5. *U.S. Protection under the Escape Clause (Section 201)*

Year	Product	Import value (millions of dollars)	Action	ISIC number	Inclusion in study as having nontariff barrier
1976	Ceramic tableware	106	Temporary increase in tariff	3610	No
1976	Specialty steel (stainless and tools)	213	Orderly marketing agreements	3811	No
1977	Footwear	981[a]	Orderly marketing agreements	3240	Yes
1977	Television sets and parts	821[b]	Orderly marketing agreements	3832	Yes
1978	Citizens' band transceivers	428[c]	Temporary increase in tariff	3832	Yes
1978	High carbon ferrochromium	70[c]	Temporary increase in tariff	3710	Yes
1978	Bolts, nuts, and large screws of iron or steel	307[c]	Temporary increase in tariff	3710 3819	Yes No
1979	Clothespins	3[c]	Global quota	3319	No
1980	Nonelectric cookware	155[d]	Temporary increase in tariff	3610, 3620, 3819	No
1980	Mushrooms	97[e]	Temporary increase in tariff	3113	No

Sources: Office of the U.S. Trade Representative, Trade Action Monitoring System, October 19, 1982; UN, *Classification of Commodities by Industrial Origin: Relationship of the Standard International Trade Classification to the International Standard Industrial Classification*, series M, no. 43, 2d ed. (UN, 1966); and U.S. Bureau of the Census, *U.S. Imports for Consumption and General Imports: TSUSA Commodity by Country of Origin*, FT 246, various years.
    a. 1974.
    b. 1976.
    c. 1977.
    d. 1979.
    e. 1978.

penetration and labor force size. Such influences are in fact confirmed in the statistical tests.

The other direction of bias occurs for very small product sectors that are protected but escape inclusion at the four-digit level of the ISIC. To examine the possible importance of this bias, table 2-5 reports all cases of protection taken under U.S. escape clause proceedings (section 201 of the U.S. trade legislation) from 1976 to 1982. These cases are judged by the U.S. International Trade Commission to determine whether "injury" exists warranting special action; for affirmative findings, the president determines what action if any should be taken, in view not only of industry conditions but also of the broader public interest. Aside from the special regimes of protection that have emerged in major sectors such as textiles and apparel, steel, automobiles, and some agricultural products, the "escape clause" mechanism is the only means of obtaining protection in the United States—assuming that the application of countervailing and antidumping duties to offset foreign export subsidies and sales below domestic price or cost are measures of fair trade enforcement, not protection.

Table 2-5 compares the cases of escape clause protection with the sectoral treatment of protection in this study. Of the ten cases of actual escape clause protection since 1976, this study accurately captures five. That is, these five are covered by the sectors identified here as having significant nontariff barrier protection. The other five cases—ceramic tableware, specialty steel, clothespins, nonelectric cookware, and mushrooms—are cases of protection omitted from the analysis here because they are subsectors that are too small to warrant designation of the parent four-digit ISIC category as being significantly protected by an NTB.

The five sectors accurately captured in the protection data base used here account for 84 percent of the total value of imports represented in table 2-5; the five sectors not captured account for only 16 percent.[27] Accordingly, though there are some small subsectors that escape inclusion in the data set using four-digit ISIC aggregation, their importance is extremely limited and becomes minimal when protection in textiles and apparel, steel, automobiles, sugar, and other sectors (see table 2-1) is added to that from escape clause actions (table 2-5). In sum, analysis at the four-digit level of the ISIC appears not only convenient from the standpoint of data availability but also broadly appropriate from a political-economic perspective, with the important adjustment of consolidation of textiles and apparel.[28]

Data for Statistical Tests

The nontariff barriers identified in table 2-2 provide the data base on the dependent variable of NTB protection for the logit tests. This depen-

27. The data for different years in table 2-5 are converted to constant dollars of 1977 for this calculation by using the U.S. wholesale price index as a deflator.

28. Note also that insofar as the four-digit level was improper for analysis, the statistical results would tend to achieve a low degree of explanation and significance. Because the final tests conducted below achieve relatively high statistical explanation and significance, they would appear to capture meaningful patterns of political-economic behavior that cannot be gainsaid on grounds of uncertainty about the appropriate level of aggregation.

dent variable is 1 for a sector in a given country listed in the table; it is zero otherwise. The data for the independent variables in the tests are drawn primarily from UN sources, supplemented by special data sources for the United States. All the variables are at the four-digit ISIC level.

The first variable, the import-penetration ratio for imports from all sources ($X1$), is taken from the import-penetration data base developed in this study, derived from UN trade and production data (chapter 1 and appendix B). The year 1978, the most recent year available in the data base, is used for this explanatory variable. The second explanatory variable, the ratio of exports to domestic production ($X2$), is also taken from the trade and production data base for 1978. For the variable change in import penetration ($X11$), the tests apply the difference between the total import-penetration ratios in 1978 and in 1970, again using the project data base on import penetration.

For each country examined, UN data are used for the following variables: $X4$ (value added per worker), $X8$ (ratio of unskilled to total employment), $X9$ (share of manufacturing labor), $X10$ (wage rate), and $X12$ (growth rate). For these variables, data for 1977 at the three-digit ISIC level are disaggregated to the four-digit level by using proportions reported in the four-digit UN data available for 1973.[29] For variables $X4$, $X8$, and $X10$, the data are normalized and expressed as ratios to the industry averages to facilitate computation of the logit function by iteration and to enhance comparison of results across countries. Thus, the wage variable is expressed as the sectoral wage divided by the average wage for all manufacturing, and so forth. The growth rate, variable $X12$, is expressed as a fraction (for example, 5 percent growth is 0.05).

Physical capital per worker ($X5$), available only for the United States, is taken from a special capital stock data base maintained by the U.S. Bureau of Labor Statistics.[30] The data refer to total stock of plant and

29. The 1977 data are from UN Statistical Office, *Yearbook of Industrial Statistics: 1978 Edition, vol. 1* (UN, 1980). The 1973 data are from United Nations, *The 1973 World Programme of Industrial Statistics: Summary of Data from Selected Countries* (UN, 1979). (For the United States, these data refer to 1972.) Proportions for four-digit detail within three-digit categories are calculated separately (from the 1973 data) for each variable—employment, wages, value added, number of operatives—and are applied to the 1977 three-digit data to estimate 1977 four-digit data. Growth rates are for 1968–77 and refer to the three-digit level. It is assumed that all four-digit components of a three-digit group had growth rates identical to that of the parent three-digit category.

30. U.S. Bureau of Labor Statistics, Office of Economic Growth.

equipment in 1972 at constant 1972 dollars, on a net basis that adjusts cumulated past investment not only for discarded assets but also for reduction in potential efficiency through aging. The capital data are at the four-digit and (principally) three-digit levels of the U.S. standard industrial classification. Corresponding employment data at the four-digit level of the SIC are obtained from the 1972 Census of Manufactures.[31] Where necessary, the capital data for three-digit SIC are disaggregated to four-digit SIC in proportion to four-digit shipment values reported in the 1972 Census of Manufactures. The capital and labor data at the four-digit SIC level are transformed into four-digit ISIC estimates by using the correspondence of the U.S. Department of Commerce. The capital–labor ratios are then calculated and normalized into relative ratios by dividing by the average capital–labor ratio for manufacturing as a whole.

For human capital ($X6$), the four-digit ISIC data for the United States in 1972 are used.[32] These data report total number of employees and total wages, as well as number of operatives and total wages of operatives. Human capital in each four-digit sector is estimated on the assumption that the wage for unskilled labor in the sector equals the average wage for operatives. Annual return to human capital, or the component of skills in the wage bill, is then calculated as the difference between total wages and the wage bill that would have been paid if all employees had received only the average wage for operatives (unskilled labor). This annual return to human capital is then capitalized to obtain the value of the stock of human capital. A 10 percent discount rate is used for this capitalization. In short, human capital stock is estimated as ten times the difference between actual wages and the wage bill that would have been paid if all employees had earned only the unskilled wage for the sector. Human capital per worker ($X6$) equals total human capital stock divided by the number of employees in the sector.

The sum of physical capital per worker ($X5$) and human capital per worker ($X6$) equals total capital per worker ($X7$). As with variables $X4$, $X5$, $X6$, $X8$, and $X10$, the total capital variable ($X7$) is normalized and expressed as a ratio to the overall average for manufacturing industry as a whole.

31. U.S. Department of Commerce, *1972 Census of Manufactures, Subject Series, General Summary* (GPO, 1975).

32. UN, *The 1973 World Programme of Industrial Statistics*, pp. 494–95. The year 1972 is used for comparability with the 1972 data on capital per worker.

Because physical capital per worker is available only for the United States, variable $X5$ is not estimated for other countries. The U.S. estimates of total capital per worker ($X7$, normalized) are applied to tests for other countries, under the assumption that sectoral differences in capital-labor combinations are relatively constant across industrial countries. Moreover, for countries other than the United States, the human capital variable ($X6$) is omitted. The influence of skill intensity is left to the variable of the ratio of unskilled labor to total labor ($X8$).[33]

The variable representing industrial concentration ($X3$) is calculated as follows. The 1972 U.S. Census of Manufactures reports the fraction of shipments represented by the four largest firms in each four-digit SIC industry.[34] These data are used, along with the U.S. Department of Commerce correspondence between SIC and ISIC, to calculate indexes of concentration at the level of four-digit ISIC industries. Specifically, the fraction of shipments coming from the four largest firms in a four-digit SIC category is applied to that category's total shipments to obtain the value of shipments from the top four firms, which may be called "affected" shipments. These values are then classified into groupings of four-digit ISIC, which are aggregated when necessary. Then the corresponding values of total shipments are obtained for four-digit ISIC categories. Finally, the "affected" shipments (that is, those from the top four SIC firms) are divided by total shipments to yield an index of concentration at the four-digit level of ISIC. This index is essentially a weighted average of four-firm concentration ratios for all SIC sectors constituting a given ISIC sector, with weighting by value of shipments.[35] Broadly, the index tells the fraction of shipment values in the ISIC category affected by potentially noncompetitive behavior by virtue of being produced by the four largest firms within the narrower, component SIC categories. The index of concentration, already stated as a fraction, is not normalized across industry sectors.

33. The primary purpose of a separate estimate of human capital per worker is to permit estimation of total capital per worker, physical and human. Otherwise the skill ratio ($X8$) should be a satisfactory measure of human capital intensity.

34. U.S. Department of Commerce, *1972 Census of Manufactures*, vol. 2, pp. SR2-6 to SR2-47.

35. Because the four-digit ISIC level is more aggregative than the four-digit SIC level, this index does not, in general, mean that the four largest firms of an ISIC grouping account for the fraction of shipments given by the concentration index.

Protection Function Estimates

Table 2-6 reports the initial estimates of protection functions for the United States, Canada, and the United Kingdom. For Japan, almost all the NTBs are in processed foods and tobacco. The simple explanation of the political power of farmers would seem to dominate the Japanese case. The measured variables for the processed agricultural products are not likely to capture the relevant differences among sectors and determine a meaningful protection function for Japan, because the political strength of farmers derives from their numbers in farm activity itself (not a part of the data set), not in the processing industries using farm inputs. For Germany, Italy, and France, inadequate data detail prevents estimation of a function at the four-digit ISIC level, although for France estimation at the three-digit level is relatively successful.

The initial, full-model estimates shown in table 2-6 provide interesting information on the relative importance of various independent variables, and their general statistical performance is not bad. However, the "percentage explanation" must be interpreted with care. Even a totally random model should be able to achieve 50 percent explanation[36] (correct choice of a binary decision half of the time), so that an explanation on the order of 90 percent is not as impressive as it would be in normal regression analysis (where a random-chance model would tend to give zero percentage explanation adjusted for degrees of freedom). More important, the explanatory power of the models reported in table 2-6 is relatively poor in predicting for actual NTB cases whether an NTB exists, and improved estimates are possible with model modifications. For policy purposes it is crucial to predict accurately cases of actual NTBs because the whole objective of forward-looking analysis is to design trade policy with a realistic view of possible protectionist obstacles in the future. This purpose would be thwarted if a model were chosen that had a high degree of general explanation but completely failed to predict the cases in which NTBs exist. The distribution of errors

36. Of course, if one category achieves, for instance, 90 percent explanation, an explanation for the remaining category of 50 percent would mean far better than random performance. Thus, in the three-country case in table 2-6, with 98.7 percent of non-NTBs explained, total performance is far better than a random 50 percent, even though for NTB cases explanation is only 47.4 percent.

Table 2-6. *Logit Functions for Nontariff Barrier Protection,*
Initial Estimates[a]

Variable	United States	Canada	United Kingdom	All three countries[b]
Constant	−1.49	−3.77	−5.87	−8.57
	(−0.21)	(−0.81)	(−0.59)	(−2.26)
Demand				
X1 Import penetration	1.62	10.15	0.07	4.58
	(0.34)	(1.75)	(0.01)	(1.47)
X2 Export/output	−12.33	−24.17	−4.70	−10.98
	(−1.22)	(−1.60)	(−0.64)	(−2.15)
X3 Concentration	4.46	c	c	c
	(1.36)			
Comparative advantage				
X4 Relative value added	−2.87	−1.41	−5.21	−7.16
per worker	(−1.22)	(−0.26)	(−1.15)	(−2.38)
X5 Relative physical	−625.70	c	c	c
capital per worker	(−0.14)			
X6 Relative total human	−437.70	c	c	c
capital per worker	(−0.14)			
X7 Relative capital per	1060.20	−1.21	0.58	0.57
worker	(0.14)	(−0.26)	(0.29)	(0.39)
X8 Skill ratio	2.28	6.93	6.34	6.03
	(0.48)	(1.75)	(0.85)	(2.04)
Supply				
X9 Share of manufacturing	52.28	45.41	53.03	79.31
labor force	(1.93)	(1.13)	(1.74)	(3.44)
X10 Relative wage rate	1.30	−2.75	1.40	4.60
	(0.46)	(−0.63)	(0.40)	(1.36)
X11 Change in import	−7.22	−16.80	2.79	0.75
penetration	(−0.74)	(−1.47)	(0.49)	(0.15)
X12 Growth rate[d]	10.03	−56.20	−50.54	−26.03
	(0.72)	(−1.68)	(−1.06)	(−1.52)
Percentage explanation	86.1	93.2	91.4	93.3
Total				
Nontariff barriers	37.5	42.9	60.0	47.4
Others	98.4	98.5	96.7	98.7
Significance level (percent)[e]	1.0	1.0	1.0	1.0

Source: Author's calculations.
a. The numbers in parentheses are *t*-statistics. Statistical significance at the 95 percent level: *t* above 1.96; at the 90 percent level: *t* above 1.65.
b. Country dummy variables were also included, but were not significant. Their coefficients were: Canada, 0.97 (1.1); United Kingdom, 0.46 (0.40).
c. Variable omitted in model estimated.
d. Note that growth rate is for 1968–77.
e. Based on chi-squared distribution of the likelihood ratio.

between the classes with nontariff barriers and those without is discussed further below.

The initial estimates for the United States[37] show the right sign on the coefficients for import penetration ($X1$), the export–output ratio ($X2$), the value added variable ($X4$), the skill variable ($X8$), and the labor variable ($X9$). The positive sign on concentration ($X3$) indicates some support for the hypothesis that industry concentration facilitates protection by making it easier to lobby successfully and reduces the problem of free-riders within the industry. However, the initial U.S. estimates show the wrong sign on several variables: relative wage ($X10$), change in penetration ($X11$), and growth rate ($X12$). The correct signs on physical capital per worker ($X5$) and human capital per worker ($X6$) are offset by the wrong sign on total capital per worker ($X7$).

More generally, the weakness of the initial U.S. estimates is shown by the fact that only one variable, share of labor force ($X9$), has a statistically significant coefficient at the 5 percent level (based on the *t*-statistic). Moreover, only 37.5 percent of the cases with NTBs, in contrast to almost all the cases without NTBs, are predicted accurately. These initial estimates show the importance of the labor-share variable, and they provide mild support for some of the other hypotheses—in particular that concerning concentration. But for more reliable estimates, additional tests and improvements are necessary.

The initial results for Canada are somewhat better.[38] They show the correct signs for all variables except the change in import penetration ($X11$). Also, the significance levels of the estimates (shown by *t*-statistics) are relatively higher for five of the variables. Again, however, the success in predicting the cases in which NTBs exist is relatively low.

For the United Kingdom the initial results show lower statistical

37. For the United States, the sector for transportation equipment (3843) is replaced by a special sector for automobiles. For this special sector, data from the U.S. International Trade Commission are used for import penetration, export–output ratio (both for January–June, 1980), change in import-penetration ratio (1975–80), and growth rate (1964–70 to 1978–79). The remaining variables are those calculated for sector 3843 from the normal sources. Also for the United States, sector 3232 (furs) is omitted for lack of data, and sector 3530 (petroleum refineries) is excluded because oil is an atypical sector. These two sectors (3232 and 3530) are also omitted in the tests for Canada and the United Kingdom.

38. For Canada, because of the consolidation of certain sectors into more aggregated groupings in the UN data on industry characteristics, the following sectors are omitted (and represented in other, merged groups): ISIC 3812, 3821, 3823, 3824, 3844, and 3902. There are seventy-three sectoral observations for Canada.

significance for most variables.[39] The important policy variable, the import-penetration ratio, shows minimal influence on protection. As in the case of the initial U.S. results, the only strong variable (based on the t-statistic) is the share of labor in the total manufacturing labor force ($X9$).

Table 2-6 also presents a pooled function for all three countries. This function achieves correct signs for all the variables except the total capital-labor variable ($X7$) and the relative wage ($X10$). Moreover, significance levels are higher for several variables.

The results in table 2-6 show a certain regularity in the sizes of coefficients across countries—especially for the skill variable ($X8$) and the labor variable ($X9$). Furthermore, the pooled function contains country dummy variables, but they are not statistically significant. The implication of both these results is that no country among the three is significantly more protective than the other two, given the underlying economic forces in each country. Interestingly, this inference is consistent with the tentative conclusion reached earlier on the broadly comparable extent of NTB protection among the industrial countries.

One source of the lack of statistical significance in the initial estimates (table 2-6) is the problem of collinearity, or very close relationship between certain independent variables, which makes it statistically difficult to ascribe the dominant influence to any one of them. Closer examination of this problem, with the use of U.S. data, shows a high correlation among the following independent variables: value added per worker ($X4$), physical capital per worker ($X5$), total capital per worker ($X7$), and wage rate ($X10$), as shown in table F-1 in appendix F. In addition, industry concentration is highly correlated with value added per worker, physical capital per worker, and the wage rate. Partially as a result of this collinearity, this complex of variables—primarily, alternative specifications of the comparative advantage influence ($X4$, $X5$, $X7$)—tends to drop out in the final protection functions estimated. The exception is in the pooled three-country model in which the increased number of observations sufficiently offsets collinearity at the national

---

39. For the United Kingdom, aggregation problems in the UN data on industry characteristics require omission of the following sectors (replaced by other, merged groups): ISIC 3114, 3691, 3813, 3819, 3849, and 3852. In addition, classification difficulties yielded unacceptable import-penetration ratios (below zero or above unity) for ISIC 3131, 3839, and 3901, which were excluded from the tests. There are seventy sectoral observations for the United Kingdom.

level to permit statistical significance for two of the comparative advantage variables (value added per worker, $X4$, and skill ratio per labor force, $X8$; table 2-6).

The problem of collinearity, especially among alternative measures of comparative advantage, means that the models estimated here may not fully capture the true influence of these variables and may correspondingly attribute excessive influence to those remaining variables found to be significant when the model is pared down to include fewer independent variables to avoid collinearity. It is important to consider the possible policy bias if overattribution to the selected variables is indeed a problem. Fortunately, if there is a bias from this source, its correction would tend to strengthen rather than undermine the policy conclusions of this study.

Foreshadowing the analysis of chapter 3, the projection of future exports from developing countries, as applied to the protection function estimates of this chapter, reveals that relatively limited new protection is likely to arise in the coming decade. If the protection functions estimated here are biased by exclusion of collinear variables, the result would be to overestimate the influence of the final chosen variables after excluding the nonsignificant collinear variables. For purposes of the policy analysis of chapter 3, the key variable is the import-penetration ratio. Increased future protection is examined by applying the projected increase in import penetration (caused by growth of developing-country exports) to the protection functions estimated in this chapter. If the coefficient relating protection to import penetration is overstated by exclusion of other variables (collinear with each other), then correction of this coefficient—if possible—would tend to show protection less responsive to import penetration. In that event, the incidence of new cases of future protection, as examined in chapter 3, would be found to be even more limited, reinforcing the policy conclusions. Thus, although collinearity may pose a problem for the precise allocation of influence among individual variables in the protection functions themselves, it would not appear to distort the eventual policy conclusions that are the principal focus of this study.

Alternative tests yielded more reliable estimates of the protection functions.[40] The best estimates found are reported in table 2-7. The

40. Typically three or four tests were conducted per country, on the basis of inclusion of the variables showing the highest significance in the initial, full model. Note that the risk of obtaining spurious significance (through "data mining") would become substantial

Table 2-7. *Logit Functions for Nontariff Barrier Protection, Best Estimates*[a]

Variable	United States[b]	Canada	United Kingdom[b,c]	France[d]	West Germany[d]	United States, United Kingdom, and Canada
Constant	−5.15	−4.26	−3.78	−5.20	−4.60	−5.88
	(−3.7)	(−1.2)	(−0.1)	(−2.0)	(−2.2)	(−4.1)
X1 Import penetration	8.00	4.69	0.44	9.94	7.96	4.06
	(1.9)	(1.2)	(0.1)	(1.3)	(1.7)	(1.9)
X2 Export/output	e	−13.97	e	e	e	−6.87
		(−1.3)				(2.3)
X4 Relative value	e	−3.89	e	e	e	−3.05
added per worker		(−0.81)				(2.6)
X7 Relative total capital	e	0.43	e	e	e	e
per worker		(0.15)				
X8 Skill ratio	e	6.09	e	e	e	5.00
		(1.7)				(3.4)
X9 Share of manufac-	82.36	45.08	52.76	30.78	20.97	59.20
turing labor force	(2.7)	(1.2)	(2.7)	(1.8)	(1.4)	(4.3)
X10 Relative wage rate	e	−0.92	e	e	e	e
		(−0.23)				
X12 Growth rate	e	−35.08	e	e	e	e
		(−1.3)				
Critical probability						
(percent)	30.0	35.0	45.0	40.0	20.0	30.0
Percentage explanation						
Total	93.0	89.7	89.6	88.9	83.3	91.3
Nontariff barriers	66.7	57.1	40.0	66.7	100.0	62.5
Others	96.1	93.0	95.3	100.0	78.9	95.3
Significance level						
(percent)[f]	1.0	1.0	1.0	1.0	1.5	1.0

Source: Author's calculations.
a. The numbers in parentheses are *t*-statistics.
b. Non-food; textiles-apparel consolidated.
c. Omits computers (3825) and aircraft (3845).
d. Calculated at three-digit international standard industrial classification (ISIC) level.
e. Variable omitted in model estimate.
f. Based on chi-squared distribution of the likelihood ratio.

improved estimates omit several variables that are statistically insignificant in the initial, full model.

In addition, improved results in table 2-7 are obtained through aggregation of all textiles and apparel (ISIC 3211–20) into a single sector

only if the ratio of tests examined to those reported were much higher. Thus, if twenty tests were conducted for each "best result" reported, spurious significance at the 5 percent level could be expected, because the meaning of this level of significance is that in one out of twenty cases purely random processes could generate the (erroneous) rejection of the hypothesis that the independent and dependent variables are unrelated.

for the United States and the United Kingdom. When the various textile sectors are included individually, with each recorded as a case of NTB protection, several register low rates of import penetration. When all textile and apparel sectors are consolidated, the resulting sector has both substantial import penetration (though lower than for apparel alone) and a very large share in total manufacturing employment—12 percent in the United States and 11 percent in the United Kingdom. Treating the entire textile-apparel complex as a single sector in terms of political economy is clearly more meaningful than applying the particular four-digit ISIC groupings as separate observations, as noted earlier.

Applying the test to industrial goods only, omitting processed foods, beverages, and tobacco, also improves the results. Such processed foods as meat, dairy products, and sugar have NTB protection that appears to reflect powerful farm-bloc pressure, despite relatively low penetration by imports. Processed foods, beverages, and tobacco are omitted from the tests for the United States and the United Kingdom on the grounds that protection response for farm-based products differs from that for industrial manufactures. However, these sectors are retained for Canada, where their presence yields better results.

For the predictions of table 2-7, special cutoff levels (typically about 35 percent) are used for the probability of an NTB—the logit measure, equation 2-5. Above this cutoff probability an NTB is predicted; below it, not. These cutoffs achieve the best distributions of errors between actual cases with an NTB and those without an NTB.[41] It is a well-established tradition in statistical analysis of binary phenomena to select the classification procedure that best achieves a balanced distribution of errors between the two categories being examined (in this case the presence of NTBs as opposed to the absence of NTBs). Thus, in discriminant analysis of the form $Z = a + \Sigma_i b_i X_i$, where a is a constant, b_i a set of parameters, and X_i a series of variables, the critical value $Z = Z^*$ is selected on grounds of minimizing the cost of misclassification. According to Anderson,

> Clearly, a good classification procedure is one which minimizes in some sense or other the cost of misclassification. . . .
>
> If we do not have a priori probabilities (on the classification between two

41. Thus, in the case of the United States, at a 50 percent cutoff, the function achieves higher general explanation (94.7 percent), but with a more imbalanced distribution (only 50 percent explanation for actual NTB cases and 100 percent for cases with no NTB).

populations) we may select log $k = c$ [for a critical cutoff level], say, on the basis of making the expected losses due to misclassification equal.[42]

In the logit analysis used here, varying the critical level of the discriminant function is analogous to varying the threshold probability for achieving optimal classification. The method used is to examine iteratively the distribution of errors by using alternative probability thresholds (at 5 percentage point intervals) and selecting that threshold that comes closest to predicting accurately an equal percentage of cases with nontariff barriers and those without. Intuitively, the "critical probability threshold" used here may be seen as an "adjusted" 50 percent dividing line, above which the case is classed as an NTB and below which it is classed as a non-NTB. It should be noted that in all the estimates of table 2-7 the critical probability is below 50 percent. This pattern reflects the fact that the underlying data are heavily weighted toward non-NTB cases, so that, without special attention to classification according to error distribution, the function does best by leaning toward prediction of no NTBs—thereby concentrating errors in the cases of actual NTBs, as occurred in table 2-6, where no special adjustment of the critical probability from a simple 50 percent was made.

In anticipation of the policy analysis of chapter 3, it is important to consider what direction of bias might exist, if any, in the use of a specially estimated cutoff threshold rather than simply a 50 percent probability. Simple use of a 50 percent cutoff would give predictions of fewer instances of protection in the projections of chapter 3. This alternative would reinforce the policy finding that future export growth from developing countries should cause relatively little incidence of new protection. However, the alternative approach would bias downward the predicted extent of protection.

For the United States, the best results (table 2-7) are achieved with a simple two-variable model relating protection to import penetration ($X1$) and the sectoral share in total manufacturing labor ($X9$). Both variables are statistically significant at the 5 percent level. This function correctly explains 93 percent of the observations, correctly predicting presence of NTBs for two-thirds of actual NTB cases and correctly predicting absence of NTBs for 96 percent of the non-NTB cases.

The two-variable model for the United States has intuitive appeal. It

---

42. T. W. Anderson, *An Introduction to Multivariate Statistical Analysis* (Wiley, 1958), pp. 127, 134.

Figure 2-2. *Protection Function for the United States*
Critical probability = 30 percent

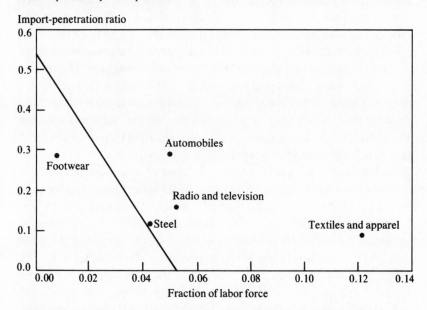

Import-penetration ratio

states that a sector representing a large number of workers has the political influence to obtain protection even if its import penetration is relatively low, but that a sector representing relatively few workers is unlikely to receive the political support for protection unless its case is compelling on economic grounds—as represented by a very high import-penetration ratio, showing substantial pressure from imports.

Figure 2-2 is a graphic representation of the U.S. protection function shown in table 2-7. The line in the graph includes all combinations of import penetration and employment share that will trigger protection (at a 30 percent probability threshold). Above the line and to its right, a sector is predicted to receive protection. Below the line and to its left, a sector is predicted not to receive protection. The figure also shows the positions of five important sectors with NTB protection. Among them, the textile-apparel sector has such a large share of national employment in manufacturing that, according to the function, it could obtain protection even if its import penetration were zero. (This finding is not auspicious for the eventual unwinding of MFA protection.) Steel, automobiles, and radio and television are all closer to the dividing line. Footwear is below it. Despite its high level of import penetration (nearly

30 percent), footwear has too small a labor force to secure protection according to the predictive function. This finding is especially telling in light of the fact that in 1981 the Reagan administration allowed the voluntary quotas on footwear against Korea and Taiwan to expire.[43]

For Canada, the best results are obtained by using all variables except the change in import penetration, which had the wrong sign. The results are also better when all sectors are included, and with original separate-sector status for textiles and apparel. In the function reported in table 2-7, statistical significance is achieved only for the skill-ratio variable ($X8$). Nevertheless, total explanation is high, and the explanation achieved for actual NTB cases is also relatively high (57 percent).

For the United Kingdom, the best estimate remains relatively weak. It achieves strong statistical significance of the labor-share variable ($X9$) and a somewhat more plausible (larger) coefficient on import penetration than in the initial estimate (but without statistical significance). Its general explanatory power is high, but explanation of the important class of actual NTB cases is relatively low (40 percent).[44] Because these results are the weakest, the projection analysis in the following chapter does not apply this function for the United Kingdom but instead applies the pooled three-country function to projections for the United Kingdom of imports from developing countries.

The best results are achieved by using the three-country pool (with all sectors for Canada and, for the United States and the United Kingdom, by omitting processed foods, beverages, and tobacco, and consolidating all textiles and apparel). This function shows the correct sign for all variables included, and all five variables included show strong statistical significance. High total explanation is achieved, and 62.5 percent of actual NTB cases are correctly explained.

The three-country model states that higher import penetration raises the probability of protection, as does a high share of manufacturing labor (as in the U.S. and the British cases). In addition, however, a higher export–output ratio alleviates protectionist pressure (given the signifi-

43. It may also have been relevant that, having just induced the Japanese to impose voluntary quotas on automobiles, the Reagan administration needed to refurbish its free-trade credentials.

44. Note that this function is estimated without sectors 3825 (computers) and 3845 (aircraft). Both are high-technology sectors with high import penetration. Both have received special government subsidies to foster competitiveness, and although the two sectors are not listed as having major NTBs, it would appear to bias the results to treat them like all other sectors.

cant negative coefficient on $X2$). This finding is important because it suggests that greater import penetration need not cause protectionist pressure if it is offset by increased exports. In particular, as developing countries penetrate industrial country markets further, some of the resulting protectionist pressures may be offset by the fact that the developing countries will become larger customers for exports from industrial countries as the developing countries respend their greater earnings of foreign exchange.

The three-country model also confirms the importance of factor intensity and (Heckscher-Ohlin) comparative advantage. Higher value added per worker, as a proxy for higher capital intensity and lower intensity of unskilled labor, is associated with less protection. The same finding is shown by the positive coefficient on the skill-ratio variable ($X8$), indicating that a higher proportion of unskilled labor in the work force is associated with greater protection.

Table 2-7 also contains estimates for France and Germany. These estimates are at the three-digit ISIC level and are based on only eighteen and twenty-four observations, respectively. They are estimated by using only two variables ($X1$ and $X9$) because of the lack of availability of several other variables. Nevertheless, they tend to confirm the importance of import penetration ($X1$) and labor-force share ($X9$) in explaining protection. Based on statistical significance (t-ratio), the import-penetration variable is more dominant for Germany and the labor-force variable more dominant for France.

Implications

The protection functions estimated for the United States, Canada, the United Kingdom, Germany, and France convey some important general implications. On the basis of the three-country model with country dummy variables, and in view of the similarity of the coefficients of individual country models, the results suggest that the protection process is relatively similar in at least the five industrial countries examined, with no significantly greater protection tendencies in one country than in another. The results show the importance of the political influence of a product sector as represented by its share in the manufacturing labor force. They show that protection tends to be against products for which the industrial countries have little comparative advantage—

products that use unskilled labor intensively. As expected, the results show the influence of high import penetration in triggering protection and the offsetting influence of exports, which help reduce protectionist pressure if located in the same industry.

At a more fundamental level, the protection functions leave unanswered questions. They do not reveal whether the measured behavior is in some way inherent or whether it is subject to change through political effort by national leaders and international negotiations. The estimates should not be interpreted as meaning that protection will inevitably come if a sector has a large labor force or a high import-penetration ratio. Rather, they record protectionist practice in the late 1970s. With committed political leadership and well-designed adjustment programs, future protection might not have to be as severe as in the past to accommodate the same levels of underlying economic variables. Nor do the functions guarantee that protection in practice will not get worse even in the absence of changes in the underlying economic variables.

Although they should not be interpreted as rigid economic laws, the protection functions do serve to capture protectionist behavior as it has recently been practiced. With this practice as the best guide to prospective problems of protection, the next chapter uses these functions to investigate the possible extent of new protection over the coming decade as industrial economies respond to greater import penetration from developing countries.

CHAPTER THREE

Prospects for Exports
of Manufactures
and for Protection

DYNAMIC performance of manufactured exports was an important ingredient in the growth record of developing countries, especially the newly industrialized ones, in the 1970s. Their economic growth in the 1980s will be strongly affected by their ability to continue to achieve rapid export expansion in manufactures. Many of these countries have substantial external debt, and rapidly growing exports are important to the orderly servicing of this debt. Many have shifted to an outward-looking development strategy based on relatively open economies and an emphasis on manufactured exports, in contrast to the regimes of industrialization based on import substitution in the 1950s and 1960s. It is widely acknowledged that the outward-looking strategy holds greater promise than import substitution as a development model that can achieve economic efficiency.

A precondition for successful implementation of this strategy, however, is a relatively open and buoyant international economy that can absorb rapid increases in manufactured exports from a growing group of developing countries following the outward-looking strategy. Yet the 1980s opened with the worst global recession since the 1930s. Although by 1983 inflation had receded sharply from double-digit levels, and significant recovery had begun in the United States, there remained serious doubts that economic growth in industrial countries for the 1980s could attain the averages of previous decades. If growth in the industrial countries is slow during the decade, their markets for manufactured imports from developing countries will not be buoyant.

Developing countries pursuing the outward-looking strategy must consider not only the macroeconomic prospects of the industrial countries but also the prospects for protection. To some extent developing countries can continue to achieve rapid export growth despite slow growth in industrial countries by increasing the penetration of manufactured exports in industrial country markets. But prudence requires a careful assessment of the extent to which continued increases in this penetration are likely to be possible without provoking new protectionist measures that stifle the growth of these exports.

The data base prepared in this study and the statistical estimates of protective behavior in chapter 2 make it possible to examine the likely incidence of future protection and its potential effect on exports of manufactures from developing countries. For this purpose, this chapter first presents alternative estimates of future growth of manufactured exports from developing to industrial countries. The analysis of this chapter then combines the export projections with projections of the future size of industrial country markets to determine whether protective responses are likely to proliferate in response to increased exports of manufactures from developing countries. The protection functions estimated in chapter 2 are applied to the projected trade and market data to determine future incidence of protection.

The analysis of this chapter considers only part of the problem. The focus on industrial country markets omits prospective growth in manufactured trade among developing countries themselves. This trade amounted to 35 percent of their manufactured exports in 1979.[1] To some extent South-South trade can alleviate obstacles posed by slow growth or increased protection in industrial country markets.[2] Nevertheless, the dominant part of the market for manufactured exports from developing countries will remain in the industrial countries, and what happens to this portion of the market will be the main force influencing the export performance of developing countries in the 1980s. Moreover, limited

---

1. However, this share has not been growing and is in fact lower now than in 1960–65 (40 percent). United Nations Conference on Trade and Development, *Trade and Development Report, 1981* (Geneva: UNCTAD, 1981), p. 49. The UNCTAD definition of manufactures is narrower than that used in this study and omits processed foods, beverages, tobacco, and nonferrous metals.

2. Some authors, such as W. Arthur Lewis, have recommended that the developing countries look to each other for expansion of trade in the 1980s, as growth at the industrial country center slows down. Lewis, "The Slowing Down of the Engine of Growth," *American Economic Review*, vol. 70 (September 1980), pp. 555–64.

success of economic integration movements among developing countries in the past, as well as the greater entrenchment of protectionism in most developing countries than in industrial countries, must give planners pause in relying too heavily, in their programs for exports of manufactures, on the growth of markets in other developing countries.

The analysis here also captures only the breadth, and not the intensity, of protectionist measures. Although the analysis makes it possible to investigate whether new product sectors are likely to face protection in the 1980s, it does not provide insight into whether the markets of currently protected items are likely to be closed more tightly or opened somewhat. This question is especially important for textiles and apparel, a major component of developing-country exports of manufactures.

Furthermore, the projections here implicitly hold constant important influences on protection that do not appear in the protection function estimates of chapter 2. Unemployment is perhaps the most important omitted variable. Because the model of chapter 2 is a cross-sectional rather than a time series analysis, it does not include the level of unemployment as an explanatory variable. Yet it is clear that in the past decade the degree of unemployment has been an important influence on protection, or at least on protectionist pressure. Other important excluded influences are exchange-rate pressure, as in the case of U.S. trade friction with Japan in 1971–72, 1977–78, and 1981–82, and the inflation rate.[3]

Export Projections for 1990

The first step in investigating the possible incidence of future protective response to developing-country exports is to consider likely levels of those exports in future years. This chapter applies two alternative sets of projections of these exports to the year 1990.

The first set of projections uses simple extrapolation of the real growth rates from 1969–70 to 1978 at the four-digit international standard industrial classification level, found in the analysis of real growth based on sectoral import price indexes (appendix table B-2). For each four-

3. C. Fred Bergsten and John Williamson, "Exchange Rates and Trade Policy," in William R. Cline, ed., *Trade Policy in the 1980s* (Washington, D.C.: Institute for International Economics, 1983), pp. 90–120.

digit sector, total exports of developing countries to the seven industrial countries are assumed to continue to grow from 1978 to 1990 at the real average annual rate from 1969 to 1978. The sector of radio, television, and communications (3832) is the only exception. Its price index (1969–78) was implausibly low, giving implausibly high real annual growth (30 percent). For a more reasonable projection, the average past rate for related electronics sectors (3831, 3833, and 3839) is applied to the radio, television, and communication sector (a rate of 18.5 percent).

Simple extrapolation of past growth rates runs the risk of overstating future growth in sectors that had high but unsustainable growth from a low base in 1969. An alternative attempt at extrapolation was made by using logistic curves, which show a deceleration of growth over time and yield total exports that rise slowly (in absolute terms) at first, then rise rapidly, and then level off, in an S-shaped curve.[4] However, because the data set contains only four benchmark years (1969, 1970, 1976, and 1978), observations for each sector were insufficient to obtain reliable estimates of logistic curves.

The second set of export projections is based on World Bank estimates. The bank estimated manufactured export growth for developing countries through 1990 at 10.9 percent annually in its 1979 report, 9.7 percent in its 1980 report, and within a range of 5.1 to 12.2 percent in its 1981 report.[5] The low end of the range stated in the 1981 report represented the possibility of increased protection.

The estimates used as the second basic set of export projections for this study assume a growth rate of manufactured exports, narrowly defined, of 10 percent annually from 1978 through 1990. This rate is a central figure in the range of World Bank projections just discussed. This rate does not apply to processed foods, beverages, tobacco, nonferrous metals, or fuels, which are not manufactures under the more narrow World Bank definition. For these products, the specific estimates in the 1980 report of the bank are used here.[6]

---

4. In a logistics curve, exports grow as follows:

$$\frac{dX}{X} = a - \frac{a}{c}X,$$

where X is the level of exports, dX is the annual change in exports, and c is the ceiling value at which exports eventually level off. With sufficient observations, such a curve may be estimated by statistical regression.

5. World Bank, *World Development Report, 1979* (Washington, D.C.: World Bank, 1979), p. 5; *1980*, p. 100; and *1981*, p. 11.

6. World Bank, *World Development Report, 1980*, p. 100.

Table 3-1. *Annual Real Growth Rates for Manufactured Exports from Developing Countries to Industrial Countries, 1978–90, World Bank Basis*
Percent

ISIC number[a]	Product sector	Growth rate
311–13	Food products and beverages	3.9
314	Tobacco	2.2
321	Textiles	4.8
322	Apparel	5.9
323–42	Leather products, footwear, wood products, furniture, paper products, and printing	9.4
351–52	Chemicals	13.0
353–54	Petroleum refineries and products	3.0
355–69	Rubber products, plastics, pottery, glass, and nonmetallic minerals	9.4
371	Iron and steel	14.2
372	Nonferrous metals	3.8
381	Metal products	9.4
382–84	Machinery, electrical machinery, and transport equipment	16.5
385	Professional goods	15.4
390	Other industries	9.4

Source: World Bank, *World Development Report, 1979, 1980, 1981* (Washington, D.C.: World Bank, 1979, 1980, 1981); and Bela Balassa, *The Newly Industrializing Countries in the World Economy* (Pergamon Press, 1981), p. 218.
a. International standard industrial classification.

Rates suggested by Bela Balassa are used to obtain product sector detail on growth rates within the group of manufactures.[7] Balassa provides separate growth rate estimates for seven broad categories. These estimates, which yield an average growth rate of 12.5 percent, are scaled down proportionately to produce an average growth of 10 percent.[8] The resulting growth rates for exports at the three-digit level of ISIC are shown in table 3-1. These three-digit growth rates are applied to exports at the level of four-digit components of the categories in question.

The growth rates in table 3-1 reflect the differing prospects of divergent product groups. The relatively slow growth of textiles and apparel reflects the influence of assumed continuation of the Multi-fiber Arrange-

7. Bela Balassa, *The Newly Industrializing Countries in the World Economy* (Pergamon Press, 1981), p. 218.
8. When the resulting growth rates of manufactures—excluding foodstuffs, beverages, tobacco, petroleum products, and nonferrous metals—are weighted by the 1978 export values in the data base of the present study, the growth rate is only 8.47 percent. Accordingly, the sectoral growth estimates based initially on Balassa's study are expanded once again by the multiple 1.18 to obtain the 10 percent average growth rate.

ment. Exports of machinery and equipment are assumed to rise considerably more rapidly than the average, reflecting the expectation of continued dynamism in products such as consumer electronics, machinery, motor vehicles, and ships and the extension of the process of manufacturing components of these and other engineering products in the developing countries. Growth rates below the average are assumed for semimanufactures and other consumer goods, given their already high shares in imports of industrial countries. The high rate for iron and steel and chemicals assumes that some of the more advanced developing countries will follow the example of Japan in exporting these products.[9]

The various assumptions made by Balassa in differentiating sectoral growth rates are optimistic about the future openness of markets in several products where protective barriers have already begun to appear, either directly against the developing countries (consumer electronics) or primarily against Japan (steel and automobiles). As for the lower growth rates for food products, beverages, tobacco, and nonferrous metals, underlying demand growth is assumed by the World Bank to be relatively slow for these products.

An important conceptual difference underlies the two sets of export projections. The extrapolations of past growth rates include many high sectoral growth rates that principally represented an outward shift in the supply of developing country exports in the 1970s. Of the eighty-one sectors at the four-digit ISIC level, thirty showed export growth rates of 20 percent or higher in 1969–78 (table B-2). Growth rates this high far exceed typical demand growth and represent instead a rapid expansion of developing-country supply and an increase in world market share from a relatively small base. The projection of such rates into the future implies a continuation of dominance of rapidly outward-shifting supply of developing-country exports, with little limitation on the side of world demand.

In contrast, the World Bank estimates were based on predictions of growth rates in income in industrial countries as applied to the "apparent income elasticities" relating the percentage growth in developing-country exports to percentage growth of industrial country income in the past. Thus Balassa cites an apparent income elasticity for these imports of 3.6 in 1963–73 and 4.1 in 1973–78, and he projects an elasticity of 3.2 for 1978–90.[10] Elasticities this high are best not interpreted as income

9. Balassa, *The Newly Industrializing Countries*, pp. 217–19.
10. Ibid., p. 217.

elasticities, however, but as the joint result of demand elasticities on the one hand and very rapid outward shifts in developing-country supply on the other.

Interpreted broadly, the extrapolative projections imply a continuation of outward-shifting supply curves for developing countries as the driving force for this trade in the coming decade, while the projections of the World Bank are geared more toward demand-determined estimates—although the income elasticities used from the World Bank estimates are so high that implicitly they also contain a large component of outward-shifting supply. The difference in conception shows up in the difference in estimates. The extrapolative estimates give much higher export figures for 1990 than the estimates derived from the World Bank figures, as is discussed below.

Allocation by Import Market

Projection of the distribution of manufactured exports from developing countries, across individual industrial country markets, is essential to an analysis of the future prospects for protection. As was shown in chapter 1, the rates of growth of imports of these goods have been substantially different among industrial countries. It would be misleading to project these imports to grow by equal proportions across all industrial countries in the future.

Differences among import markets stem from differences in their income growth and differences in their apparent income elasticity of demand for these goods—which, again, is really a hybrid reflecting differences in supply conditions as well.

Most forecasts of economic growth show Europe and North America growing at roughly comparable rates in the 1980s, at rates of about 3.0 to 3.5 percent, with Japan growing somewhat faster (5.5 to 6.0 percent). When the apparent income elasticities for imports of manufactures from developing countries during the 1970s (table 1-2) are applied to the range of growth rates, the market growth falls into two distinct categories. In an upper tier, the United States, Canada, Germany, and Japan have a prospective growth of 7 to 12 percent annually in imports from developing countries. Japan's market growth is high because of high income growth; for the other three countries, high market growth derives from a high income elasticity. A second, lower tier of countries includes

France, Italy, and the United Kingdom. For this group the demand for imports from developing countries appears likely to grow at 4 percent annually or less—the result of a combination of moderate growth with low (past) income elasticities for these imports.

On the basis of these differences, the projections incorporate a rising share of the market allocated to the United States, Canada, Germany, and Japan, and a declining share to France, Italy, and the United Kingdom. Accordingly, given the general expansion of developing countries' manufactured exports by 1990 (under either set of projections), for the first tier of industrial countries the projected trade is expanded further by 10 percent, while for the second tier the projected trade is reduced by one-third.[11]

To recapitulate, the export projections for 1990 are estimated as follows:

$$(3\text{-}1) \qquad M_{ik} = M_{ik}(1 + g_k)^{12}(1.102),$$

for i = the United States, Canada, Germany, and Japan, and

$$(3\text{-}2) \qquad M_{ik} = M_{ik}(1 + g_k)^{12}(0.67),$$

for i = France, Italy, and the United Kingdom, where M = imports, i is the importing country, k is the product sector, and g is the sectoral growth rate of the imports in question. The exponent 12 is for growth over the twelve-year period 1978–90. Two sets of estimates are obtained, one using the extrapolation basis for sectoral export growth rates (g_k), and the other using the World Bank estimates as the basis for these growth rates. Table 3-2 shows the total values of imports of manufactures from developing countries by industrial country market, for the base year 1978 and for 1990 under the two alternative sets of export projections. The projections derived from extrapolation of past growth rates are considerably higher than those based on the World Bank estimates. Under the extrapolative projections, the real annual growth rate for these imports in the aggregate is 14.1 percent. This rate is much higher than the average in the period 1969–78 on which the extrapolation

11. These adjustments are approximately the expansion or reduction required to adjust the shares of the upper and lower tiers of industrial country markets in exports of manufactures from developing countries from their 1978 base (76.6 percent and 23.4 percent, respectively) to their 1990 levels in view of the divergent import growth rates between the two groups of industrial countries.

Table 3-2. *Alternative Projections of Exports of Manufactures from Developing Countries to Major Industrial Countries, 1990*
Billions of 1978 dollars

Importing country	1978 actual	Extrapolation of 1968–78 growth	World Bank basis
United States	29.9	217.1	106.2
Canada	1.8	12.9	5.6
West Germany	8.5	45.8	21.9
France	4.8	9.6	6.8
Italy	3.2	7.4	5.3
United Kingdom	6.9	26.9	13.0
Japan	10.6	45.4	26.6
Total	65.7	365.1	185.4

Source: See text.

is based (7.5 percent). This apparent paradox is explained by the fact that the weight of the rapidly growing sectors rises over time and boosts the overall growth rate. The average annual growth rate for the World Bank–based projections is considerably lower, at 10 percent annually in real terms.[12]

The extrapolative projections are sufficiently high to be viewed as an upper-bound estimate. For purposes of predicting future protective response, the extrapolative estimates should represent an upper-bound case for the incidence of new protection; showing high expansion of imports of manufactures into industrial countries, they are relatively likely to trigger protection as estimated by the protection functions. In contrast, the World Bank–based projections are moderate-case estimates that are less likely to yield predictions of new protection in the future because of their more modest estimates of future levels of imports of manufactures from developing countries.

12. The average growth rate of 10 percent is somewhat surprising since the sectoral growth rates in the World Bank–based projections are designed to average 10 percent for manufactures more narrowly defined and are lower, about 3 to 4 percent, for processed foods, beverages, tobacco, petroleum products, and nonferrous metals. That the weighted average growth nevertheless equals 10 percent appears to result from the expansion procedure; the expansion of the estimates for the United States, Canada, Germany, and Japan and the shrinkage of the estimates for the other three markets may mean that greater weight is being given to higher-growth sectors by virtue of their concentration in the first tier of markets.

Projections of Independent Variables

The key variable for projecting future protective response to manufactured imports from developing countries is the import-penetration ratio—the ratio of imports to apparent consumption. This ratio requires estimation of 1990 levels for domestic consumption in the industrial countries at the four-digit ISIC level. It also requires estimation of total imports, as opposed to those from developing countries alone.

To project domestic consumption, the projections estimate per capita income growth in each industrial country and apply this growth to sectoral income elasticities for domestic consumption. In addition, consumption is assumed to grow proportionately with population. Thus, for a given product sector and country, 1990 consumption is estimated as:

$$(3\text{-}3) \qquad C_{ik}^{90} = C_{ik}^{78} (1 + g_i^{E_k})^{12} (1 + \dot{n}_i)^{12},$$

where C is apparent consumption, the superscripts 90 and 78 are for 1990 and 1978, i is the country, k is the product sector, g is the growth rate of per capita income, E_k is the income elasticity of product sector k, and $\dot{n}$ is the annual growth rate of population. The exponent 12 is for growth over the twelve-year period.

The population growth rates for the seven major industrial countries for 1978–90 are calculated as the average of 1970–79 and projected 1980–2000 population growth rates as reported by the World Bank.[13] Per capita income growth for each country is projected as follows. The World Bank has projected economic growth from 1980 to 1990 at 3.9 percent annually for North America and Japan and at 3.3 percent for Western Europe (high case; the low case growth rates are 3.1 and 2.4 percent, respectively).[14] These growth rates are converted to per capita growth rates and disaggregated between Japan and North America (following Balassa's forecast that Japanese growth will exceed that in the United States by 2.5 percent annually).[15] In the regional disaggregation, relative size of GNP is taken into account. Actual growth rates from 1978 to 1980 are combined with these projected rates from 1980 to 1990 to obtain the

13. World Bank, *World Development Report, 1981*, p. 167.
14. Ibid., p. 10.
15. Balassa, *The Newly Industrializing Countries*, p. 213.

projections for the full period 1978–90.[16] Appendix table F-3 summarizes the projected growth rates.

The sectoral income elasticities (E_k) are derived from four sources.[17] The simple average estimate across these four studies is used for each sector without any attempt to obtain differing elasticities across the individual industrial countries. However, the elasticities are normalized so that their sum when weighted by apparent consumption equals unity. The rationale for normalization is that it makes little sense to project that the total apparent consumption for all industries will grow other than proportionately with income over the coming decade. Because the sectoral consumption weights vary by country, the resulting normalizing factor varies by country, making the sectoral elasticities used vary as well.[18] Table F-4 reports the sectoral elasticities before country normalization.

Two sets of estimates of apparent consumption for 1990 are made using equation 3-2: one applying the high alternative for industrial country growth and one applying the low alternative. Given the consumption estimates, the import-penetration ratio is projected in the following way. From the projections of developing-country exports in 1990 (on both the extrapolative and World Bank bases), the import-penetration ratio for developing-country supply is known. The total import-penetration ratio is then calculated by adding the import-penetration ratio for imports from all other countries (that is, developed countries) in the base year, 1978. Thus, for each product sector and importing industrial country

$$(3\text{-}4) \qquad \left(\frac{M}{C}\right)^{90} = \left(\frac{M}{C}\right)^{78}_{O} + \left(\frac{M}{C}\right)^{90}_{LDC},$$

where M/C is the import-penetration ratio, the superscripts 90 and 78

16. Actual growth rates are from International Monetary Fund, *World Economic Outlook* (Washington, D.C.: IMF, 1981), p. 111.

17. Balassa, *The Newly Industrializing Countries*, p. 225; Clopper Almon, Jr., and others, *1985: Interindustry Forecasts of the American Economy* (Lexington, Mass.: Lexington Books, 1974), p. 37 ("choice" elasticities); H. S. Houthakker and Lester D. Taylor, *Consumer Demand in the United States, 1929–1970: Analyses and Projections* (Harvard University Press, 1966), pp. 166–67; and calculations from Wharton Econometric Forecasting Associates, "The Wharton Annual Model: Post-Meeting Forecast, June 1981" (Washington, D.C.: WEFA, 1981), vol. 1, pp. 1–21.

18. The consumption weighted sums of elasticities (used for normalization) range from 1.07 for France to 1.12 for Japan.

refer to 1990 and 1978, subscript O refers to "other" countries, and subscript LDC refers to less developed countries. Because of rapid growth in some of the extrapolative estimates, these projections of import penetration occasionally exceed 100 percent (imports exceed apparent consumption). If so, a ceiling of 100 percent is applied to the projected penetration ratio.

The projections of import penetration assume that only the penetration by developing countries will change over the next decade. Penetration by other (industrial) countries will remain unchanged at its base level in 1978. The assumption of constant penetration by other countries reflects the absence of any detailed basis for projection. This assumption implies that import penetration will stop its upward trend of recent decades, except for the possibility of rising penetration by developing-country supplies. Because the phase of postwar trade liberalization is broadly completed, this source of rising penetration should be minor. The possible impact of high income elasticity for imports is already taken into account insofar as high elasticity represents concentration of imports in products with high demand elasticities, because sectoral demand elasticities are already incorporated into the consumption projections. The main remaining source of rising import penetration would seem to be the continuation of outward-shifting supply from developing countries, and this force is measured by the specific estimates of future penetration by developing countries.

Perhaps in some sectors the penetration of imports from other countries would decline in the future if penetration by developing countries grows rapidly. It is often asserted that penetration of markets by imports from developing countries is not as troublesome as it might appear because their imports are mainly displacing previous supply from other countries (such as Japan). However, no systematic evidence indicates a negative relationship between past growth in developing-country penetration and in penetration by other countries. On the contrary, regressions relating changes in the two penetration ratios from 1970 to 1978 for each industrial country market (using the eighty-one sectors of four-digit ISIC as observations) find that they are positively, not negatively, correlated.[19] As these tests indicate, the assumption that

19. The regression is of the form $dZ_O = a + b(dZ_L)$, where dZ is the change in import penetration ratio for developing-country supply and dZ_O is the same change for supply from other countries, 1970 to 1978. The coefficients b are 0.21 (United States); 0.22 (Canada); 0.68 (Germany); 0.90 (France); 0.93 (Italy); 1.76 (United Kingdom); and

some portion of the expected increase in developing-country supply will be offset by a reduction in supply from other countries would be misleading. Indeed, if past relationships were to continue in the future, the projections may underestimate rather than overestimate future penetration from other countries, because the estimates assume constant penetration from other countries.

The absence of offsetting substitution between developing and other country penetration in the tests for 1970–78 suggests that the replacement of Japanese supply by developing-country supply, noted in chapter 1, was not typical. Indeed, it appears to have been confined to a limited number of product sectors that, however, were important in value terms. As a more general rule, offsetting substitution for existing supply by industrial country trading partners cannot be assumed to soften the adjustment effect of increased market penetration by developing countries.

A second independent variable for which projection is necessary is the ratio of exports to output ($X2$ in the protection functions). In the absence of any detailed basis for projecting either exports or output at the sectoral level, one approach would be to assume that the sectoral ratios of exports to output in 1990 will be the same as in the base year, 1978. However, for policy purposes it is important to capture one effect that could cause the export–output ratio to vary. As import penetration by developing countries rises, these countries earn the foreign exchange to become bigger customers for exports from industrial countries. Because this induced expansion of exports can help alleviate protectionist pressure, it would bias the future estimates of protection upward if no account were taken of induced increases in the export–output ratio resulting from higher developing-country earnings of foreign exchange from their higher penetration into industrial country markets.

Although there is little basis for projecting completely new export–output ratios for 1990, there is a reasonable basis for calculating how much the effect of induced exports to developing countries should change these ratios from their levels in the base year. The 1990 projection may then be estimated as the 1978 ratio of exports to output, plus the change in this ratio attributable to induced exports to developing countries.

0.10 (Japan). All are significant at the 5 percent level except the coefficients for Canada and Japan.

The extra exports to developing countries expected as a consequence of higher developing-country demand may be estimated (for a given industrial country) as

(3-5) $$\Delta X_k = \Phi_k \left\{ \Sigma_j \left[\left(\frac{M}{C} \right)_j^{90} - \left(\frac{M}{C} \right)_j^{78} \right] C_j \right\},$$

where ΔX_k is the induced increase in exports in product sector k, Φ_k is the fraction accounted for by sector k in total manufactured exports of the country to developing countries in the base year, the subscript j refers to sector j, Σ refers to summation, and the other variables are as before. The difference between the import-penetration ratio in 1990 and 1978 in sector j, multiplied by sectoral consumption, identifies the extra export earnings of developing countries in 1990 attributable to increased import penetration. (Note that because penetration from other sources is held constant, the entire increase in penetration represents extra export earnings for developing countries.) When these sectoral amounts of extra exports by developing countries are summed, the total increase in these exports is obtained (that is, the entire bracketed expression in equation 3-5 following the initial term). This total of extra export earnings by developing countries is then distributed across sectors in proportion to each sector's share in manufactured exports from the industrial country in question to all developing countries. This procedure assumes (1) that all induced exports are in manufactures, (2) that the developing countries respend in the industrial country in question the entire amount of their extra export earnings obtained from increased import penetration into that country, and (3) that the sectoral allocation of induced exports is identical to the average sectoral allocation of the industrial country's manufactured exports to developing countries in the base year. These assumptions, which include one providing for continuation of the current trade balance between the industrial countries and developing countries (relative to consumption), are reasonable, simplifying assumptions necessary to provide a basis for determining induced exports by sector.

So that the ratio of exports to production can be obtained, the induced sectoral exports for 1990 are normalized for comparison with the 1978 level of apparent consumption and then added to both the numerator and denominator of the 1978 export–output ratio. Thus

(3-6) $$\left(\frac{X}{Q} \right)_k^{90} = \frac{X_k^{78} + \Delta X_k'}{Q_k^{78} + \Delta X_k'},$$

where X is exports, Q is domestic production, k refers to sector k, $\Delta X_k'$

is normalized value of induced exports in 1990 rescaled to 1978 levels, and the superscripts 90 and 78 refer to 1990 and 1978.

The normalized value of induced exports, $\Delta X'$, equals the 1990 value for induced exports scaled down by the ratio of total consumption in 1978 to total consumption in 1990 ($\Delta X'_k = \Delta X_k [C^{78}/C^{90}]$, where C^{78} and C^{90} refer to total consumption across all sectors in 1978 and 1990). This scaling down is necessary to make the 1990-based estimate of induced exports comparable to the 1978 estimates of exports and output.

The rationale for adding induced exports (appropriately scaled) to both numerator and denominator of the export–output ratio is the following. Other things being equal, domestic output in a sector will rise by the amount of induced exports to meet the additional export demand. The new export–output ratio will have a higher total of exports in the numerator as well as a higher level of output in the denominator.

Equations 3-1 through 3-6 complete the special calculations used to project values of the independent variables in the protection function. For the other variables required—$X4$, relative value added per worker; $X7$, relative total capital per worker; $X8$, skill ratio; $X9$, share of labor force; $X10$, relative wage; and $X12$, growth rate—the analysis assumes that the sectoral values remain unchanged from their 1978 levels. These variables are industry characteristics, specified in most cases as relative to the industry-wide average. There is little if any basis for projecting changes in these industry characteristics, especially since the relative specification for most of them means that industry-wide trends would be omitted in any event. The growth rate is an exception. It is required only for the Canadian projections, and without additional information the analysis assumes that the sectoral growth rates for the 1990 projections are identical to those in the base period, 1968–77.

Protection Estimates for 1990

Given the projections of independent variables to 1990, the best estimates of the protection function (table 2-5) are applied to these variable values to estimate the incidence of protection in 1990. For the United States, the function used involves only two variables, import penetration and sectoral share of the total labor force in manufacturing. For Canada, an eight-variable function is applied, with 1990 projections for the import-penetration ratio ($X1$) and the export–output ratio ($X2$) and base period values for the other variables.

For the United Kingdom, the best function estimated had a positive but not a statistically significant coefficient on import penetration. Projections using that function would have little meaning. Instead, the projections for the United Kingdom apply the pooled model estimated jointly for the United Kingdom, Canada, and the United States. This function uses five independent variables, including the import-penetration ratio and the export–output ratio. For France and Germany, the projections use the functions estimated at the three-digit ISIC level, and these projections correspondingly apply variables and obtain results at the three-digit level.

Tables 3-3 through 3-8 report the results of projections of NTB protection to 1990. Sectors not appearing in the tables do not have major known NTBs currently and are not predicted to have them in the future. Table 3-3 summarizes the U.S. projections. It shows that nontariff protection is expected to continue in the consolidated sector of textiles and apparel (3211–20), in iron and steel (3710), in radio, television, and communication equipment (3832), and in automobiles. Future protection is predicted in footwear (3240), although the function did not predict the actual protection that existed in the base period.

The U.S. projections indicate that new protection may be expected to arise in the following sectors, regardless of the basis used for projecting import penetration: motorcycles and bicycles (3844), clocks and watches (3853), and jewelry (3901).[20] In addition, under the variant with high growth rate of imports from developing countries based on simple extrapolation of past growth, new protection by 1990 may be expected for leather products (3233), furniture (3320), rubber products (3559, but only under the low-consumption variant), pottery and china (3610), and sporting goods (3903). New protection is also projected for other machinery (3829) and printing (3420), although erroneous prediction of protection for these two sectors already in the base period suggests that future protection may also be falsely predicted (especially for printing, where the import penetration rises little and the dominant influence is the large labor force, which does not change in the projections).

Table 3-4 shows the levels of import penetration behind these projections, as well as the actual probabilities estimated for the logit function (equation 2-5). Because the function used applies only import penetration

20. Subsequent to the completion of these calculations, the Reagan administration did in fact impose special protection on imports of motorcycles in 1983.

Table 3-3. *Projections of Major Nontariff Barriers for the United States, 1990*

ISIC number	Product sector[a]	1978 actual	1978 predicted	High consumption	Low consumption	High consumption	Low consumption
				Extrapolation		World Bank basis	
3211–20	Textiles and apparel	1	1	1	1	1	1
3233	Leather products (except footwear)	0	0	1	1	0	0
3240	Footwear	1	0[c]	1	1	1	1
3320	Furniture	0	0	1	1	0	0
3420	Printing	0	1[d]	1	1	1	1
3559	Rubber products not elsewhere classified	0	0	0	1	0	0
3610	Pottery, china, and earthenware	0	0	1	1	0	0
3710	Iron and steel	1	1	1	1	1	1
3829	Machinery not elsewhere classified	0	1[d]	1	1	1	1
3832	Radio, television, and communication equipment	1	1	1	1	1	1
3841	Shipbuilding	1	0[c]	0	0	0	0
3843[e]	Motor vehicles	1	1	1	1	1	1
3844	Motorcycles and bicycles	0	0	1	1	1	1
3853	Watches and clocks	0	0	1	1	1	1
3901	Jewelry	0	0	1	1	1	1
3903	Sporting goods	0	0	1	1	0	0

Source: Author's calculations.
a. Model not applied to foods, beverages, and tobacco (3111–40).
b. 1 = presence of NTB; 0 = absence of NTB.
c. Type 2 error: failure to predict presence of NTB where one existed.
d. Type 1 error: prediction of NTB where none existed.
e. Special sector for automobiles, narrowly defined.

and labor-force share and because the labor-force share is assumed not to change, new cases of protection are predicted solely as the result of estimates of higher import penetration.

The figures in table 3-4 generally show much higher import penetration in 1990 from the extrapolation of past growth of imports from developing countries than from the projection of these imports based on the growth rates anticipated for broad categories by the World Bank. In some cases (footwear, clocks and watches, and sporting goods) simple extrapolation

Table 3-4. Import Penetration and Protection Probabilities Predicted for the United States, 1990
Percent

ISIC number	Product sector[a]	1978 actual	Import penetration 1990				1978 predicted	Probability of protection[b] 1990			
			Extrapolation		World Bank basis			Extrapolation		World Bank basis	
			High consumption	Low consumption	High consumption	Low consumption		High consumption	Low consumption	High consumption	Low consumption
3211–20	Textiles and apparel	9.7	25.9	28.6	12.4	13.5	99.6	99.9	99.9	99.7	99.7
3233	Leather products (except footwear)	14.2	96.6	100.0	27.0	29.7	2.3	94.2	95.6	6.0	7.4
3240	Footwear	29.3	100.0	100.0	47.2	50.1	10.7	97.1	97.1	33.1	38.4
3320	Furniture	6.8	30.4	33.6	9.3	9.9	6.2	30.1	35.6	7.4	7.8
3420	Printing	2.0	4.9	5.2	3.0	3.1	47.3	53.1	53.8	49.2	49.5
3559	Rubber products not elsewhere classified	11.5	42.4	46.5	17.6	19.0	2.9	25.8	32.6	4.6	5.1
3610	Pottery, china, and earthenware	34.1	91.9	98.0	41.8	43.1	9.6	91.3	94.5	16.3	17.8
3710	Iron and steel	11.7	14.9	15.4	14.6	15.2	32.9	38.7	39.8	38.3	39.3
3829	Machinery not elsewhere classified	5.4	16.6	18.4	7.3	7.7	40.1	62.6	65.8	44.4	45.0
3832	Radio, television, and communication equipment	16.1	38.2	44.4	32.9	38.0	60.7	89.9	93.6	85.5	89.8
3841	Shipbuilding	3.3	6.2	6.7	6.3	6.9	0.2	0.2	0.3	0.2	0.3
3843[c]	Motor vehicles	29.5	29.5	29.5	29.5	29.5	81.1	81.1	81.1	81.1	81.1
3844	Motorcycles and bicycles	50.4	56.2	57.4	60.0	61.8	25.7	35.3	37.7	42.6	46.2
3853	Watches and clocks	35.3	100.0	100.0	74.4	81.4	10.2	95.2	95.2	71.9	81.8
3901	Jewelry	49.4	67.7	73.0	67.0	72.2	27.3	61.9	71.2	60.5	69.8
3903	Sporting goods	16.8	100.0	100.0	28.3	31.7	2.8	95.6	95.6	6.8	8.7

Source: Author's calculations.
a. Model not applied to foods, beverages, tobacco (3111–40).
b. Probability cutoff for prediction of nontariff barrier: 30 percent.
c. Special sector for automobiles, narrowly defined. With minimal imports of completely assembled automobiles from developing countries, 1990 estimates are unchanged from 1978.

causes imports to grow to levels above domestic apparent consumption, forcing a ceiling of 100 percent for import penetration.

In contrast to the assumption about import growth rates, the assumption about the rate of economic growth in industrial countries influencing the level of consumption in 1990 has little effect on the projections. In almost all cases, if a sector is predicted to have NTB protection in 1990 under the high-consumption variant, it is also predicted to have protection under the low-consumption variant. This finding suggests that the possible range of variation in the growth of developing-country exports of manufactures will be much more important in determining future protection than will the range of likely variation in the size of industrial country markets.

The U.S. results do not indicate a massive wave of new protection in the future. New protection appears to be confined to a limited number of additional product sectors that are not of great importance. This conclusion is especially true if the more realistic World Bank–based estimates of future imports of manufactures are used instead of the much higher estimates based on extrapolation of past growth. Specifically, under the World Bank–based growth rates for this trade, the only sectors predicted to incur new protection are motorcycles and bicycles, clocks and watches, and jewelry. Though these sectors are of interest to developing countries, they do not amount to a major portion of the total market.

One way to interpret the results for the United States is that the product sectors with political muscle by virtue of their large labor force already have protection: textiles and apparel, steel, and automobiles. Few additional sectors are likely to obtain protection because the remaining sectors affected by imports are modest in size individually and lack the worker base—and therefore the political influence—to obtain protection. The exceptions illustrate the point further: clear instances of new protection occur only in sectors where the import penetration is projected to rise to very high levels—above 60 percent for motorcycles and bicycles, clocks and watches, and jewelry. Having small labor forces, these sectors have been too weak politically to secure protection in the past despite relatively high import penetration (averaging 45 percent), but the extremely high penetration projected for the future indicates that they are becoming likely candidates for protection despite limited political influence.

The important influence of size of labor force in explaining protection is at once a source of cynicism and of hope. One may rather cynically conclude that product sectors with a large work force have the political clout to obtain protection even when the underlying import threat is limited. At the same time, one may conclude more hopefully that most protection for such sectors is already in place and that there are few sectors left with the labor force size and political strength to secure new protection. This optimistic view is nevertheless tempered by the qualification that existing protection in the sectors with large labor forces may be difficult to dismantle. Protection in steel and automobiles could become locked into the trading system just as textile protection has been, despite the best intentions of policymakers to make this protection temporary.

Tables 3-5 and 3-6 report the projections estimated for Canada and the United Kingdom. For Canada, the projections show a continuation of NTB protection in knitting, apparel, and footwear. The only clear prediction of new protection is for sporting goods (furniture and leather goods are ambiguous because they were falsely predicted to have protection in the base period), and even this prediction holds only for the case of extrapolative growth of imports from developing countries. Strikingly, there are projections of sectors where existing protection may be dismantled. In spinning and weaving, protection is correctly predicted for the base period, 1978, yet the projections show no protection for 1990.

Table 3-6 reveals the influences driving the forecasts for Canada. In sporting goods a sharp rise occurs in import penetration (especially under extrapolative import growth). For leather products, rising import penetration pushes the probability of protection higher, suggesting future protection despite the erroneous prediction of protection in the base period.

The most intriguing findings for Canada are the sharp drops in probability of protection for spinning and weaving (3211) and radio, television, and communication equipment (3832). The driving force behind these predictions of liberalization is the rise in the ratio of exports to output projected for these sectors. These products show a relatively high propensity for exports to developing countries, and a significant portion of the extra export earnings of developing countries from rising import penetration *in other sectors* is respent on Canadian exports in these two sectors. With a higher export–output ratio, each sector shows a substantial decline in the likelihood of protection. This finding suggests

Table 3-5. *Projections of Major Nontariff Barriers for Canada and the United Kingdom, 1990*

				Presence of nontariff barrier[a]			
				1990			
Importing country and ISIC number	*Product sector*	*1978 actual*	*1978 predicted*	Extrapolation		World Bank basis	
				High con-sumption	*Low con-sumption*	*High con-sumption*	*Low con-sumption*
Canada							
3211	Spinning and weaving	1	1	0	0	0	0
3212	Made-up textiles	1	0[b]	0	0	0	0
3213	Knitting	1	1	1	1	1	1
3214	Carpets	1	0[b]	0	0	0	0
3220	Apparel	1	1	1	1	1	1
3233	Leather products (except footwear)	0	1[c]	1	1	1	1
3240	Footwear	1	1	1	1	1	1
3320	Furniture	0	1[c]	1	1	1	1
3832	Radio, television, and communication equipment	1	0[b]	0	0	0	0
3903	Sporting goods	0	0	1	1	0	0
United Kingdom[d]							
3211–20	Textiles and apparel	1	1	1	1	1	1
3233	Leather products (except footwear)	0	0	1	1	0	0
3240	Footwear	1	0[b]	0	1	0	0
3710	Iron and steel	1	1	0	0	0	0
3832	Radio, television, and communication equipment	1	0[b]	0	0	0	0
3843	Motor vehicles	1	1	0	0	0	0

Source: Author's calculations.
a. 1 = presence of NTB; 0 = absence of NTB.
b. Type 2 error: failure to predict NTB where one exists.
c. Type 1 error: prediction of NTB where none exists.
d. Model not applied to foods, beverages, and tobacco (3111–40). Textiles and apparel consolidated.

that there are liberalizing feedback effects from increased import penetration by developing countries. In other words, increases in that penetration does not lead only to more protection; instead, by providing the foreign exchange for increased imports by developing countries, that rising penetration boosts industrial country exports in other sectors and may well reduce protectionist pressures in those other sectors.

For the United Kingdom, the projections show that protection is expected to continue in the consolidated sector of textiles and apparel

Table 3-6. *Import Penetration, Export Ratios, and Protection Probabilities Predicted for Canada and the United Kingdom, 1990*
Percent

Importing country and ISIC number	Product sector	Import penetration			Export ratio			Protection probability[a]		
		1978	1990[b] Extrapolation	World Bank basis	1978	1990[b] Extrapolation	World Bank basis	1978	1990[b] Extrapolation	World Bank basis
Canada										
3211	Spinning and weaving	34.0	32.5	35.2	8.1	24.9	23.8	39.0	5.4	7.0
3212	Made-up textiles	12.8	17.1	13.3	3.6	9.0	8.6	16.3	10.0	9.0
3213	Knitting	8.0	10.8	8.2	0.7	5.5	5.1	56.5	43.4	41.6
3214	Carpets	11.0	11.8	11.3	6.3	13.8	13.3	5.5	2.0	2.1
3220	Apparel	18.4	50.2	23.2	4.6	6.8	6.7	92.6	97.6	92.2
3233	Leather products (except footwear)	18.6	93.5	30.1	4.0	4.8	4.7	70.0	98.6	78.3
3240	Footwear	30.0	100.0	41.7	7.4	9.0	8.9	68.0	97.8	75.0
3320	Furniture	15.8	27.6	17.0	7.0	11.3	11.0	50.4	49.3	38.3
3832	Radio, television, and communication equipment	55.6	67.3	64.6	17.3	42.9	41.5	14.0	0.8	0.8
3903	Sporting goods	52.1	100.0	71.7	8.3	11.2	11.0	17.6	57.3	26.8
United Kingdom										
3211–20	Textiles and apparel	26.6	33.1	26.0	21.7	30.8	30.2	90.8	97.2	96.4
3233	Leather products (except footwear)	20.3	71.2	25.4	12.8	17.8	17.4	14.8	49.3	13.5
3240	Footwear	22.4	47.2	25.1	11.2	18.0	17.5	20.9	31.1	16.1
3710	Iron and steel	16.1	16.6	16.6	17.7	30.9	30.0	34.1	17.7	18.6
3832	Radio, television, and communication equipment	26.7	32.3	30.8	31.2	52.0	50.7	8.4	2.7	2.8
3843	Motor vehicles	30.3	31.2	30.5	36.3	54.1	53.0	31.5	12.3	12.9

Source: Author's calculations.
a. Probability cutoff for prediction of nontariff barrier: Canada, 35 percent; United Kingdom, 30 percent.
b. Low-consumption variant.

(3211–20). The only sector with new protection predicted is leather products (3233), and this protection occurs only in the extrapolative case, not when World Bank growth rates for imports are used. Instead of new protection, the more striking results for the United Kingdom are a reduction in protectionist pressures in iron and steel (3710), radio, television, and communication equipment (3832), and automobiles (3843), as shown by both tables 3-5 and 3-6. These three sectors show elimination of protection (iron, steel, and automobiles) or further reduction in probability of protection (radio, television, and communication equipment, from, however, an underpredicted base level). As with spinning and weaving and radio, television, and communication equipment in Canada, the influence causing reduction of protectionist pressures is induced export activity. Broadly, increased import penetration by developing countries of a variety of other products provides foreign exchange that the developing countries then respend on such products as iron and steel, radio, television, and communication equipment, and automobiles. This raises British exports of these products by enough to reduce the protectionist forces affecting them (primarily forces derived from import competition from Japan).

The message of import liberalization that emerges from the results for Canada and the United Kingdom is perhaps too good to be true. It strains credulity to maintain that the principal result of an onslaught of imports from developing countries in products such as leather goods and sporting goods will not be increased protection in these products but decreased protection in automobiles and steel as the industrial country exports more of those products to the developing countries. As a control on the projections, sensitivity analysis is conducted by holding the export–output ratio constant at its base-period level rather than by permitting it to rise in response to induced exports to developing countries. Table 3-7 reports the results of this sensitivity analysis. The projections in these forecasts apply base-period (1978) values to all variables except the import-penetration ratio.

As would be expected, in the sensitivity analysis liberalization no longer occurs. Protection is now predicted to continue into the future, instead of disappearing for spinning and weaving in Canada and for steel and automobiles in the United Kingdom; though not high enough to predict actual protection, the probability of protection is predicted to rise rather than fall in radio and television products in both countries.

In this sensitivity analysis, more sectors are predicted to have future

Table 3-7. *Alternative Projections of Protection for Canada and the United Kingdom, 1990*[a]

| Importing country and ISIC number | Product sector | Presence of nontariff barrier[b] | | | | Probability of nontariff barrier (percent)[c] | | |
| | | | | 1990[a] | | | 1990 | |
		1978 actual	1978 predicted	Extrapolation	World Bank basis	1978	Extrapolation	World Bank basis
Canada								
3211	Spinning and weaving	1	1	1	1	39.0	37.4	40.4
3212	Made-up textiles	1	0[e]	0	0	16.3	19.2	16.6
3213	Knitting	1	1[e]	1	1	56.5	59.8	56.8
3214	Carpets	1	0[e]	0	0	5.5	5.7	5.5
3220	Apparel	1	1	1	1	92.6	98.2	94.0
3233	Leather products (except footwear)	0	1[f]	1	1	70.0	98.7	80.1
3240	Footwear	1	1[f]	1	1	68.0	98.3	78.6
3320	Furniture	0	1[f]	1	1	50.4	63.9	51.8
3610	Pottery, china, and earthenware	0	0	1	0	13.0	38.3	17.2
3819	Metal products not elsewhere classified	0	1[f]	1	1	35.0	45.6	37.2
3832	Radio, television, and communication equipment	1	0[e]	0	0	14.0	22.0	19.9
3903	Sporting goods	0	0	1	0	17.6	66.9	34.9

United Kingdom

3211–20	Textiles and apparel	1	1	1	98.0	98.5	98.0
3233	Leather products (except footwear)	0	0	0	14.8	57.8	17.6
3240	Footwear	1	0[e]	1	20.9	41.8	22.7
3710	Iron and steel	1	1	1	34.1	34.7	34.6
3824	Industrial machinery	0	0	1	26.2	45.3	44.4
3829	Machinery not elsewhere classified	0	1[f]	1	40.2	46.6	41.2
3832	Radio, television, and communication equipment	1	0[e]	0	8.4	10.4	9.8
3843	Motor vehicles	0	1	1	31.5	32.3	31.8
3853	Watches and clocks	0	0	0	5.3	42.4	10.6

Source: Author's calculations.

a. Sensitivity analysis using 1978 value for export–output ratio instead of 1990 projection.

b. 1 = presence of NTB; 0 = absence of NTB.

c. Probability cutoff for prediction of NTB: Canada, 35 percent; United Kingdom, 30 percent.

d. Low-consumption variant.

e. Type 2 error: failure to predict NTB where one exists.

f. Type 1 error: prediction of NTB where none exists.

Table 3-8. Projections of Major Nontariff Barriers for France and West Germany, 1990

Importing country and ISIC number	Product sector	Presence of NTB[a]				Import penetration (percent)			Probability of protection		
		1978 actual	1978 predicted	1990[b] Extrapolation	1990[b] World Bank basis	1978	1990[b] Extrapolation	1990[b] World Bank basis	1978	1990[b] Extrapolation	1990[b] World Bank basis
France											
321–22	Textiles and apparel	1	1	1	1	26.1	26.0	25.0	67.8	68.5	66.0
351	Industrial chemicals	1	1	1	1	38.6	40.0	40.0	41.4	45.0	44.0
371	Iron and steel	1	0[c]	0	0	32.6	33.0	33.0	29.8	31.8	31.6
382	Machinery not elsewhere classified	0	1[d]	1	1	41.2	44.0	42.0	88.7	91.2	89.5
383	Electrical machinery	1	1	1	1	16.8	18.0	18.0	40.1	43.8	42.6
384	Transport equipment	1	1	1	1	19.7	20.0	20.0	70.1	71.4	70.8
West Germany											
321	Textiles	1	1	1	1	34.3	38.0	37.4	29.6	36.0	34.9
322	Apparel	1	1	1	1	48.6	96.6	57.5	49.4	97.8	66.5
324	Footwear	0	0	1	1	37.6	58.8	41.2	19.0	55.9	23.8
361	Ceramics	1	1	1	1	41.2	66.3	44.8	23.1	68.8	28.5
371	Iron and steel	1	1	1	1	21.0	22.4	22.3	20.9	22.8	22.6
382	Machinery not elsewhere classified	0	1[d]	1	1	18.9	22.0	20.0	52.0	58.2	54.2
383	Electrical machinery	0	1[d]	1	1	13.6	18.2	17.0	31.2	39.4	37.2
384	Transport equipment	1	1	1	1	22.7	28.3	24.8	39.5	50.4	43.4
385	Technical instruments	0	1[d]	1	1	51.3	100.0	63.3	48.9	99.0	71.2
390	Other manufactures	0	1[d]	1	1	61.2	92.4	76.9	61.0	94.9	84.5

Source: Author's calculations.
a. 1 = presence of NTB; 0 = absence of NTB; probability cutoff for prediction of NTB: France, 40 percent; Germany, 20 percent.
b. Low-consumption variant.
c. Type 2 error: failure to predict NTB where one exists.
d. Type 1 error: prediction of NTB where none exists.

protection. In Canada, besides the new protection predicted in the main analysis for leather products (extrapolative case), the sensitivity analysis predicts new protection for furniture (3320), china and pottery (3610), metal products not elsewhere classified (3819), and sporting goods (3903). However, these new predictions are only for the case of extrapolative import growth (china and pottery, sporting goods), or else they occur in sectors in which protection was mistakenly predicted for the base period (furniture, metal products). In general, the sensitivity tests for Canada confirm the pattern of the main analysis: the incidence of new protection by 1990 appears to be limited. The sensitivity tests and the main analysis differ largely in that when the export–output ratio is held constant (sensitivity case), liberalization of existing protection does not occur.

The same findings emerge for the United Kingdom. Table 3-7 shows that with the export–output ratio held constant, protection continues into the future for iron and steel (3710) and automobiles (3843), instead of disappearing. Besides the protection predicted in the main analysis (leather products, extrapolative case), new protection is now predicted for special industrial machinery (3824), machinery not elsewhere classified (3829), and watches and clocks (3853). The sensitivity analysis thus confirms the main analysis that widespread proliferation of protection is not expected for the United Kingdom.

The projections for France and Germany appear in table 3-8. These projections are at the three-digit level of the ISIC (twenty-nine sectors), the only level at which data are available for estimation. As a result, the projections are less significant than those for the United States, Canada, and the United Kingdom. Sometimes the three-digit classification is so broad that product subsectors with problems of future protection may be missed because the broader, parent sector is found to be not likely to experience protection difficulties.

For France, the results in table 3-8 indicate that no three-digit product sectors are predicted to encounter new protection by 1990. Protection is predicted to continue in textiles and apparel (321–22); industrial chemicals (351), where quotas currently restrict dyestuffs; electrical machinery (383), where protection restricts radio and television receivers; and transport equipment (384), where voluntary export restraints limit imports from Japan. In iron and steel, the probability of protection is predicted to remain constant in the future (at a fairly high level, although not high enough to have predicted accurately the presence of NTB protection in the base period). Because the remaining sector, machinery

(382), is erroneously predicted to have protection in the base period, the future protection predicted should not be construed as a case of likely new protection. In short, at the three-digit level protection in France is projected to hold constant, with no instance of new protection by 1990. Compared with the projections for the United States, Canada, and the United Kingdom, this result appears to be biased toward an absence of new protection. Broad aggregation masks high import-penetration ratios that could occur in more narrow sectors as future exports of manufactures from developing countries grow rapidly, biasing the projections toward failure to predict new protection in the future.

To gauge the general significance of the increase in protection predicted in this study, table 3-9 summarizes the extent of market coverage represented by the product sectors that are predicted to have protection in 1990 but have no protection in the base period. The table shows two alternative measures of market coverage: the percentage share of the sector in total consumption of industrial products and the percentage share of the sector in imports of manufactures from developing countries (both in 1978).

The low estimates shown in table 3-9 refer to the narrowest concept of prediction of new protection. These estimates refer to new protection projected when the lower of the two export projection methods (usually the World Bank basis) and the high-consumption variant are used. They exclude predictions of future protection if in the base period protection was also predicted but did not exist. The high estimates are based on the most comprehensive inclusion of predicted new protection. Typically they apply the case of export growth extrapolated at the 1969–78 rate and the low variant for future consumption. They include cases of predicted protection even if protection was already predicted for the base period but did not exist.

For the United States, predicted new protection by 1990 ranges from as low as 0.92 percent of the market (consumption weights) to 11.12 percent (import weights). The simple average of all four alternative estimates is 6.96 percent. In the broader estimates, the most important sectors of new protection (based on share of total market for manufactures) are furniture, printing, machinery not elsewhere classified, and jewelry. Even the more comprehensive estimates of new protection do not imply an overwhelming closure of the U.S. market.

For Canada, there are no low-case predictions of new protection (leather products other than footwear are excluded because they were

Table 3-9. *Market Coverage of Product Sectors for Which New Protection Is Predicted by 1990*
Percent

		Low estimate		High estimate	
Importing country and ISIC number	Product sector	Share of consumption[a]	Share of imports from developing countries	Share of consumption[a]	Share of imports from developing countries
United States					
3233	Leather and substitutes (except footwear)	0.16	0.76	0.16	0.76
3320	Furniture	. . .	. . .	1.22	1.16
3420	Printing	. . .	. . .	3.83	1.22
3559	Rubber	. . .	. . .	0.57	1.29
3610	Pottery, china, and earthenware	. . .	. . .	0.14	0.35
3829	Machinery not elsewhere classified	. . .	. . .	3.84	0.96
3844	Motorcycles and bicycles	0.17	0.21	0.17	0.21
3853	Watches and clocks	0.18	1.05	0.18	1.05
3901	Jewelry	0.41	3.08	0.41	3.08
3903	Sporting goods	. . .	. . .	0.21	1.04
	Total	0.92	5.10	10.73	11.12
Canada					
3233	Leather and substitutes (except footwear)	. . .	. . .	0.13	0.83
3320	Furniture	. . .	. . .	1.37	0.98
3610	Pottery, china, and earthenware	. . .	. . .	0.14	0.54
3819	Other metals	. . .	. . .	1.44	1.62
3903	Sporting goods	. . .	. . .	0.12	1.42
	Total	. . .	. . .	3.20	5.39
United Kingdom					
3233	Leather	. . .	. . .	0.12	0.44
3824	Industrial machinery	. . .	. . .	1.69	0.22
3829	Machinery not classified elsewhere	. . .	. . .	2.19	0.38
3853	Watches and clocks	. . .	. . .	0.29	1.11
	Total	. . .	. . .	4.29	2.15
West Germany					
324	Footwear	0.80	0.71	0.80	0.71
385	Professional goods	. . .	. . .	1.25	1.71
390	Other industries	. . .	. . .	0.73	3.51
	Total	0.80	0.71	2.78	5.93

Sources: Tables 3-3 through 3-8.
a. Percent of total apparent consumption of four-digit ISIC industries in 1978, excluding petroleum products.

falsely predicted as being protected in the base year). The high-case estimates apply the alternative projections that hold the export–output ratio constant (table 3-7). On this basis, between 3.20 and 5.39 percent of the market for manufactures comes under new protection by 1990. If these estimates are averaged with zero new protection in the low-case alternatives, 2.15 percent of the market is predicted to encounter new protection.

For the United Kingdom, there are also no low-case instances of new protection; those predicted in table 3-5 do not occur under the high-consumption variant (not shown in the table). In the high case (which applies the alternative holding the export–output ratio constant, table 3-7) between 2.15 and 4.29 percent of the market for manufactures experiences new protection. Averaged with zero new protection on the low-case basis, overall coverage of U.K. protection is predicted to rise by 1.61 percent of the market.

In Germany, the projected incidence of new protection by 1990 ranges from three-fourths of 1 percent of the market to slightly more than 4 percent under the low and high cases (and with the import and consumption bases averaged for each). The simple average of the four alternative estimates gives 2.6 percent of the market as the breadth of new protection that might be expected by 1990, approximately the same magnitude as for Canada and the United Kingdom.

By all counts, the central finding in these estimates is that no massive surge of future protection is projected when the prospective exports of manufactures from developing countries are confronted with the statistical functions for protective response. The greatest incidence of projected new protection is in the United States, and even there the extent of the increase in protection is limited: 7 percent market coverage, compared with an already existing average coverage of 39 percent of the market (consumption and developing-country export weights, table 2-3). In a broad sense, and one that admittedly defies real quantification in more normal terms (for want of tariff equivalent measures of the severity of protection rather than just its product coverage), U.S. protection facing manufactures from the developing countries might rise by about one-fifth between now and 1990 (that is, 7 percent additional coverage as a fraction of the 39 percent base period). This prospect should not be too discouraging for developing-country exporters, and the prospects are better for the other industrial country markets. Given the somewhat lower base-period coverage of protection in Canada (22 percent average, consumption and developing-country export bases, table 2-3), protection there might rise by about one-tenth by 1990 (2 percent/22 percent); the corresponding figure for the United Kingdom is only one-fourteenth (1.6 percent/23 percent), and for Germany, one-tenth (2.6 percent/25.2 percent).

An important caveat to these findings is that they do not take into account the possibility of a generalized shift toward more protection in all industries because of unusually high and protracted unemployment in industrial countries. The analysis here is based on the patterns established in the period broadly from 1976 through 1981. In this period the unemployment rate in OECD countries averaged 6.0 percent, and real growth of GNP averaged 3.1 percent yearly. By 1982, however, the slowdown in world growth that began in 1980 had reached severe proportions, causing the most serious three-year stagnation since the 1930s. OECD growth in 1982 averaged only one-half a percentage point and unemployment 8.5 percent (with unemployment of approximately 10 percent in the United States and Europe).[21] In this environment protectionist pressures intensified. For example, in the United States considerable congressional pressure arose for a new form of "reciprocity" action whereby punitive protection would be imposed if foreign countries did not reduce their protection and for "local content" legislation effectively screening out large portions of automobile imports from Japan.[22] Similar pressures for new protection were present in Europe.

If economic growth remains unusually sluggish and unemployment extremely high during the rest of the decade, it is likely that protection affecting exports from developing countries will be greater than that predicted in this study on the basis of comparative experience among industries in the base period 1976–81. There is no inherent reason why stagnation should dominate the 1980s, however, although the widespread decline in productivity growth beginning in the 1970s does give cause for concern over long-run trends in global economic growth. From the vantage point of the experience of 1980–83, however, the likelihood

21. Organization for Economic Cooperation and Development, *Economic Outlook: July 1982* (Paris: OECD, 1982), pp. 14–21; and OECD, *Historical Statistics, 1960–1980* (Paris: OECD, 1982), pp. 37–40.

22. See C. Fred Bergsten and William R. Cline, "Trade Policy in the 1980s," *Policy Analyses in International Economics,* no. 3 (Washington, D.C.: Institute for International Economics, 1982).

seems to be that growth and employment in the 1980s are most likely to be on the low side of that experienced in the late 1970s rather than on its high side. This suggests that if bias exists in the projections here at an aggregate level, it is toward excessive optimism about maintaining open markets.

Finally, another major factor in the international economic environment will also play a role in the openness of markets to exports from developing countries. The financial system of industrial countries has become highly dependent on the debt owed to their banks by developing countries. At the end of 1981 the nine largest U.S. banks had exposure in nonoil developing countries equal to 221 percent of their capital.[23] With their banking systems increasingly vulnerable to default by developing countries, policymakers in industrial countries will have an additional reason to attempt to keep open their markets for exports from developing countries. If these markets become more closed, the chances of defaults or at least disruptive debt reschedulings will rise. Increasingly, the developing countries may expect a new alliance with the bankers in industrial countries to keep markets open so that the developing countries can earn the foreign exchange they need to make payments on their external debt. The clear risks of financial crisis in the North as a result of any paralysis of exports from the South may act as an important deterrent to protection in the 1980s and may offset, at least in part, a tendency toward greater protection because of possibly higher global unemployment and slower growth.

Conclusion

Manufactured imports from developing countries have grown rapidly in the last decade, exceedingly rapidly in many product sectors. It is possible to investigate the prospects for future protection by projecting these imports and applying to them the statistical protection functions calculated in chapter 2. Projections of this type affirm the general conclusion that no widespread surge in protection appears to await exports of manufactures by developing countries. To be sure, the projections indicate that in the future protection is likely to exist for

23. Board of Governors of the Federal Reserve System, "Country Exposure Lending Survey" (Washington, D.C.: The Board, 1982).

several major product sectors already restricted by nontariff barriers. That finding should come as no surprise, particularly after the experience of the Multi-fiber Arrangement. The brighter side of the projections is that cases of new protection appear to be limited. The industrial countries may be closer to the "standstill" in protection requested by the developing countries than either group realizes.

These broad conclusions are strengthened if moderate export growth rates expected by the World Bank are applied, but the general nature of the findings holds true even if exports are projected by simple extrapolation of past growth rates, of which many are remarkably high—in excess of 20 percent annually in a large number of the product sectors.

The projections here tend to single out common sectors in which new protection is a risk in various industrial countries: leather products (3233), furniture (3320), china and pottery (3610), machinery not elsewhere classified (3829), clocks and watches (3853), and sporting goods (3903). Other things being equal, developing countries might do well to approach these markets with caution. Even if things are not equal and developing countries might have to give up some cost advantages by diversifying to other products in which comparative advantage is less favorable, diversification away from these products might be worth consideration as a second-best strategy.

The best strategy would be to avoid new protection altogether by pursuit of appropriate adjustment policies in industrial countries and to dismantle gradually the existing protection in major sectors such as textiles and apparel, steel, footwear, radio and television receivers, and automobiles. The protection function estimates and projections suggest that a broad liberalization of this sort is unlikely to occur in the current political climate. But with sufficient political will, considerable liberalization might be possible. Although this study provides no basis for considering the forces that might make possible such a political effort, one that essentially would change the parameters of the protection functions, there is clearly a precedent in the process of postwar tariff liberalization for an opening of trade that goes beyond the political limitations of preceding decades. The counterpart of more open markets for exports from developing countries would be an increase in their ability not only to service their external debt but also to purchase more goods and services from industrial countries. The nonoil developing countries already account for 32 percent of U.S. exports, 25 percent of those from the European Community (excluding exports within the

Community), and 35 percent of exports from Japan.[24] Dynamic expansion of these export markets could contribute importantly to future growth in industrial countries in a mutually beneficial process of specialization favorable to both industrial and developing countries.

Even without a major new phase of liberalization of this sort, however, it would appear that the prospects for continued market access of manufactured imports from developing countries are relatively favorable, even if these imports grow rapidly. Nonetheless this optimistic outlook is premised on the successful avoidance of any massive shift toward protection in the 1980s (North-North as well as North-South) that might occur as a consequence of protracted global recession and unemployment. If macroeconomic policies in industrial countries cannot avoid a return to the global recession of 1980–82, the prospects for open markets for the exports of developing countries could be considerably dimmer than those estimated in the analysis of this study, which is largely based on experience from the period 1976–81.

24. Calculated from OECD, *Statistics of Foreign Trade: Monthly Bulletin*, series A (Paris: OECD, 1982).

CHAPTER FOUR

Conclusion and Policy Implications

So THAT the findings of this study can be put in perspective, it is useful first to consider the importance of exports to the economic growth of developing countries. Export earnings enable developing countries to import capital goods for the investment necessary for economic growth and to purchase the intermediate inputs required to keep the economy producing at its full potential. Postwar experience has shown that countries that achieve higher export growth have also been able to attain higher levels of economic growth. Figure 4-1 presents summary evidence demonstrating this point for forty developing countries. The figure shows that when these countries are grouped according to ascending rates of export growth (horizontal axis), the groups with higher export performance also have higher growth of gross domestic product. Technically the causal relation between export and GDP growth is complicated because exports are included in GDP and therefore a correlation exists between the two even if higher export earnings do not facilitate faster growth of other components of GDP. But more detailed analyses have shown that, after accounting for this inherent relationship, export growth has a stimulative effect on GDP.[1]

The importance of exports has been heightened in recent years by the growing external debt of developing countries. From 1973 to 1983 the external debt of non-OPEC developing countries rose from $130 billion to $664 billion. Approximately 62 percent of the debt is owed to Western banks and other private creditors and the rest to governments and

---

1. See for example, Bela Balassa, "Exports and Economic Growth: Further Evidence," *Journal of Development Economics,* vol. 5 (June 1978), pp. 181–89.

Figure 4-1. *Relation between the Average Growth of Gross Domestic Product and the Average Growth of Exports, Forty Developing Countries, 1960–80*

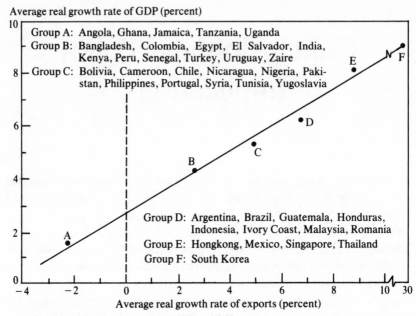

Average real growth rate of GDP (percent)

Group A: Angola, Ghana, Jamaica, Tanzania, Uganda
Group B: Bangladesh, Colombia, Egypt, El Salvador, India, Kenya, Peru, Senegal, Turkey, Uruguay, Zaire
Group C: Bolivia, Cameroon, Chile, Nicaragua, Nigeria, Pakistan, Philippines, Portugal, Syria, Tunisia, Yugoslavia

Group D: Argentina, Brazil, Guatemala, Honduras, Indonesia, Ivory Coast, Malaysia, Romania
Group E: Hongkong, Mexico, Singapore, Thailand
Group F: South Korea

Average real growth rate of exports (percent)

Source: World Bank, *World Development Report, 1982*, pp. 112–25.

multilateral agencies.[2] The single most important factor determining the ability of the developing countries to make orderly payments on this growing debt is the growth of their export earnings. The decline of their exports in 1982 played an important role in precipitating major debt reschedulings and serious strain on the international financial system, and the recovery of exports will be essential to the future servicing of this debt. Together with Eastern Europe and non-capital-surplus OPEC countries, the nonoil developing countries account for 183 percent of the capital reserves of U.S. banks (283 percent for the nine largest),[3] and any widespread defaults on this debt (especially defaults such as those that occurred in the 1930s) would pose a severe test for the viability of

2. International Monetary Fund, "World Economic Outlook," IMF Occasional Paper 21 (1983), p. 200.
3. William R. Cline, *International Debt and the Stability of the World Economy*, Policy Analyses in International Economics 4 (Washington, D.C.: Institute for International Economics, 1983), p. 33.

private banks and the adequacy of defense mechanisms of central banks. More likely than any catastrophic event for world banking, however, is a prolonged and painful cutback in domestic economic growth in developing countries if their exports remain stagnant and they continue to be forced to reduce the level of their imports.

If exports are important to developing-country growth, manufactured exports are especially important. The patterns of demand are such (with low income elasticities of demand for raw materials) that in general the developing countries cannot anticipate relying on the rapid growth of raw material exports to create export expansion, as the severe declines in commodity prices in 1981–82 vividly illustrated. The importance of manufactures is shown by the fact that in 1978 they already accounted for 30 percent of exports for low-income countries and 52 percent for middle-income countries (excluding those exporting oil), even when the narrow definition of manufactures from the standard international trade classification is used.[4]

Export performance, in manufactures and generally, reflects to an important degree the practices that developing countries follow. The policies of high protection and overvaluation of exchange rates frequently followed in the 1950s and early 1960s caused poor export performance for many developing countries.[5] Development theory has shifted from an emphasis on import substitution to outward-looking growth based on dynamic export performance and relatively open trading policies. But much work remains to be done on the design of optimal trade policies for rational development of infant industries with good prospects for long-run comparative advantage.[6]

Although policies inside developing countries clearly affect their export performance, so do the trade policies adopted by industrial countries, where the largest markets for these exports are found. The new protectionism of the 1970s showed a tendency for industrial countries to close off markets to developing countries as they became proficient in producing the goods in question. The popular impression

4. World Bank, *World Development Report, 1981* (Washington, D.C.: World Bank, 1981), p. 150.

5. See for example, Anne O. Krueger, *Liberalization Attempts and Consequences,* Studies in International Economic Relations, vol. 10 (Ballinger for the National Bureau of Economic Research, 1978).

6. For one of the few recent attempts to analyze infant industry development, see Larry E. Westphal, "Empirical Justification for Infant Industry Protection," World Bank Staff Working Paper 445 (World Bank, March 1981).

has been that products from developing countries have been responsible for widespread loss of jobs in industrial countries, even though research has consistently shown that job losses are usually attributable to slow growth in domestic markets and rising labor productivity, and that trade in manufactures with developing countries has generated many more export jobs in industrial countries than it has cost in jobs lost to imports.[7] A continuation and intensification of the protectionist response in industrial countries to manufactured exports from developing countries could severely limit the future growth of these exports. This would reduce the prospects for economic growth in developing countries and not only risk an induced slowdown in jobs and production associated with exports to developing-country markets but also intensify strains on the international financial system as developing countries become less able to manage the burden of their external debt.

Export Performance

This study analyzes the actual performance of manufactured exports from developing countries in the 1970s and considers the future prospects for growth of these exports—in particular the likelihood of intensified protection against them in the future. As seen in chapter 1, these exports grew rapidly in the 1970s. From 1969 to 1978 their average real growth rate in the markets of the seven largest industrial countries was 7.6 percent a year. If the narrower definition of manufactures used by the General Agreement on Tariffs and Trade and the World Bank is considered (excluding processed foods and nonferrous metals), the average growth rate was an even more impressive 15.6 percent annually from 1965 to 1973 and 12.4 percent from 1973 to 1980.[8]

More recently this export growth has slowed down. Under the narrow World Bank definition, manufactured exports from developing countries

---

7. Anne O. Krueger, "LDC Manufacturing Production and Implications for OECD Comparative Advantage," paper prepared for the Conference on Prospects and Policy for Industrial Structure Change in the United States and Other OECD Countries (University of Minnesota, January 1979); Bela Balassa, "The Changing International Division of Labor in Manufactured Goods" (World Bank, 1979); Errol Grinols and Erik Thorbecke, "The Effects of Trade Between the U.S. and Developing Countries on U.S. Employment," Working Paper 171 (Cornell University, Department of Economics, 1978).

8. World Bank, *World Development Report, 1983* (World Bank, 1983), p 10.

grew by only 4.1 percent annually in 1980–82.[9] Recession in Europe and the United States has played an important role in this slowdown. In the more recent statistics the influence of protection is difficult to determine, but cyclical factors would seem more important because the principal sectoral trade barriers against developing countries after 1979 were already largely in place by the mid-1970s.[10]

The detailed trade data for the 1970s used in this study show a concentration of growth in several product sectors with remarkably high real export growth rates. Among eighty-one four-digit categories of the international standard industrial classification, growth of exports to industrial countries exceeded 20 percent annually (1969–70 to 1978) for thirty categories. The more important of these, by value, include leather products; footwear; furniture; plastics; tires; other rubber products; ceramics; hardware; metal structures; machinery; radio, television, and communication equipment; motor vehicle parts; scientific equipment; watches and clocks; and sporting goods. The concentration of export values and growth in a limited number of product sectors (including textiles and apparel) has meant that the pressures for protectionist response have been higher than would have been expected from the extremely modest overall average presence of manufactured imports from developing countries, which accounted for only about 2 to 3 percent of market supply in the late 1970s.

Concentrated and rapid growth has led to significant increases in import penetration from developing countries in selected product sectors. Important categories with increased penetration by developing countries in the U.S. market, in the period 1970–78, include leather products (5.4 to 11.1 percent), apparel (3.4 to 12.4 percent), footwear (0.8 to 14.0 percent), radio, television and communication equipment (1.5 to 6.8 percent), watches and clocks (0.6 to 13.8 percent), and jewelry (5.0 to 18.2 percent).

Today's protection is not necessarily caused by market penetration from developing countries, however. In the key sectors of steel and automobiles, protection is North-North rather than North-South. Japan

9. Ibid.
10. With respect to imports of industrial countries from all sources, virtually all the slowdown in 1980 and 1981 can be explained statistically by the recession in the industrial countries. C. Fred Bergsten and William R. Cline, "Trade Policy in the 1980s: An Overview," in William R. Cline, ed., *Trade Policy in the 1980s* (Washington, D.C.: Institute for International Economics, 1983), pp. 72–78.

(automobiles) or Japan and Europe (steel) provide the source of import pressure. In these two sectors in particular, market penetration by developing countries remained negligible as of the late 1970s (although by 1983 imports from developing countries had increased to a sizable share of total imports in steel).

The United States, Germany, and Japan have been the most dynamic markets for exports of manufactures from developing countries. In the United States and Germany, these exports have grown at a high rate relative to market growth, while in Japan the market itself has grown rapidly because of high GNP growth. For the seven major industrial countries, penetration by manufactured imports from developing countries ranges from 1.62 percent of apparent consumption (Canada) to 3.1 percent (Germany), averaging 2.46 percent. Despite its restrictive image, Japan (with a penetration ratio of 2.61) shows no less import penetration by developing-country manufactures than the other industrial country markets, under the broad definition of manufactures used in this study.

Exports of manufactures from developing countries have tended to shift away from traditional products (such as processed foods, nonferrous metals, textiles, clothing, and footwear) to nontraditional products such as machinery; radio, television, and communication equipment; and watches and clocks. However, the evidence does not support the hypothesis that the lower-income developing countries are replacing the middle-income newly industrialized countries as suppliers of traditional manufactures in a process of "stages of comparative advantage" whereby the low-income countries would take the place of those countries on the lower rungs as they move up the ladder of product sophistication. Some evidence indicates that the developing countries have replaced Japan as a supplier of certain manufactured exports to industrial country markets. However, more generally there appears to be no systematic decline of import penetration by industrial country suppliers to offset rising penetration by developing countries. On the contrary, across sectors the instances of rising penetration tend to come from imports from both sources.

Explaining Protection

The statistical estimates of protectionist behavior (chapter 2) show that for the United States the key determinants of protection are the absolute size of the labor force and the level of import penetration (total imports relative to apparent consumption) in the sector in question. These are classic political variables in explaining protection (appendix C). More technical considerations, such as minimization of labor adjustment costs, would cause protection to be related to the change in import penetration, not its level, and to such variables as skill ratio or wage rate, but not the absolute size of employment (an indicator of political clout).

The best statistical results are obtained by using a joint test for the United States, Canada, and the United Kingdom. In this model, protection is related to the size of sectoral employment, the import-penetration level (but not its change), industry concentration (facilitating mobilization for lobbying), the ratio of exports to output (negative sign, showing that export-oriented industries are less protectionist), value added per worker (negative sign, indicating less protectionist pressure in industries that are relatively intensive in physical and human capital), and share of unskilled labor in the work force (positive sign, or more protection in unskilled sectors). These variables are among those commonly found to have an influence on protection (appendix C).

The three-country model does not find a statistically significant difference in the protectionist forces among the three countries, indicating that the underlying political and economic determinants are similar in those countries and that none of the three is significantly more protectionist in its behavior than the others. More generally, the estimated parameters of the more important variables are surprisingly similar across the five countries for which estimates are available, indicating uniformities in the political-economic process of protection.

Quantitative analysis of protection requires a focus on major nontariff barriers if it is to address the principal locus of protection today. Since the Tokyo Round of negotiations in the 1970s, tariffs have been low, and the significant protection is that provided by nontariff barriers (NTBs) such as quotas and voluntary export restraints. Yet because tariffs are much more easily measured than NTBs, most empirical studies have carried out tests that use tariffs as the variable to be explained. This study chooses for analysis the protection by major NTBs (using logit analysis, which considers a dependent variable that takes on a value of either zero—for no barrier—or 1—for the presence of a barrier). Although this approach may sacrifice some precision, it should more than compensate by achieving greater relevance to current protection than would be possible with an investigation of tariffs. In addition to the choice between tariffs and NTBs, the choice of sectoral aggregation is important in the quantitative analysis of protection. In particular, the results of chapter 2 suggest the importance of considering the textile-apparel complex as a single large sector in order to capture accurately the influence of the political variable of employment size.

The data base on major NTBs indicates that industrial countries typically protect from 25 to 40 percent of their markets. Although the differing intensity of NTB protection among different countries makes these "coverage" figures ambiguous for comparing their relative degree of protection, the NTB coverage estimates suggest that the United States is not necessarily less protectionist than other countries (including Japan and France), popular impressions notwithstanding.

Prospects for Future Protection

Whereas past studies of protectionist behavior have generally been limited to estimates of models of existing protection, the analysis of chapter 3 attempts to project future protection under alternative scenarios for exports of manufactures from developing countries. The policy objective of this analysis is to determine whether rapid growth of these exports can continue into the future without provoking a proliferation of restrictive barriers in the markets of industrial countries. The projections apply the estimated statistical protection functions (from chapter 2) to the projected import-penetration ratios (and other variables) expected by 1990 to determine what additional sectors may be subject to protection at that time.

Two alternatives are used for the projections. The first assumes that manufactured exports from developing countries continue to grow at the same rates in real terms as they did during the 1970s, for each of eighty four-digit ISIC categories. This scenario gives a high average growth rate of 14 percent annually for these exports from 1978 to 1990. The second alternative applies the annual growth rates to 1990 expected by the authors of recent World Bank projections; these growth rates give a considerably lower average, 10 percent.

The most important independent variable for the projections of protection is the future level of import penetration. This variable requires an assumption about future supply from sources other than developing countries, in addition to the estimated future exports from developing countries. The analysis assumes that the present ratios of imports to consumption remain constant into the future for supplies from non-developing-country sources.

The broad conclusion from these projections is that no great increase in the incidence of protection above its current base is likely. The largest potential increase in the incidence of protection is for the United States, where the market coverage by NTBs would rise from about 40 percent now to 47 percent by 1990. The projections for Canada, the United Kingdom, France, and Germany show considerably smaller incidence of new protection by 1990.

Nevertheless, certain product sectors consistently appear in some or most of the individual country projections as prime candidates for new protection in response to higher future import penetration. These problem sectors include leather products, furniture, china and pottery, machinery not elsewhere classified, clocks and watches, and sporting goods.

Moreover, the analysis does not address the possibility that the severity of protection could intensify in those sectors where it already exists. In apparel, for example, exports of developing countries to the major industrial countries grew in real terms by 15 percent annually from 1969–70 to 1978, and two out of six other textile sectors grew at rates of over 13 percent (appendix B). But the new Multi-fiber Arrangement for 1982–85 promises to be considerably more restrictive than the previous MFA. In the discussions on the new MFA, negotiators for the European Community insisted on the right to impose actual reductions in imports while U.S. negotiators supported limitation of import growth to the rate of domestic market growth, a much slower rate than the 6 percent growth ceiling under the previous MFA.[11] Similarly, protection in steel could intensify and thwart nascent export efforts by developing countries.

The sectors with major nontariff barriers have demonstrated that they have the political influence to obtain protection. The developing countries would do well to avoid concentrating future export growth efforts in these sectors because increased market penetration is likely to be met with increased intensity of protection. The principal sectors in this

11. Brij Khindaria, "U.S. Takes a Tougher Stance on MFA Negotiations," *Financial Times* (London), December 15, 1981, p. 9. Even though the umbrella MFA will provide the same 6 percent ceiling as before, the bilateral agreements are likely to call for lower growth, related to the slow rate of growth of domestic demand.

category are textiles, apparel, footwear, television sets, and steel. (The expiration of U.S. escape clause protection of television sets and footwear in 1981 does not mean that these sectors are good prospects for rapid future growth of developing-country supply; such growth would invite renewal of protection.) In automobiles, the other major protected sector, there is probably more scope for growth of developing-country supply, which is primarily in automobile parts. In this trade the developing countries have the multinational corporations as allies, with production organized on a world basis. Even in this sector labor opposition to imported components is growing, however.

If the developing countries are to avoid rapid expansion of exports in sectors with strong existing protection (especially textiles, apparel, footwear, television sets, ships, and steel) as well as other sectors that seem most likely to confront new protective barriers in the future (ceramics, watches and clocks, leather products, furniture, certain machinery, and sporting goods), they will need to diversify their manufactured exports. Sectors that hold promise of remaining relatively open include processed foods, beverages, wood products, pulp and paper, chemicals, fertilizers, plastics, rubber products, nonferrous metals, engines, a broad range of machinery and equipment, domestic electrical appliances, aircraft parts, and photographic goods—broadly, the ISIC categories not showing major protection currently nor projected to do so in the future. Diversification would probably mean some sacrifice in comparative advantage. But a more diversified export profile has greater security. In terms of concrete policy measures, these considerations imply that in their design of special export incentives, planners in developing countries should avoid including the sectors vulnerable to protection in their list of sectors to receive such incentives.

Merits of a Moderate Course

Appendix D examines an extreme scenario for manufactured exports from developing countries. It asks, what would happen to protection if all developing countries tried to emulate the East Asian export-oriented economies (Hong Kong, Korea, Singapore, and Taiwan) and reach the same relative intensity of manufactured exports as this "Gang of Four" (G-4)? The analysis uses cross-country patterns relating manufactured exports to GDP as a function of developmental level (per capita income) and country size (population). The manufactured exports of the East Asian economies are found to be far above the cross-country pattern while many other developing countries, especially in Latin America, are found to lie below it. Simulations indicate that if all other developing countries increased their exports of manufactures to levels comparable with those of the G-4, the total of manufactured exports from developing countries would rise more than sevenfold. Such an increase would mean that approximately 80 percent of the value of manufactured exports of developing countries would be in products with resulting import penetration of 15 percent or higher in industrial country markets (not including imports provided by other industrial countries). This high penetration (frequently much higher than the 15 percent threshold examined) would pose substantial risk of provoking new protection.

The G-4 analysis in appendix D suggests that there are limits to the absorptive capacity of markets for exports of manufactures from developing countries, even though these limits may be high. If the G-4 export expansion (by a multiple of 7.5) were phased in by 1990 (a period of eight years), the ratio of manufactured exports to GDP for developing countries would have to grow by 29 percent a year. Adding a GDP growth rate of 4 percent a year, the manufactured exports would have to grow by 34 percent annually. (The resulting import penetration would still be comparable to that in the once-for-all static shift examined in appendix D if income also grew at 4 percent in industrial countries; the penetration would be even higher if income grew more slowly in industrial countries than in developing countries.) This growth would far exceed the range of prospective export growth considered in chapter 3, from 10 to 14 percent annually. Although export growth averaged 30 percent in 1960–79 in the exceptional case of South Korea,[12] the analysis of appendix D suggests that the generalization of such growth rates to all developing countries would cause such a large rise in the penetration of industrial country markets that a protectionist response would be likely.

When the findings of chapter 3 and appendix D are considered together, the policy implication is that there is a speed limit on the expansion of manufactured exports that developing countries would do well to observe if they wish to avoid a protectionist reaction. In the aggregate, developing countries can probably expand their manufactured exports at real rates of 10 to 15 percent annually without provoking a

12. World Bank, *World Development Report, 1981*, p. 149.

strong protectionist response (chapter 3), but expansion at rates of 30 percent or higher would be much more likely to provoke problems of market absorption and protection (appendix D). Even an expansion of 15 percent would represent a relatively buoyant market for developing countries, however, and an expansion that in most cases would be sufficient for the achievement of relatively high domestic growth rates. Moreover, because some developing countries are unlikely to achieve export growth this high, others would have room to expand exports somewhat more rapidly.

For most developing countries, expansion of manufactured exports within a "safe" range of up to 15 percent annually would be consistent with liberalization of the external sector through lower protection and increased exchange-rate realism. But that might be a slower rate than would result from reversing the policy regime toward a strong bias in favor of exports (through export subsidies, for example). Although there appears to be an upper speed limit on the growth of manufactured exports in view of the absorptive capacity of markets, this limit is higher than planners in some developing countries might think. It would be a mistake for policymakers in developing countries to turn back to inward-looking policies, to fail to adopt outward-looking reforms, or to limit export growth to rates well below target rates of growth for national income because of a pessimistic expectation of severe market limitations on export expansion.

Further Policy Implications

The findings of chapter 3 and results of parallel work by other authors (appendix C) indicate a need to reexamine policies of import restraint in industrial countries. The statistical analyses show that political influence, not economic criteria, dominates the process of decisionmaking on protection. Thus the consistent influence of the employment size of an industry, a variable representing political strength, dominates variables—such as the skill ratio, wage rate, and change in import penetration—that are more relevant to the economic question of adjustment cost. Accordingly, a reexamination of current protection by policymakers and the public would be likely to expose a set of blatantly political policies that need to be reformed if trade policy is to be based on economic criteria rather than on special interests.

Protection in textiles offers a good example. Because of a firm political coalition between the producers of textiles and the manufacturers of apparel (and their respective labor unions), both sectors gain from severe import restraints under the MFA. Yet on economic criteria protection of textiles is an anomaly. Textiles (ISIC sectors 3211–19) have shown a trade surplus for several years in the United States and some other industrial countries, making this industry the only one that receives major protection and yet exports more than it imports. A trade policy based on economic rather than on political criteria would begin at once to dismantle the protection that the textile industry has been able to secure through its alliance with the apparel industry (where technical economic criteria would be more likely to provide for at least temporary protection).

Ideally, protection in industrial countries would begin to evolve toward a structure based on rational economic criteria that weigh costs and benefits. Protection costs for consumers would be compared with the benefit to labor and producers of avoiding adjustment costs. In most but probably not all cases, policymaking on a basis of such cost-benefit analysis would yield much less protection than currently exists.

A fundamental question is whether the political factors that explain protection can be changed. Their importance is shown by the statistical analysis of trade policy. But the strength of political influences need not be immutable. The industrial countries have passed through phases of protectionism and liberalization. The surge in protectionist pressures in the United States in 1981–83 appeared to be closely related to the strength of the dollar, a consequence largely of the particular mix of loose fiscal and tight monetary policy pursued by the Reagan administration and the Federal Reserve. Protectionist pressures more generally were aggravated by recession and high unemployment in Europe and the United States. Under different cyclical and exchange-rate circumstances protectionist pressures could decline. Moreover, in other fields of economic policy past patterns of political interest have been challenged. Recent deregulation of the airlines, trucking, and banking industries in the United States has been a triumph of rational economic considerations over vested political interests.

By early 1982 the climate for changing protectionist measures was conducive to still more severe protection rather than toward liberalization. The U.S. trade representative judged that "the trade pressures are the most intense we've had since the early 1970s," and a former U.S.

deputy special trade representative reflected that "there hasn't been as great a risk to the world trading system in the postwar period."[13] In the U.S. Congress there was a growing movement to enact new legislation calling for retaliatory trade barriers against countries judged to be keeping their markets closed to U.S. exports,[14] although this approach would break the tradition of "most favored nation" treatment for all suppliers, a keystone of the success of trade liberalization in the postwar period. Nevertheless, the Reagan administration remained ideologically committed to an open trading posture; in 1981 it had allowed import quotas on footwear and television sets to expire even though it succumbed to pressure for protection of automobiles and induced the Japanese government to adopt voluntary export restraints.

At best the prospects for changing the political factors determining protectionism are mixed. Policymakers in developing countries cannot count on any general shift away from protectionism in industrial country markets. Nevertheless, they can take comfort from the fact that even under the present political-economic relationships that influence protection, the manufactured exports of developing countries should be able to grow at reasonably brisk rates without provoking a widespread protectionist response.

Certain policy measures could help improve the environment for open trade. Improved adjustment assistance to workers and firms is one such policy. After a long period of ineffectiveness because of overrestrictive requirements for eligibility,[15] the U.S. Trade Act of 1979 liberalized adjustment assistance so much that in 1980–81 massive expenditures were being incurred for automobile workers under the program, even though the U.S. International Trade Commission concluded that the automobile industry did not warrant special escape-clause protection (under section 201 of the trade law) because its difficulties were not attributable mainly to imports. Adjustment assistance was a natural candidate for the budgetary ax during the severe fiscal cutbacks of 1981. The program was largely gutted, which left domestic workers without a cushion for the adjustment process. The virtual absence of an adjustment assistance program invites greater protectionist pressure. Labor can

13. *Wall Street Journal,* January 5, 1982.
14. Hobart Rowen, "Brock Says U.S. Will Not Tolerate Barriers to Trade," *Washington Post,* February 1, 1982.
15. Charles R. Frank, Jr., *Foreign Trade and Domestic Aid* (Brookings Institution, 1977).

more credibly argue that import restrictions are the only policy instrument available to deal with pressures from imports. Revitalizing the program of adjustment assistance would require restricting its availability to cases where imports are the cause of the industry's difficulty, yet making the instrument less rigid than in the 1960s and early 1970s. A revived program of adjustment assistance would ideally go much further than past programs toward promoting actual adjustment—through planned closure of plants, relocation of workers, or programs for increased competitiveness.

The development of an international code on protection to "safeguard" threatened domestic industries is another area of priority for policy. At present there is little international discipline to govern the network of protective quotas imposed under this broad concept to defend jeopardized domestic industries. Voluntary export restraints adopted by suppliers under pressure from governments of importing countries are outside any GATT rules. A safeguards code would impose certain limitations on these practices, such as time limits and provisions for gradual liberalization. Negotiations on a safeguards code broke down in the Tokyo Round in the late 1970s, largely because of the conflict between the European countries, which sought the right of imposing safeguard protection selectively (on a few supplier countries only), and the developing countries, which opposed "selectivity" on the grounds that it would greatly weaken the bargaining strength of supplier countries by isolating them from potential allies among other suppliers. Because quantitative limitations under safeguard protection are an increasingly dominant component of protection, especially the protection facing developing countries, the achievement of a code disciplining these measures would be an important breakthrough in favoring prospects for exports from developing countries.

Policymakers in developing countries may also be able to improve access to foreign markets by entering into bilateral negotiations and offering liberalization of their own markets in return. The past practice of nonreciprocity, whereby developing countries offered little liberalization of their own in multilateral trade negotiations, has tended to limit the extent of liberalization in those negotiations on products of interest to the developing countries. Besides inducing liberalization of markets in industrialized countries, liberalizing offers by developing countries would typically have the secondary benefit of reducing distortions in their own economies.

Notwithstanding the uncertain outlook for protection in the world economy, the principal conclusion of this study is that developing countries appear to have considerable scope for continued expansion of their exports of manufactured goods at relatively rapid rates. But either a generalized move to extremely high growth rates for these exports (similar to the exceptional Korean performance in the 1960s and 1970s) or a concentration of exports in the most sensitive products would run the risk of a protective response from industrial countries.

That the industrial country markets can absorb a relatively brisk growth of diversified manufactured exports from developing countries is important because the developing countries are experiencing intense pressure on their balance of payments, and steady growth of manufactured exports will be an important instrument for their continued economic growth. Their export performance and economic growth will have consequences for the industrial countries in terms of future markets and the capacity of developing countries to meet their obligations of payments on external debts.

Appendixes

Estimates of Import Penetration

A MAJOR difficulty for policy analysis of exports of manufactures from developing countries has been the lack of detailed data on import-penetration ratios that relate manufactured imports from developing countries to production and consumption in industrial countries. Sufficiently detailed data could reveal patterns of high and rapidly growing import-penetration ratios in industrial product sectors despite a relatively low level of import penetration from developing countries for manufactures in the aggregate.

This statistical note attempts to advance the state of trade and production data for North-South trade by providing standardized and detailed estimates of import-penetration ratios.[1] The underlying data are from UN sources. The industrial disaggregation used is the four-digit level of the international standard industrial classification, representing eighty-one manufactured product categories. The estimates are for seven industrial country markets: the United States, Canada, Japan, France, West Germany, Italy, and the United Kingdom. These countries accounted for 88 percent of total imports of the seventeen industrial country members of the Organization for Economic Cooperation and Development from non-oil-exporting developing countries in 1978.[2] The estimates are for 1978 (the latest year with production data available)

I am indebted to William Hutton for able research assistance and to the U.S. Department of Commerce for financial support.

1. Estimates from related work at the World Bank were not available at the time of preparation of this study.

2. Calculated from International Monetary Fund, *Direction of Trade Yearbook, 1979* (Washington, D.C.: IMF, 1979).

and 1969, 1970, and 1976, as other benchmark years for assessing growth rates in the 1970s.

Trade Data and Correspondence

The trade data are from the computerized trade data base of the United Nations. These data are at the five-digit level of the standard international trade classification, representing 1,585 product categories.

For conversion of the SITC trade data into four-digit ISIC categories, the two sets of classifications are linked by the official UN correspondence.[3] Use of the UN correspondence is complicated by the fact that many of the five-digit SITC categories (approximately 21 percent) have multiple listings of ISIC categories. Therefore, only a part of the trade data may be unambiguously put into ISIC production categories. Nevertheless, analysis with U.S. data indicates that the great bulk of manufactured trade by value is in SITC categories that do have unique correspondences with ISIC categories. Of all U.S. imports of manufactures in 1976, 85 percent by value were in products for which there was an unambiguous correspondence with a single ISIC category.

For the minor part of trade with multiple ISIC categories corresponding to a given SITC category, the following method is used. On the side of exports, for the SITC category in question, the country's export value is allocated among the corresponding ISIC production categories in proportion to the relative size of production among these categories in the country. For example, if an SITC category has two corresponding ISIC categories, the export value is allocated between them in proportion to their respective values of domestic production. Thus

(A-1) $E_i^j = \phi_i^j E_j$,

where E_i^j is the amount of exports allocated from SITC category j to ISIC category i, E_j is the total value of exports in SITC category j, and

(A-2) $\phi_i^j = \dfrac{Q_i}{\Sigma_{i \in j} Q_i}$,

where ϕ_i^j is the share of exports in SITC category j to be allocated to

---

3. United Nations, *Classification of Commodities by Industrial Origin: Relationship of the Standard International Trade Classification to the International Standard Industrial Classification*, series M, no. 43, 2d ed. (UN, 1966).

ISIC category i, Q_i is domestic production in ISIC category i, and $i \in j$ means the set of ISIC industries, i, that are included in the multiple correspondence listing for SITC category j.

The logic behind allocation of exports based on domestic production shares is that the profile of a country's exports of manufactures by individual product sector is likely to resemble the profile of its domestic production of the same products. An important practical consequence of this allocation is that it avoids the arbitrariness of category width: some categories may be trivial in size and others large, and in such cases it would be misleading to allocate exports evenly across a number of ISIC categories merely because these various categories had all been listed in the correspondence for the SITC category in question.

For imports, the allocational procedure used is somewhat more complicated. It is based again on production weights but uses the production of the trading partners rather than of the importing country itself. The principle of using production weights for the correspondence allocation remains necessary to avoid the problem of arbitrarily disparate size across classifications. Use of domestic production weights, however, makes less sense for imports than for exports. The country may be importing a product precisely because it does not have significant domestic production. It is therefore more meaningful to base the allocations of import data on the production values for trading partners as a proxy for the relative weights of various sectors in the home country's imports.[4]

The allocation used for imports for a given SITC category in which multiple corresponding ISIC categories are listed is as follows:

$$(A\text{-}3) \qquad\qquad M_i^j = \lambda_i^j M_j,$$

where M_i^j is the value allocated to imports in ISIC sector i out of total imports in SITC category j (M_j), and

$$(A\text{-}4) \qquad\qquad \lambda_i^j = \Sigma_k \theta_{ik}^j \Psi_{jk},$$

where θ_{ik}^j is, for partner country k, the share of production in ISIC category i out of production in the ISIC sectors listed as corresponding to the SITC category j in question, and Ψ_{jk} is the share of partner country

---

4. Direct information on these imports by ISIC category is of course not available; the import data are by SITC, giving rise to the allocational problem in the first place.

k in the home country's imports of SITC product j. These two variables are calculated as

(A-5)
$$\theta_{ik}^j = \frac{Q_{ik}}{\Sigma_{i\in j}Q_{ik}},$$

where Q_{ik} is the value of production in ISIC sector i in partner country k, and $i\in j$ refers to the set of ISIC sectors listed as corresponding to SITC category j; and

(A-6)
$$\Psi_{jk} = \frac{M_{jk}}{\Sigma_k M_{jk}},$$

where M_{jk} is the value of imports in SITC category j from partner country k.

For this allocational computation, only the sixteen industrial countries for which ISIC production data are available are considered as partner countries k in obtaining import shares. Moreover, the weight λ_i^j is normalized by the constraint that it sum to unity for all ISIC categories i corresponding to a given SITC category j.[5]

In summary, for each SITC category with multiple ISIC corresponding categories listed, the allocation of trade data across these ISIC categories is based on (1) domestic production shares for exports and (2) trade-weighted production shares of trading partners for imports. As mentioned earlier, these allocational procedures are necessary for only a relatively small portion of trade, however (for U.S. imports, only 15 percent of value). For the bulk of trade, a unique correspondence exists between each SITC category and a single ISIC category.[6]

---

5. This is done so that the import value M_j is fully allocated into the i sectors of ISIC, and not over- or understated. Thus the weights used are normalized as

$$\lambda_i^{j*} = \lambda_i^j\left[\frac{1}{\Sigma_i\lambda_i^j}\right].$$

The need for normalization arises because, while for a single partner country $\Sigma_i\theta_{ik}^j = 1$, when the parameters θ_{ik}^j are weighted by SITC partner trade weights Ψ_{jk} (equation A-4) the result may be that the summation of the ISIC sector weights, $\Sigma_i\lambda_i^j$, exceeds or falls short of unity.

6. For U.S. imports of footwear, direct information on the division between nonrubber (82 percent) and rubber (18 percent) footwear is used to allocate the trade data on footwear (SITC 85102, 85103) between ISIC categories for nonrubber footwear (3240) and rubber products industries (3559), respectively. U.S. International Trade Commission, *Non-rubber Footwear: U.S. Production, Exports, Imports for Consumption, Apparent U.S. Consumption, Employment, Producers' Price Index, and Consumer Price Index*, Second Calendar Quarter 1978, no. 1019, and Third Calendar Quarter 1979,

Finally, the correspondence between SITC and ISIC leads to some overinclusion of essentially raw materials in certain sectors for processed trade. This problem is most serious in ISIC 3116 (grain mill products), 3119 (confectionery), and 3121 (foods not elsewhere classified), where the procedure described above leads to incorporation of coffee (SITC 07110), cocoa (07210), and tea (07410). Although some portions of these SITC categories are indeed manufactured in some way (for example, SITC 07110 contains coffee substitutes and roasted coffee as well as raw coffee), more detailed trade data for the United States indicate that the bulk of imports in these categories is in raw products. Accordingly, the basic data set of this study is adjusted to exclude these three important raw materials from the ISIC categories where they would normally be placed following the general correspondence and allocational procedure described above.[7] This exclusion significantly affects the total magnitude estimated for manufactured imports into the seven largest industrial countries from developing countries, since total imports of coffee, cocoa, and tea in 1978 were about $10 billion and manufactured imports were $66 billion (table 1-1). For additional discussion of the product inclusion of manufactures as defined in this study, see appendix E.

Production Data

The basic source for production data is the United Nations. These data are available at the three-digit ISIC level for 1970, 1976, and 1978.[8] For 1973, the UN data are available at the four-digit level.[9] For purposes

---

no. 909 (Washington, D.C.: USITC, 1978, 1979). For other countries the entire value of footwear trade is allocated to nonrubber footwear.

For apparel, the entire value of SITC categories 84141, -43, -44 is allocated to ISIC 3220. Although the UN correspondence also lists ISIC 3213, analysis of U.S. Department of Commerce data shows that application of the general allocating formula in the text gives excessive assignment to ISIC 3213 and insufficient assignment to ISIC 3220. Department of Commerce, *U.S. Commodity Exports and Imports as Related to Output, 1976 and 1975* (Washington, D.C.: Department of Commerce, 1979), pp. 46–49.

7. Note, however, that the analysis of appendix D applies an earlier version of the data base not excluding coffee, cocoa, and tea, as did the protection functions estimated in chapter 2, where, however, the entire range of processed foods is omitted from the tests in the sectoral estimates for the United States and the United Kingdom.

8. United Nations, *Yearbook of Industrial Statistics: 1975 Edition,* vol. 1, and *Yearbook of Industrial Statistics: 1976 Edition,* vol. 1 (UN, 1977 and 1979). Unpublished 1978 data were provided by the UN.

9. United Nations, *The 1973 World Programme of Industrial Statistics: Summary of Data from Selected Countries* (UN, 1979).

of obtaining the four-digit estimates for 1970 and 1976, the national shares of four-digit ISIC categories within each three-digit grouping for the 1973 data base are applied to the more aggregative three-digit figures available for 1970, 1976, and 1978. To the extent that actual four-digit production shares within three-digit groupings changed from 1970 to 1978, discrepancies between estimated and actual shares should be relatively evenly split between the 1970 and 1976 estimates because of the use of the intermediate year 1973 as the base for four-digit sectoral shares.

The industrial production data used are for the following countries: (1) for both import-penetration ratios and import shares, Canada, France, Germany, Italy, Japan, the United Kingdom, and the United States; and (2) for import shares, Austria, Belgium, Australia, Denmark, Finland, New Zealand, Norway, Sweden, and the Netherlands.

For certain countries, four-digit ISIC detail was not completely available from the UN data for 1973. In those cases, additional national sources were used to disaggregate three-digit ISIC data into four-digit categories.[10] For all countries, production data are expressed in national currencies. For comparability with the trade data expressed in dollars, national currency values are converted into dollars at the average exchange rate for the year in question.[11]

Ratios Calculated

Two basic ratios indicate the role of trade in domestic supply. The first is an import-penetration ratio, defined as the ratio of imports to apparent domestic consumption. Apparent consumption equals domestic production plus imports minus exports. Thus the import penetration ratio m is

---

10. For France: Office Statistique des Communautés Européennes, *France, 1970: Tableau Entrées-Sorties* (Bruxelles: Communautés Européennes, 1974). For the United Kingdom: for ISIC group 382, Organization for Economic Cooperation and Development, *Industrial Production, 1978-1* (Paris: OECD, 1978), p. 19, and IMF, *International Financial Statistics,* vol. 31 (April 1978), pp. 368–69.

11. International Monetary Fund, *International Financial Statistics,* selected issues.

(A-7)
$$m = \frac{M}{Q + M - E},$$

where M is the value of imports, Q the value of production, and E the value of exports in the ISIC sector. This ratio reflects the relative importance of imports in meeting domestic demand. For purposes of protection patterns, for most manufactures in advanced countries, the higher the import-penetration ratio, the greater the pressure for protection will be in the industry.

For this appendix, a second ratio calculated is the net import ratio: imports minus exports divided by apparent consumption. Thus the net import ratio n is calculated as

(A-8)
$$n = \frac{M - E}{Q + M - E}.$$

This ratio differs from the import-penetration ratio in that it subtracts the ratio of exports to apparent consumption. This second ratio is of interest because in sectors with relatively high exports the pressures for protection may be lower than in other sectors with an equally high import-penetration ratio but relatively lower exports. Producers in sectors with well-developed export interests may be more concerned about foreign retaliation and therefore less inclined toward protectionism than producers in sectors with limited export interests. Because the producers of exports may not be the same firms (or even in the same products when defined narrowly enough) as producers of import substitutes, however, a high import-penetration ratio may be a source of protectionist pressure even when exports in the same industry are relatively high.

Both sets of ratios are calculated for total trade as well as for trade with developing countries alone. In this way it is possible to identify the specific role of developing countries in the level and growth of import penetration and net trade.

Estimates for the United States

Chapter 1 reports the principal findings of the estimates of import penetration. The discussion here provides further detail of those estimates. Table 1-7 shows selected product sectors with high import penetration in the United States. Table A-1 shows the principal devel-

Table A-1. *Principal Developing Countries Supplying*
Imports to Nonfood, High-Penetration Sectors,
United States, 1976

ISIC number	Product sector	Supplier	Import-penetration ratio (percent)
3215	Cordage, rope, and twine	Brazil	4.74
		Mexico	6.52
		Taiwan	1.30
3220	Apparel (except footwear)	Korea	2.20
		Hong Kong	2.92
		Taiwan	2.08
3231	Tanneries and leather finishing	Argentina	8.57
		Brazil	2.60
		India	4.80
3233	Leather products (except footwear)	Brazil	0.57
		Colombia	0.50
		Mexico	1.42
		Korea	4.96
		Hong Kong	3.24
		Taiwan	5.21
3240	Footwear (except rubber and plastic)	Brazil	2.29
		Mexico	0.42
		Korea	4.06
		Taiwan	2.12
		Yugoslavia	0.42
3832	Radio, television, and communication equipment	Mexico	1.08
		Korea	0.89
		Hong Kong	0.81
		Taiwan	1.47
		Singapore	0.81
		Malaysia	0.57
3853	Watches and clocks	Mexico	0.85
		Korea	0.94
		Hong Kong	3.96
		Taiwan	2.31
		Singapore	2.07
		Malaysia	0.91
3901	Jewelry and related articles	Colombia	0.51
		Hong Kong	1.43
		India	1.73
		Israel	4.97

Source: Author's calculations.

oping countries that supply these high-penetration products (for nonfood sectors) for 1976. The penetration ratios confirm certain stylized facts about manufactured imports from developing countries. The East Asian "export platforms" and Mexico are important in radio and television equipment and in watches and clocks; Hong Kong, Korea, and Taiwan are important in wearing apparel, leather manufactures, and footwear (for which Brazil is also important); Argentina stands out in the supply of leather.

For selected product sectors, special industry studies provide the basis for verifying the import-penetration ratios estimated here. For nonrubber footwear, studies by the U.S. International Trade Commission report data indicating an import-penetration ratio in 1977 of 23.4 percent for value and 47 percent for number of pairs.[12] The value-penetration ratio is close to the estimate here for 1976 (21.3 percent). The large divergence between the value- and the physical-penetration ratio reflects the much lower price, and to some extent the quality, of imports than of domestic nonrubber footwear production.

Apparel and steel are two other major sectors in which U.S. nontariff protection is important. On the basis of U.S. Department of Commerce estimates for thirty-five detailed categories of apparel and eleven detailed categories for steel and iron (all at the four- or five-digit standard industrial classification level), the 1976 import-penetration ratios in these sectors (imports to apparent consumption) are 15.6 percent for apparel and 8.7 percent for iron and steel.[13] The corresponding estimates obtained from the present analysis of ISIC data are 11.9 percent for apparel and 6.5 percent for iron and steel.

In short, for these important and sensitive import sectors—footwear, apparel, and steel—supplementary information provides estimates of import-penetration ratios close to those estimated from the United Nations trade and production data, although in all three cases the UN-based estimates are somewhat lower than those from the alternative sources.

---

12. The physical import-penetration ratio is given in *Non-rubber Footwear*, Third Calendar Quarter 1979, p. 6. The same source reports exports and import value, pp. 6, 8. The value of domestic shipments for 80 percent of shipments is reported in U.S. International Trade Commission, *Non-rubber Footwear: First Annual Surveys of Producers and Importers, Calendar Years 1976 and 1977* (USITC, 1978).

13. Calculated from U.S. Department of Commerce, *U.S. Commodity Exports and Imports as Related to Output, 1976 and 1975* (Department of Commerce, 1979), pp. 47–49, 59–62.

Net Import Ratios

Import-penetration ratios overstate the severity of vulnerability to imports in those sectors where imports are offset by substantial export sales. One of the high import-penetration sectors listed in table 1-7 has a low net import ratio (imports minus exports, relative to apparent consumption). In the United States for 1976, radio, television, and communication equipment showed net import penetration of − 1.4 percent as opposed to gross import penetration of 6.1 percent. This difference reflects U.S. exports in more sophisticated electronic equipment, which offset imports in basic electronic components manufactured mainly in foreign export platforms such as Taiwan, Korea, and Mexican border industries. For the other sectors listed in the table, however, even the net import ratios remain relatively high, indicating that export sales are insufficient to remove the market pressure experienced from import competition.

Estimates for Other Countries

The United States is the largest single market for manufactured exports from developing countries, accounting for 42 percent of the total exported by developing-market-economy countries.[14] Europe, Japan, and Canada are also important markets. The estimates based on UN trade and production data provide an assessment of the extent to which manufactured exports from developing countries have penetrated these markets.

Table A-2 presents selected import-penetration ratios for developing-country manufactures in the markets of Canada, Japan, Italy, France, Germany, and the United Kingdom in 1976, supplementing corresponding estimates for 1978 as shown in chapter 1. The sectors included in the table are those in which at least one country has imports from developing countries in excess of 7 percent of apparent consumption.[15] For com-

14. Calculated from UNCTAD, *Handbook of International Trade and Development Statistics, 1979* (UN, 1979), pp. 102–03.
15. The sector of radio, television, and communication equipment (3832) is included as well because of rapid growth of penetration in the U.S. market, and iron and steel (3710) is included because of its significance as an import-sensitive industry in the United States.

parison, the table shows the corresponding penetration ratios for the United States.

Data on the overall extent of import penetration provide information on the relative degree of openness of the various industrial countries to manufactured exports from developing countries. This concept of openness does not necessarily refer to the degree of freedom from import protection, because it also includes structural factors such as the size of the economy (the larger the economy, the lower imports relative to production are likely to be, as a whole and from developing countries) and its factor endowments (for example, the more abundant in unskilled labor, the less an industrial country is likely to rely on imports from developing countries).

Three indicators of overall market penetration by manufactures from developing countries appear in table A-3. The first indicator is the average import-penetration ratio (from developing countries) for all four-digit ISIC sectors, weighted by sectoral gross output. The second indicator is the median of these sectoral-penetration ratios. The third measure of openness is the percentage of total gross manufacturing output represented by those sectors in which import penetration from developing countries is at least 7 percent of the market.

The low levels of aggregate penetration ratios for imports from developing countries have already been discussed. The third indicator in table A-3 provides a different type of assessment of the market presence of these imports. It shows that if a penetration of 7 percent or higher is taken as the basis for signaling potentially sensitive sectors, then approximately 6 percent of industrial output in these countries is in such sectors. This estimate includes sectors oriented toward raw materials needed from abroad (for example, foodstuffs sectors, leather tanneries, and fur finishing), so that the true incidence of commercial policy problems caused by imports from developing countries is probably even smaller than these figures suggest. Considering that typically 20 to 30 percent of the market is protected by nontariff barriers in industrial countries (table 2-3), the relatively small coverage of sectors with high penetration from developing countries (6 percent, table A-3) reinforces the view that much of current protection is primarily North-North rather than North-South.

On the basis of all three measures, the United Kingdom stands out with the highest degree of import penetration from developing countries, and France the lowest. The others are relatively comparable in degree

Table A-2. *Penetration Ratios for Imports from Developing Countries into High-Penetration Sectors in Seven Industrial Countries, 1976*
Percent

ISIC number	Product sector	United States	Canada	West Germany	France	Italy	United Kingdom	Japan
3113	Preserved fruits and vegetables	1.7	3.6	11.3	5.9	4.2	4.7	6.7
3114	Canned fish	17.4	5.3	3.4	6.8	8.2	2.0	15.6
3115	Agricultural oils	3.9	7.9	19.9	13.8	16.6	13.5	4.8
3116	Grain mill products	0.2	0.4	2.9	2.4	8.6	1.7	3.3
3118	Sugar	13.7	7.9	1.4	12.7	3.0	27.4	16.3
3119	Confectionery	6.4	2.2	1.5	5.8	1.6	3.5	1.7
3121	Food not elsewhere classified	3.6	2.4	6.0	2.2	1.4	6.5	3.1
3140	Tobacco	3.7	0.4	2.4	3.0	2.2	8.9	1.1
3211	Spinning and weaving	3.4	5.9	10.1 }	}	13.3 }	8.8	6.8
3212	Made-up textiles (except apparel)	0.7	2.0	2.2 }	}	0.7 }	1.6	2.3
3214	Carpets and rugs	1.4	0.9	21.1 }	4.5[a] }	2.0 }	4.6	1.8
3215	Cordage and rope	21.6	26.8	1.0 }	}	0.6 }	2.3	0.8
3220	Apparel (except footwear)	9.5	13.2	13.3 }	}	3.4 }	16.3	8.2

SIC	Industry							
3231	Tanneries and leather finishing	18.2	5.8	8.8		32.7	22.2	7.8
3232	Fur dressing	0.1	4.2	10.4	4.6[a]	1.7	3.4	3.5
3233	Leather products (except footwear)	18.0	8.9	8.4		0.7	7.1	1.8
3240	Footwear (except rubber and plastic)	9.7	6.4	2.4		0.4	3.7	3.8
3311	Sawmills	2.2	1.8			4.8	5.3	1.4
3319	Wood and cork not elsewhere classified	3.5	2.6	2.0	3.0[a]	2.6	3.7	1.7
3540	Miscellaneous petroleum and coal products	6.3	1.2	1.8	1.3	6.8	3.9	13.1
3710	Iron and steel	0.6	0.8	0.4	1.1	0.8	0.3	0.3
3720	Nonferrous metals	3.4	0.7	7.4	6.7	13.7	7.5	5.4
3832	Radio, television, and communication equipment	6.1	4.0	2.7	1.5	1.8	2.2	2.0
3853	Watches and clocks	11.8	10.0	8.2	n.a.	2.6	10.3	2.7
3901	Jewelry	11.8	8.8	n.a.	n.a.	0.0	n.a.	28.2
3903	Sporting goods	5.2	15.4	11.4	n.a.	3.6	7.0	2.4
3909	Manufactures not elsewhere classified	5.2	3.0	n.a.	n.a.	6.7	5.8	2.2

Source: Author's calculations.
n.a. Not available.
a. See notes to table 1-10.

Table A-3. *Indicators of Overall Market Penetration*
by Manufactured Products from Developing Countries
into Seven Industrial Countries, 1976
Percent

Importing country	Import-penetration ratios (four-digit ISIC numbers)		Percentage of gross industrial output in sectors with 7 percent or higher import penetration
	Average[a]	Median	
United States	1.91	0.85	1.6
			(4.9[b])
Canada	1.44	0.77	3.6
West Germany	1.98	0.65	8.4
France	1.57	0.38	1.4
Italy	2.12	0.49	6.1
United Kingdom	2.58	0.98	9.8
Japan	2.31	0.74	8.8

Source: Author's calculations.
a. Weighted by sectoral gross output.
b. Including sector 3832: radio, television, and communication equipment.

of penetration, although under the third criterion the United States has low penetration unless the sector of radio, television, and communication equipment (6.1 percent penetration ratio) is included among the high-penetration sectors.

The current stylized facts of commercial policy tend to depict the United Kingdom as increasingly protective, Japan and to some extent France as tacitly restrictive, the United States as relatively liberal, and Germany as highly liberal. The high degree of revealed openness of the British market to manufactured products from developing countries is at odds with the image of British protectiveness (although increasing protection might be explained as being caused by high penetration), and to some extent the same may be said for Japan. Otherwise, the estimates of total penetration are relatively consistent with these stylized facts of commercial policy.

Penetration at the Three-Digit Level

For some purposes it is useful to consider import penetration at a level of aggregation in between the detailed four-digit categories of the

ISIC and the total aggregates for all manufacturing. Tables A-4 and A-5 present estimates of import penetration in 1978 for the twenty-nine groupings at the three-digit level of the ISIC. The data for penetration by developing countries (table A-4) show that at this more aggregate level penetration is considerably lower than in the high-penetration sectors at the four-digit level shown in tables A-2 and 1-10. Only five sectors stand out with high penetration at this level: diverse foods (312), apparel (322), leather products (323), footwear (324), and other manufactures (390). Table A-5 reports the corresponding penetration estimates for imports from all sources in 1978. In these estimates a relatively large U.S. market share of imports is also apparent in wood products (331), rubber products (355), ceramics (361), iron and steel (371), nonferrous metals (372), electrical machinery (383), transport equipment (384), and technical instruments (385). For Canada, Germany, France, Italy, and the United Kingdom, the three-digit estimates for total imports show a generally high level of import presence in domestic markets. Higher trade shares in these economies reflect their smaller size and, in the case of the European countries, the level of integration within the European Community market.

The three-digit estimates for Japan show that its total import penetration is consistently lower than that of any other major industrial country. This pattern contrasts with the pattern of imports from developing countries alone, where Japanese penetration is more comparable to that of other industrial markets. Lower total penetration in the Japanese market reflects influences of comparative advantage, with reliance on imports of raw materials (given scarce natural resources and emphasis on manufactured exports). Distance may also help explain low total penetration in Japan. Finally, some would argue that the Japanese pattern also results from protection of the market either by overt nontariff barriers or tacit administrative guidance or by sociocultural factors inhibiting imports, such as an antiquated distributional system, a "buy Japan" mentality among consumers, and oligopolistic practices by Japanese manufacturers.

Table A-4. *Import Penetration by Developing Countries into Seven Industrial Countries, Three-Digit Estimates, 1978*

Percent

ISIC number	Product sector	United States	Canada	West Germany	France	Italy	United Kingdom	Japan
311	Food products	2.3	1.8	3.8	4.4	4.2	4.6	5.0
312	Food products, diverse	2.0	1.6	3.4	1.4	1.0	4.0	1.6
313	Beverages	0.2	0.7	0.2	0.9	0.0	0.2	0.1
314	Tobacco	3.9	0.3	3.4	2.3	1.3	10.4	0.8
321	Textiles	2.3	3.4	7.7	4.4	7.7	5.6	5.2
322	Apparel	12.5	10.9	13.9	0.0[a]	7.2	15.2	7.8
323	Leather products (except footwear)	10.3	9.5	8.5	5.2	15.0	9.4	7.1
324	Footwear	14.0	9.8	2.4	0.0[b]	0.5	4.9	5.8
331	Wood products	2.6	1.7	1.9	1.7	8.6	5.4	1.3
332	Furniture	2.3	1.1	0.0[c]	0.0[c]	0.9	0.7	1.4
341	Paper	0.1	0.0	0.3	0.3	0.2	0.2	0.1
342	Printing	0.8	0.7	0.9	0.3	0.6	0.9	0.2
351	Industrial chemicals	1.2	1.7	0.4	1.1	0.9	1.1	0.8
352	Other chemical products	0.5	0.2	0.0[d]	0.7	0.0[d]	0.7	0.7
353	Petroleum refineries	6.1	1.4	2.1	1.0	7.6	2.2	13.1

354	Petroleum and coal products	0.1	1.0	0.0[e]	0.0[e]	0.0[e]	0.6	0.2
355	Rubber products	3.2	1.1	0.7	1.0	0.8	1.2	0.7
356	Plastic products	4.2	2.1	1.1	0.0[f]	1.4	2.3	0.5
361	Pottery, china, and earthenware	6.1	6.0	2.3	0.4	0.5	1.6	0.4
362	Glass products	0.8	0.7	0.5	0.2	0.0[g]	0.3	0.3
369	Other nonmetallic minerals	0.8	0.5	0.5	0.0[g]	0.0[g]	0.4	0.7
371	Iron and steel	1.2	0.5	0.4	0.6	0.4	0.4	0.3
372	Nonferrous metals	4.0	1.4	6.1	5.6	14.4	5.3	5.6
381	Fabricated metal products	1.0	0.6	0.5	0.2	0.4	0.5	0.1
382	Machinery (nonelectrical)	0.6	0.5	0.3	0.5	0.5	0.4	0.2
383	Electrical machinery and equipment	4.1	1.6	1.1	0.8	1.2	1.4	0.5
384	Transport equipment	0.3	0.1	0.6	0.2	0.6	2.9	0.1
385	Technical instruments	2.0	2.1	3.6	0.0[h]	0.9	4.4	1.4
390	Manufactures not elsewhere classified	9.3	4.7	12.8	0.0	9.9	4.6	6.8

Source: Author's calculations.
a. Included in 321.
b. Included in 323.
c. Included in 331.
d. Included in 351.
e. Included in 353.
f. Included in 355.
g. Included in 361.
h. Included in 382.

Table A-5. *Import Penetration from All Sources into Seven Industrial Countries, Three-Digit Estimates, 1978*
Percent

ISIC number	Product sector	United States	Canada	West Germany	France	Italy	United Kingdom	Japan
311	Food products	5.3	11.4	20.0	16.4	28.7	21.7	12.0
312	Food products, diverse	3.0	8.6	14.6	7.8	12.0	14.2	3.2
313	Beverages	7.7	10.7	8.1	10.1	9.1	4.9	2.3
314	Tobacco	5.7	2.0	11.2	8.1	26.2	31.6	4.3
321	Textiles	5.1	23.4	34.3	26.1	25.1	24.3	8.6
322	Apparel	15.3	18.4	48.6	0.0[a]	34.5	31.9	10.4
323	Leather products (except footwear)	14.3	33.4	39.2	22.9	29.7	22.5	11.3
324	Footwear	29.3	30.0	37.6	0.0[b]	1.9	22.4	7.4
331	Wood products	11.5	9.9	17.7	14.5	74.2	29.4	5.2
332	Furniture	6.8	15.8	0.0[c]	0.0[c]	15.3	13.8	2.5
341	Paper	6.8	7.8	23.1	20.4	19.2	24.5	3.0
342	Printing	2.0	18.7	13.4	13.2	8.3	7.6	1.2
351	Industrial chemicals	8.4	42.0	17.2	38.6	23.9	22.3	6.6
352	Other chemical products	3.2	16.5	0.0[d]	15.5	0.0[d]	15.3	5.5
353	Petroleum refineries	9.7	4.1	28.5	10.2	26.9	19.2	15.0
354	Petroleum and coal products	1.5	18.8	0.0[e]	0.0[e]	0.0[e]	6.6	0.8

355	Rubber products	11.4	22.3	23.2	32.2	17.3	14.4	2.3
356	Plastic products	9.2	47.9	29.5	0.0[f]	43.7	33.8	2.4
361	Pottery, china, and earthenware	34.1	69.6	41.2	12.6	12.4	12.0	1.8
362	Glass products	7.1	46.9	23.8	24.4	0.0[g]	22.3	2.1
369	Other nonmetallic minerals	3.9	11.3	13.2	0.0[g]	0.0[g]	7.3	1.9
371	Iron and steel	11.7	23.4	21.0	32.6	16.1	16.1	0.9
372	Nonferrous metals	12.5	19.3	33.2	29.4	58.9	32.6	12.8
381	Fabricated metal products	4.0	15.4	14.1	14.3	16.0	9.5	1.1
382	Machinery (nonelectrical)	7.3	62.5	18.9	41.2	37.2	26.4	3.2
383	Electrical machinery and equipment	10.5	36.0	13.6	16.8	18.8	16.6	1.9
384	Transport equipment	12.6	45.5	22.7	19.7	26.7	32.8	2.6
385	Technical instruments	11.1	60.2	51.3	0.0[h]	37.6	45.8	12.8
390	Manufactures not elsewhere classified	23.0	25.1	61.2	0.0[c]	53.7	n.a.	11.9

Source: Author's calculations.

n.a. Not available.
a. Included in 321.
b. Included in 323.
c. Included in 331.
d. Included in 351.
e. Included in 353.
f. Included in 355.
g. Included in 361.
h. Included in 382.

Price Indexes for Imports of Manufactured Goods from Developing Countries, 1969–78

THIS appendix presents estimates of price indexes for imports of manufactures from developing countries for the years 1969, 1970, 1976, and 1978. The indexes are based on unit values of imports for five-digit categories of the standard industrial trade classification for the United States, Canada, France, Italy, the United Kingdom, and Japan. The data are from UN trade data tapes. The individual unit values are weighted to obtain indexes for broader categories: four-digit categories of the international standard industrial classification.

Method

The basic data are for import values and quantities for five-digit SITC categories in 1969, 1970, 1976, and 1978. These series are converted to detailed SITC price categories as follows:

(B-1) $$P_i^t = \frac{U_i^t}{U_i^{70}},$$

where P_i^t is the detailed price index for year t (1969, 1976, 1978) and U_i^t, U_i^{70} are unit values (import value divided by import quantity) in year t and 1970, respectively.

The weights for aggregating these detailed price indexes into four-digit ISIC indexes are derived from the process of allocating import data at the five-digit SITC level into the broader four-digit ISIC groups (appendix A).

The basic weights used for this process are

(B-2) $$\phi_{ij} = \frac{M_{ij}}{\Sigma_i M_{ij}}, i\in j,$$

where M_{ij} is the value of imports from developing countries allocated from a five-digit SITC category i into four-digit ISIC category j. Note that M_{ij} is not necessarily the full value of SITC category i; in many cases, different portions of the SITC category are allocated to different ISIC categories.

These weights are calculated for 1969 and for 1978. The 1969 weights are used to calculate a Laspeyres price index as follows:

(B-3) $$P_j^L = \Sigma_{i\in j}\phi_{ij}^{69}P_i,$$

where P_j^L is the Laspeyres price index for ISIC sector j, P_i is the price index at the detailed (five-digit SITC) level, and ϕ_{ij}^{69} indicates the weight from 1969 data.

A Paasche price index, using terminal period weights, is calculated as

(B-4) $$P_j^P = \frac{1}{\Sigma_{i\in j}\phi_{ij}^{78}(1/P_i)},$$

where ϕ_{ij}^{78} indicates weights from 1978 data.

A Fisher ideal price index, combining the Laspeyres and Paasche indexes, is then calculated as

(B-5) $$P_j^F = (P_j^L P_j^P)^{\frac{1}{2}}.$$

In preparation of the indexes, missing data and unacceptable data were treated in the following way. First, for those categories missing unit value information, the price index was calculated as

(B-3') $$P_j^L = \frac{\Sigma_{i\in j}\phi_{ij}^{*69}P_i}{\Sigma\phi_{ij}^{*69}},$$

where the asterisk indicates only those SITC categories for which unit values are available. This process normalizes the weighted sum of detailed price indexes to account for the fact that otherwise the sum of weights for the categories with unit values available would be less than unity whenever unit values were missing. For the Paasche index, the corresponding treatment gives

$$(\text{B-4}') \qquad P_j^P = \frac{\Sigma_{i \in j} \phi_{ij}^{*78}}{\Sigma_{i \in j} \phi_{ij}^{*78} \, (1/P_i)}.$$

A related problem is that in some cases the unit values change severalfold between years, indicating either changes in national definition of quantity units or else major change in the qualitative nature of the products actually entering under the SITC category in question. The following criteria were used to screen the data for this type of unacceptable case: any detailed price index exceeding 25.0 or below 0.25 was rejected and the category treated as one with missing data. These bounds are sufficiently wide to permit large variation in prices but sufficiently narrow to screen out observations in which the unit value data imply extremely implausible price changes.

No price index is computed at the four-digit ISIC level if the fraction of trade covered by valid detailed price indexes ($\Sigma_{i \in j} \phi_{ij}^*$) is less than 15 percent. In this way, the calculations avoid accepting for an entire four-digit ISIC category a price index that may be highly unrepresentative because it covers only a small fraction of trade in the category.

Once the Fisher ideal price indexes are calculated individually for the seven industrial countries, a set of aggregate indexes is calculated for these countries taken as a group. These aggregate indexes are calculated as

$$(\text{B-6}) \qquad P_j^{FA} = \Sigma_k \theta_{kj} P_{kj}^F,$$

where P_j^{FA} is the aggregate Fisher ideal price index for four-digit ISIC category j, θ_{kj} is the share of industrial country k in the total imports (from developing countries) of the seven industrial countries in product category j, and P_{kj}^F is the Fisher ideal price index in product sector j for industrial country k.[1] If insufficient country-level indexes are available for a particular product category to cover 15 percent or more of total

1. For country-product categories in which either a Laspeyres or Paasche index is available but the other is not (because matching SITC categories exist for one weighting year but not the other), the calculation applies whichever index is available instead of the Fisher index.

imports from developing countries into the seven industrial countries in that category, no price index is calculated for the product in question.

For comparison, similar aggregate price indexes are calculated with the unit values of inputs from all sources, including industrial countries. All the calculations are analogous to those of the equations given above, except that the prices used in equations B-1 and B-3 through B-6 refer to prices of imports from all sources, not just from developing countries. Note that for these total-source price indexes, the weights applied (equations B-2 through B-4) still refer to imports from developing countries only. If the weights are kept unchanged, comparison of sectoral price indexes for imports from developing countries with those from all sources is possible without introducing disturbance by changing the weighting attributed to each detailed category.[2]

Sectoral real values of imports from developing countries are obtained by dividing the sectoral price indexes into nominal values of imports in each sector in the years in question:

$$\text{(B-7)} \qquad\qquad M^*_{jt} = \frac{M_{jt}}{P^{FA}_{jt}},$$

where M_{jt} is the value of imports into the seven industrial countries from developing countries in sector j and year t (1969, 1970, 1976, and 1980), M^*_{jt} is the corresponding real value in 1970 sectoral prices, and P^{FA}_{jt} is the aggregate Fisher ideal price index (equation B-6) for the sector j and year t in question.

Once sectoral real import figures are calculated, it is possible to calculate a single aggregate implicit deflator for manufactured imports from developing countries by comparing the total nominal value of all these imports to their total real value obtained by summing the sectoral real values from equation B-7. Thus,

$$\text{(B-8)} \qquad\qquad P^*_t = \frac{\Sigma_j M_{jt}}{\Sigma_j M^*_{jt}},$$

where P^*_t is the single, overall deflator for manufactured imports from developing countries. Because of the sharp and unrepresentative rise in

2. This procedure does mean, however, that the total-source indexes are not as appropriate for the direct purpose of measuring import prices for manufactured imports from all sources as these indexes would be if in equations B-2 through B-4 the weights referred to imports from all sources instead of those from just the developing countries.

petroleum prices over the period, petroleum refining (ISIC 3530) is excluded from the calculation.

It is also possible to use the sectoral real import estimates (equation B-7) to calculate real sectoral growth rates of imports of manufactures from developing countries. Using the average between 1969 and 1970 as the base period, real sectoral growth rates are calculated from the base to 1976 and to 1978.[3]

As with sectoral price indexes, sectoral real imports and the overall deflator (equations B-7 and B-8), as well as sectoral real growth rates, may be calculated for manufactured imports from all sources. For this purpose, nominal import values from all sources into the seven industrial countries are applied to equations B-7 and B-8, and the price indexes for imports from all sources are applied to equation B-7.

Results

At the aggregate level, the prices of imports of manufactures (excluding refined petroleum) from developing countries behaved similarly to those of imports from industrial countries (table B-1). From 1970 to 1978, these prices rose by somewhat more than twofold. As shown in the table, the deflator for manufactured imports from developing countries rose from 100 to 223 from 1970 to 1978. Correspondingly, these imports grew in value from $18.1 billion in 1970 to only $34.2 billion in 1978 at constant sectoral prices, compared with $76.4 billion at 1978 prices.[4]

Table B-1 also reports two price indexes that reflect corresponding prices for manufactured exports of industrial countries. The first, the deflator from all sources, is the alternative estimate discussed above. It is heavily influenced by supplies coming from industrial countries because the developing countries account for only about 17 percent of

---

3. Calculated as

$$g = \frac{\log M_t^* - \log M_o^*}{n} \times 100,$$

where log is the natural logarithm, M_o^* is the average of 1969 and 1970 real imports, M_t^* refers to real imports in 1976 or 1978, and $n = 6.5$ for 1976, 8.5 for 1978.

4. This includes the value of coffee, cocoa, and tea eliminated in the basic data set used for the main analysis of this study. See appendix A.

Table B-1. *Aggregate Price Index and Nominal and Real Values of Imports of Manufactured Products from Developing Countries into Seven Industrial Countries, Selected Years, 1969–78*[a]
1970 = 100

Item	1969	1970	1976	1978
Nominal imports (billions of dollars)	16.3	18.1	51.2	76.4
Real imports (billions of dollars, 1970 sectoral prices)	17.4	18.1	28.7	34.2
Overall deflator	93.2	100.0	178.5	223.2
Addenda				
Deflator for imports from all sources	94.3	100.0	171.7	217.9
UN price index, exports of manufactures from developed countries	94.1	100.0	185.2	231.5

Source: Author's calculations.
a. Excluding petroleum refineries, ISIC 3530.

total supply of these imports.[5] The second is the UN index of unit values for manufactured exports from developed market economies.[6]

If the deflator for imports of manufactures from developing countries is compared with that for imports from all sources, a slight gain appears in terms of trade for developing countries between 1970 and 1978. That is, the price index for manufactured imports from developing countries rose to 223 by 1978 while that for imports from all sources rose to only 218, and therefore prices of imports from industrial countries (the dominant, non-developing-country component of the total index) must have risen to a level somewhat lower than 218. However, if the same comparison is made between the deflator for imports from developing countries and the UN price index for manufactured exports from developed countries, the opposite trend is shown (223 as opposed to 232 for 1978, respectively). The results shown in table B-1, therefore, seem to indicate that no significant trend is present in the terms of trade of manufactured products for developing countries relative to that for industrial countries. Moreover, because the conclusion is based on prices excluding refined petroleum, there should be no upward bias in the manufacturing terms of trade from the sharp rise in petroleum prices

5. Note that the nominal values of manufactured imports from all sources into the seven industrial countries were $117.1 billion in 1970 and $443.1 billion in 1978.
6. United Nations, *Monthly Bulletin of Statistics*, vol. 34 (March 1980), p. xxii, and vol. 26 (March 1972), p. xiv.

and their influence on refined petroleum exports from developing countries.[7] Of course, the calculations here are not direct measures of total terms of trade for developing countries, which would require price data on all imports and exports of the developing countries themselves. Nonetheless, the price data developed here shed additional light on the terms-of-trade issue because they do not show any systematic trend of manufactured export prices for developing countries relative to those of industrial countries.

The information in table B-1 indicates that, with the overall deflator for imports of manufactures from developing countries, the average real growth rate of these imports from 1969–70 to 1978 was 7.7 percent a year. However, for a large number of important individual sectors, the real growth rates were much higher (table B-2). Even excluding sectors with small import magnitudes, for which growth rates may be extremely high but not particularly meaningful, the growth performance of many sectors is impressive. If only those categories with 1978 exports to industrial countries exceeding $100 million (column 1) are considered, nineteen product sectors had annual real growth rates exceeding 20 percent (1969–70 to 1978), accounting for $12.6 billion in 1978 (or approximately one-sixth of total developing-country exports of nonoil manufactures to the seven industrial countries).[8] Among these nineteen fastest growing sectors, the largest trade values are in footwear and in radio and television. The other fast-growing sectors represent a broad range of largely nontraditional products, including watches and clocks, motor vehicle parts, machinery, rubber products, furniture, and photographic and scientific equipment. In the face of the sharp advance over this range of products, it was only the extremely slow growth of such major products as nonferrous metals (3720) and important categories of processed foods that held down the growth rate of manufactured exports to less than 8 percent.

The price indexes at the sectoral level show few surprises. Petroleum refineries (3530) and derivatives (3540) show the sharpest price increases.

---

7. Although price indexes are included for refined petroleum in table B-2, they do not enter into the general indexes presented in table B-1.

8. A twentieth sector, aircraft (3845), also exceeds 20 percent growth, but here the data appear not to reflect meaningful developing-country exports. The 1978 figure comes almost entirely from imports into the United Kingdom from such unlikely manufacturers of aircraft as Saudi Arabia, and the trade in question may refer to secondhand equipment rather than actual production.

The indexes for textiles and apparel show no pronounced divergence from the general index. Some observers have hypothesized that developing countries may be worsening their terms of trade in these traditional products by exporting so much of them; other observers emphasize that the presence of physical import quotas induces developing countries to upgrade sharply the quality of these products and cause a spurious rise in unit values. Neither tendency is evident in the indexes here, which show neither a substantial lag behind the general price index nor an advance ahead of it.[9] The price index for footwear shows a substantial rise above the general price index, although the rise may be attributable more to rising leather prices (also high in the table) than to upgrading in the face of protection, since quota protection against footwear did not begin until late in the 1970s.[10]

The price index for nonferrous metal reflects the severe loss in terms of trade for copper in this period. More puzzling is the extremely low rise in prices for radio, television, and communication products (3832), which show a nearly stable nominal price level over the period. This anomaly seems to be confirmed by the corresponding price index calculated for imports from all sources (table B-3). Although it is plausible that rapidly declining prices from technological change played a role in restraining these prices, the index may nevertheless be biased downward by compositional changes, causing the extremely high real growth rate (30 percent annually) to be overstated.

The price indexes and real growth rates for manufactured imports from all sources (table B-3) show generally comparable price behavior but lower growth rates than those for manufactured imports from developing countries alone. For example, footwear imports show a real growth of 12 percent (all sources) rather than 23 percent (developing countries); radio and television products, 14 percent instead of 30 percent (although the difference may be affected by bias in the developing-country price index); watches and clocks, 12 percent instead of 42

9. There are twenty-two separate SITC price indexes that enter into the price indexes for apparel (3220). This degree of detail seems sufficient to avoid at least a considerable part of the spurious price increase observed when unit values are calculated for more aggregative categories. That is, compositional shift among those twenty-two subcategories, toward categories with higher unit values, would not by itself cause the measured price index for the sector to rise.

10. The United States negotiated orderly marketing agreements limiting shoe imports in 1977. Bahram Nowzad, *The Rise in Protectionism* (Washington, D.C.: IMF, 1978), p. 26.

percent; rubber products, 8 percent instead of 20 percent; and so forth. The comparison is especially suggestive for apparel (3220), where imports from all sources grew almost as fast (12 percent) as those from developing countries (15 percent). This experience implies that, although protection did not succeed in holding down to a low rate the real growth of apparel imports from developing countries, protection may have played a role in dampening the growth of developing-country supply relative to that from industrial countries; the divergence between the two growth rates is far lower than in most of the other manufacturing sectors in which developing-country suppliers became important in this period.

At the aggregate level, manufactured imports (nonoil) grew from $103 billion in 1969 to $443 billion in 1978. Deflated by the overall deflator for these imports (table B-1), from the 1969–70 base to 1978 they grew at an annual rate of 6.9 percent in real terms. Thus, with 7.7 percent real growth, imports of these goods from the developing countries grew somewhat faster than the corresponding imports from all sources, raising the developing countries' share in the total from 15.6 percent in 1969–70 to 17.2 percent in 1978.

Conclusion

The estimates presented here suggest no significant change in terms of trade in manufactured goods between industrial and developing countries over the 1970s. The estimates also highlight the sharp cleavage between two sets of manufactured exports from developing countries. In one, processed foodstuffs and nonferrous metals, real growth was extremely slow, and because these products account for a large portion of the total, their low growth held back total manufactured export performance. In a second group, however, real export growth was phenomenal, ranging above 20 percent annually for a wide spectrum of primarily nontraditional manufactured goods.

Table B-2. Price Indexes and Annual Average Real Growth Rates for Imports of Manufactured Products from Developing Countries into Seven Industrial Countries, 1969, 1976, and 1978[a]

ISIC number	Product sector	1978 imports (millions of dollars) (1)	Price index (1970 = 1.0000)			Real growth rate (percent)	
			1969 (2)	1976 (3)	1978 (4)	1969–70 to 1976 (5)	1969–70 to 1978 (6)
3111	Meat	2116.3	0.9332	1.8624	2.2326	-3.14	-2.15
3112	Dairy	178.1	0.9350	2.1217	3.7438	4.65	10.14
3113	Preserved fruits and vegetables	1791.1	0.9431	1.6324	2.3576	7.42	8.48
3114	Canned fish	3590.4	0.9245	1.8921	2.3865	12.56	10.80
3115	Agricultural oils	2379.7	0.8666	1.6825	2.2805	5.60	4.07
3116	Grain products	3656.1[b]	0.8077	2.3138	3.5160	0.37	0.64
3117	Bakery	38.8	1.0071	1.6040	2.1340	25.14	23.13
3118	Sugar	1560.8	0.9423	2.3626	2.1408	-2.71	-3.96
3119	Confectionery	3195.5[c]	1.0549	2.0455	3.7329	1.69	1.81
3121	Food not elsewhere classified	7100.5[d]	0.8295	2.1241	3.2416	1.87	0.69
3122	Prepared animal foods	37.9	0.8658	2.0207	2.5662	-16.05	-9.44
3131	Spirits	121.0	1.0479	1.6468	1.8431	5.91	6.19
3132	Wine	53.6	0.9891	1.9642	2.4601	-28.68	-20.10
3133	Malt liquors	19.9	0.9720	1.7614	1.5999	20.60	20.12
3134	Soft drinks	3.4	1.1771	3.0897	1.9467	24.80	31.93
3140	Tobacco	960.3	0.9967	2.1349	2.3060	6.90	7.26
3211	Textile spinning	5088.7	0.9927	1.9466	2.7257	2.19	0.18
3212	Made-up textiles	235.2	0.9512	2.1026	2.4999	13.14	13.52

3213	Knitting	211.0	0.9293	1.5848	2.0196	18.84	15.03
3214	Carpets and rugs	841.9	0.9302	2.1952	2.8911	5.20	7.13
3215	Cordage, rope, and twine	120.1	1.0347	2.3318	2.8455	5.98	4.95
3219	Textiles not elsewhere classified	101.0	0.9720	1.8017	1.9282	1.71	5.20
3220	Apparel	9219.5	0.9855	2.0561	2.4806	16.87	15.09
3231	Tanneries and leather finishing	666.4	1.0274	2.3846	2.9786	5.57	3.74
3232	Fur dressing	117.9	0.7986	2.3954	3.6484	10.35	6.35
3233	Leather products (except footwear)	412.8	0.9528	1.9083	2.1502	21.61	22.59
3240	Footwear	1287.3	1.0223	2.8774	3.1938	21.68	22.67
3311	Sawmills	1966.6	1.0393	2.0200	2.3324	5.33	6.51
3312	Wood containers	86.3	0.9670	1.3458	1.5985	24.18	23.42
3319	Wood products not elsewhere classified	282.9	1.0753	1.6071	1.4786	16.02	19.05
3320	Furniture	599.8	0.9043	1.3750	1.8825	28.18	26.00
3411	Pulp and paper	161.4	0.8932	1.9612	2.0347	9.74	14.24
3412	Containers and boxes	6.2	0.9629	1.4369	1.8018	12.46	15.05
3419	Paper products not elsewhere classified	19.6	0.9114	1.5833	2.1713	21.10	18.35
3420	Printing	708.3	0.9038	1.7901	2.2317	14.57	16.59
3511	Industrial chemicals	1645.1	0.9751	2.0169	2.1332	7.34	13.30
3512	Fertilizers	92.7	0.9637	2.3615	2.3358	15.86	14.13
3513	Plastics	129.6	0.9723	1.6031	1.4971	16.02	28.23
3521	Paints	3.8	1.6244	2.0165	2.0364	10.99	14.74
3522	Drugs	312.9	0.7193	1.5892	2.0241	9.44	10.09
3523	Soaps	19.4	1.0086	2.9198	2.7677	6.11	7.58
3529	Chemical products not elsewhere classified	345.4	0.9555	1.7150	2.4562	5.58	3.83
3530	Petroleum refineries	13274.2	0.9552	5.1016	6.1813	0.17	0.12

Table B-2 (continued)

ISIC number	Product sector	1978 imports (millions of dollars) (1)	Price index (1970 = 1.0000)			Real growth rate (percent)	
			1969 (2)	1976 (3)	1978 (4)	1969–70 to 1976 (5)	1969–70 to 1978 (6)
3540	Petroleum and coal products	32.6	1.0590	6.0745	9.6651	−15.07	−32.44
3551	Tires	178.0	1.3610	1.1513	2.0417	27.08	21.01
3559	Rubber products not elsewhere classified	579.1	1.0067	2.3528	2.3503	19.65	20.39
3560	Plastics not elsewhere classified	1532.0	1.0043	1.1973	2.5426	22.95	15.22
3610	Pottery, china, and earthenware	190.4	1.0367	1.6320	2.5211	25.81	24.40
3620	Glass	138.4	1.0167	1.4249	2.4616	18.62	12.75
3691	Clay	58.2	1.0790	1.5461	1.9095	24.20	26.61
3692	Cement	57.2	0.0000	0.0000	0.0000	−10.69	4.15
3699	Nonmetallic products not elsewhere classified	421.5	0.9679	1.5260	1.9339	5.14	6.36
3710	Iron and steel	1502.7	0.8544	1.8495	2.1241	12.61	14.65
3720	Nonferrous metals	4664.0	0.9198	1.3297	1.5662	−0.87	0.52
3811	Hardware	333.3	0.9413	1.4404	1.7114	21.60	22.38
3812	Furniture (metal)	15.5	0.9968	1.3559	1.6043	20.88	26.87
3813	Structural metal products	109.8	0.9183	1.6949	2.0379	23.68	27.66
3819	Other metals	792.6	0.9250	1.5732	1.8335	17.34	19.61
3821	Engines	24.3	0.8895	1.2503	2.1257	33.49	25.45
3822	Agricultural machinery	23.0	0.0000	4.1218	4.3441	9.85	14.48
3823	Metal- and woodworking machinery	109.5	1.2875	2.7077	1.9433	18.05	29.60

Code	Description						
3824	Industrial machinery	159.3	1.3789	1.3668	2.3673	32.47	22.99
3825	Computing machinery	626.9	1.0040	1.7494	3.4175	20.50	12.23
3829	Machinery not elsewhere classified	509.1	0.9746	2.2590	2.0536	30.25	32.64
3831	Electrical machinery	250.2	0.0000	1.1246	1.6174	30.08	23.10
3832	Radio, television, and communication equipment	5239.7	1.0214	1.0110	1.0815	33.54	29.86
3833	Appliances	71.2	1.0055	0.0000	2.1973	35.40	35.99
3839	Electrical appliances not elsewhere classified	362.5	0.0000	2.2914	2.9265	11.52	12.16
3841	Shipbuilding	254.2	0.9282	4.2204	0.0000	2.81	16.13
3842	Railroad equipment	45.3	0.5489	0.0000	2.7103	2.73	24.16
3843	Motor vehicles	646.2	0.8829	2.9328	2.6154	24.37	26.77
3844	Motorcycles and bicycles	96.6	0.8847	1.8605	0.0000	15.83	13.06
3845	Aircraft	836.9	1.0070	0.0000	2.3573	14.40	25.93
3849	Transport equipment not elsewhere classified	3.4	0.4853	3.2472	2.6701	35.77	46.14
3851	Scientific equipment	227.7	0.9939	1.6177	1.3842	22.03	25.26
3852	Photographic equipment	325.4	0.7028	3.4340	3.4172	17.84	20.06
3853	Watches and clocks	708.9	0.0000	0.0000	0.0000	47.68	41.62
3901	Jewelry	1919.4	0.0000	0.0000	0.0000	8.93	9.62
3902	Musical instruments	135.6	0.9187	1.2996	1.2436	2.14	7.51
3903	Sporting goods	579.4	0.9475	1.9175	2.1354	23.35	23.98
3909	Manufactures not elsewhere classified	1145.0	0.9807	1.6265	2.1907	2.95	4.59

Source: Author's calculations.

a. Entries of 0.0000 indicate absence of relevant index. For these cases, real growth rate calculations apply the overall UN price index of manufactured exports from developed countries (table B-1).

b. Excluding coffee: $457.2 million.

c. Excluding cocoa: $1,182.3 million.

d. Excluding coffee: $1,723.0 million.

Table B-3. *Price Indexes and Annual Average Real Growth Rates for All Imports of Manufactured Products into Seven Industrial Countries, 1969, 1976, and 1978*[a]

ISIC number	Product sector	1978 imports (millions of dollars) (1)	Price index (1970 = 1.0000)			Real growth rate (percent)	
			1969 (2)	1976 (3)	1978 (4)	1969–70 to 1976 (5)	1969–70 to 1978 (6)
3111	Meat	17015.9	0.9419	1.8083	2.2699	2.10	2.00
3112	Dairy	5436.0	0.9383	2.0365	3.0334	5.44	3.27
3113	Preserved fruits and vegetables	4376.8	0.9388	1.6387	2.3184	6.83	5.56
3114	Canned fish	8372.0	0.9019	2.1465	2.8125	5.52	5.60
3115	Agricultural oils	4766.3	0.8714	1.6849	2.3014	4.98	3.99
3116	Grain products[b]	4672.9	0.8089	2.3132	3.5087	0.96	0.42
3117	Bakery	640.9	0.9709	1.7987	2.0534	9.42	12.96
3118	Sugar	2578.0	0.9169	2.5062	2.2674	-0.61	-2.10
3119	Confectionery[c]	4751.0	1.0534	2.0125	3.7117	2.65	2.02
3121	Food not elsewhere classified[d]	9875.0	0.8327	2.1203	3.2132	2.16	1.04
3122	Prepared animal foods	560.4	0.8266	2.0286	2.7224	-0.78	0.10
3131	Spirits	1959.1	1.0664	1.6137	1.8690	2.71	4.34
3132	Wine	2217.3	0.9894	1.7316	2.2766	4.90	6.70
3133	Malt liquors	809.4	0.9635	1.7522	1.6028	11.54	14.37
3134	Soft drinks	98.2	0.9303	1.7636	1.4775	15.63	20.54
3140	Tobacco	2869.1	1.0024	1.9491	2.0684	4.05	6.36
3211	Textile spinning	16671.1	0.9869	1.8511	2.5529	4.05	2.76

Code	Industry						
3212	Made-up textiles	973.8	0.9771	1.8843	2.4622	7.49	7.40
3213	Knitting	1140.1	0.9898	1.4417	1.8165	5.38	4.25
3214	Carpets and rugs	1992.7	0.9400	2.1937	2.8841	4.52	4.87
3215	Cordage, rope, and twine	260.1	1.0174	2.1594	2.7897	1.65	2.06
3219	Textiles not elsewhere classified	844.4	1.0010	2.6277	2.2741	-1.79	4.30
3220	Apparel	17708.5	0.9941	1.6589	2.1677	13.49	11.56
3231	Tanneries and leather finishing	1599.6	1.0372	2.2483	2.6743	4.20	3.97
3232	Fur dressing	525.8	0.9762	2.0564	2.8323	5.94	4.68
3233	Leather products (except footwear)	756.7	1.0026	1.7273	2.3117	12.86	13.04
3240	Footwear	4331.2	1.0211	1.3747	2.0935	13.82	12.40
3311	Sawmills	10368.7	1.0343	2.1878	2.4677	2.56	5.06
3312	Wood containers	268.0	0.9985	1.3444	1.5577	9.66	11.54
3319	Wood products not elsewhere classified	789.0	1.0810	1.5946	1.4285	8.13	12.06
3320	Furniture	4427.9	0.9439	1.3234	1.8332	16.17	13.36
3411	Pulp and paper	11881.0	0.8822	2.0943	2.0852	1.37	3.02
3412	Containers and boxes	399.8	0.8952	1.8351	2.4030	8.68	6.90
3419	Paper products not elsewhere classified	728.0	0.9571	1.6328	1.9814	13.19	12.91
3420	Printing	5429.7	0.9219	1.7194	2.1156	6.03	6.59
3511	Industrial chemicals	21320.6	1.0347	1.8247	2.0900	9.61	10.53
3512	Fertilizers	1429.5	0.9726	2.3463	2.3936	8.12	11.28
3513	Plastics	6192.2	1.0144	1.4231	1.5302	12.29	12.30
3521	Paints	481.5	1.0596	2.4856	2.6260	4.49	7.41
3522	Drugs	4343.8	0.8815	2.0334	2.8078	5.28	5.80
3523	Soaps	1034.1	0.9249	1.9058	2.3250	9.10	9.18
3529	Chemical products not elsewhere classified	4353.0	0.9830	1.7032	2.3352	7.60	6.17
3530	Petroleum refineries	32130.7	0.9747	5.0353	6.1282	1.46	1.87

Table B-3 (continued)

ISIC number	Product sector	1978 imports (millions of dollars) (1)	Price index (1970 = 1.0000)			Real growth rate (percent)	
			1969 (2)	1976 (3)	1978 (4)	1969–70 to 1976 (5)	1969–70 to 1978 (6)
3540	Petroleum and coal products	570.9	0.9455	3.5368	2.8877	-2.77	-2.24
3551	Tires	2958.3	0.9944	2.9924	2.0785	6.66	12.74
3559	Rubber products not elsewhere classified	2528.1	0.9820	1.5006	2.2232	11.69	7.70
3560	Plastics not elsewhere classified	10023.5	0.9885	1.9435	2.1663	9.07	10.28
3610	Pottery, china, and earthenware	1649.0	0.9690	1.9353	2.3215	5.87	8.36
3620	Glass	3142.1	0.9467	1.3822	2.1616	9.74	6.88
3691	Clay	979.6	0.9957	1.7061	1.9000	8.70	9.87
3692	Cement	420.4	0.0000	0.0000	0.0000	2.21	9.67
3699	Nonmetallic products not elsewhere classified	3577.8	0.9843	1.6454	2.0858	5.06	4.36
3710	Iron and steel	25580.8	0.8313	1.9496	2.0918	2.93	6.35
3720	Nonferrous metals	17739.1	0.9187	1.3636	1.6057	2.89	3.35
3811	Hardware	2822.3	0.9122	1.5348	1.9498	7.83	7.86
3812	Furniture (metal)	192.6	0.8717	1.2553	1.3979	13.53	16.08
3813	Structural metal products	3431.7	0.8306	1.5306	1.7864	7.96	8.36
3819	Other metals	7045.6	0.9127	1.5025	1.7953	10.02	10.39
3821	Engines	817.3	1.0205	1.8039	2.4761	8.33	7.64
3822	Agricultural machinery	2880.3	0.7622	1.6255	2.1576	8.46	5.52
3823	Metal- and woodworking machinery	4070.3	1.1950	1.0792	2.2322	10.05	3.72

3824	Industrial machinery	12787.8	0.9716	1.9407	2.5419	4.62	4.56
3825	Computing machinery	9698.6	0.8837	0.8477	1.6456	17.21	9.52
3829	Machinery not elsewhere classified	13596.5	0.8385	1.6553	1.8705	7.86	8.61
3831	Electrical machinery	3136.4	0.0000	1.3478	1.5913	11.70	12.04
3832	Radio, television, and communication equipment	22722.1	1.0031	1.2927	1.5551	15.82	14.38
3833	Appliances	1040.1	0.9777	0.0000	2.4028	10.99	9.90
3839	Electrical appliances not elsewhere classified	3076.6	0.9128	1.5453	2.1241	8.63	7.71
3841	Shipbuilding	3427.5	0.9437	2.1236	3.2259	9.96	7.25
3842	Railroad equipment	338.2	1.0636	2.1638	3.1455	7.60	7.38
3843	Motor vehicles	52194.8	1.0033	1.9108	2.6102	8.19	7.01
3844	Motorcycles and bicycles	2328.8	0.8957	2.0430	0.0000	6.31	9.63
3845	Aircraft	7787.3	0.8970	1.9441	2.8195	−0.04	1.68
3849	Transport equipment not elsewhere classified	41.8	0.9084	2.0409	2.3309	4.81	4.27
3851	Scientific equipment	5382.0	0.9418	1.6712	2.0545	7.86	8.09
3852	Photographic equipment	5519.3	0.9458	2.4078	2.8949	5.68	9.06
3853	Watches and clocks	2277.5	0.0000	0.0000	0.0000	10.45	11.51
3901	Jewelry	10227.7	0.0000	0.0000	0.0000	5.33	9.81
3902	Musical instruments	1072.6	0.9001	1.2345	1.1854	5.58	9.01
3903	Sporting goods	1162.1	2.1014	2.0050	2.7149	14.36	13.42
3909	Manufactures not elsewhere classified	3592.6	0.9756	1.4930	2.1432	7.78	7.85

Source: Author's calculations.

a. Entries of 0.0000 indicate the absence of a relevant index. For these cases, real growth rate calculations apply the overall UN price index of manufactured exports from developed countries (table B-1).
b. Excluding coffee: $1,379.5 million.
c. Excluding cocoa: $2,691.5 million.
d. Excluding coffee, tea: $4,269.6 million.

Quantitative Studies of Protectionist Response

SINCE the mid-1970s a burgeoning new literature has developed on quantitative explanations of import protection. This literature has tended to build in successive layers that reinforce preceding analysis, rather than to swing between opposing views. Accordingly, certain stylized facts of protectionist behavior are gradually emerging. At the same time, the various studies frequently differ considerably in the data sets analyzed, in the statistical techniques used, and in the degree of formalization of the theoretical models underlying statistical tests. The bulk of this literature concerns the cross-sectional analysis of protection across industries rather than the level of protection over time. This survey examines several of the studies on this subject in the order of their appearance. It omits the segment of the literature that discusses whether U.S. protection favors labor or capital.[1] Instead, the literature reviewed here examines the various forces leading to protection.

1. An early analysis by Vaccara found that nominal tariffs for the United States were positively related to labor intensity, measured by the ratio of employees to value added or of labor costs to gross output. Using these results, Travis proposed that tariff impediments blocking normal comparative advantage explained the Leontief paradox (whereby U.S. exports were found to be more labor intensive than imports). However, Basevi found that there was no significant relationship between labor intensity and effective rate of protection for U.S. tariffs in 1958. Arguing that effective, not nominal, rates were relevant for resource allocation, Basevi disputed Travis's explanation of the Leontief paradox. Nevertheless, subsequent research by Ball found a strong negative relationship between both effective and nominal U.S. tariffs and wages per employee, indicating that protection benefits unskilled labor. Cheh introduced another layer of inconclusiveness: he found that although 1964 tariff rates were positively related to labor use (ratio of employees to value added), confirming Vaccara's earlier findings, when nontariff barriers were included with tariffs a significant relationship between

Two authors working independently, John Cheh and J. J. Pincus, helped institute the recent surge of quantitative literature analyzing protection.[2] As a historical analysis of the U.S. Tariff Act of 1824—a piece of legislation considered by historians to have been especially dominated by special interest groups—the study by Pincus provides an appropriate starting point. He examines the variation of tariffs across industries in terms of the interplay between the intensity of pressure from special interest groups and the responsiveness of Congress to that pressure. Like some subsequent authors, he cites previous literature in the field of public choice (including Mancur Olson[3]) as a basis for formulating hypotheses about the behavior of pressure groups.

Pincus argues that because the magnitude of the benefits of protection to producers depends on the absolute size of their output, lobbying efforts will be greater the larger the output of an industry. He proposes that industries facing higher tariffs on their intermediate inputs will secure higher protection in compensation. Invoking the free-rider problem, he expects higher protection for industries with fewer establishments and higher industrial concentration. Considering ease of communication among firms, he anticipates higher protection for industries that are more concentrated geographically, although for this variable the historical period is important because of the limited relevance of geographic dispersion for modern communication. Arguing that quasi rents of proprietors stand to rise proportionately more when their income is a

---

protection and labor use no longer existed. This left the Travis hypothesis once again without support. To complete the confusion, the NTB tariff equivalents Cheh used (from Baldwin) are so incomplete and rough that it should not be surprising that they do not perform well statistically. Beatrice N. Vaccara, *Employment and Output in Protected Manufacturing Industries* (Brookings Institution, 1960); William Penfield Travis, *The Theory of Trade and Protection,* Harvard Economic Studies, vol. 121 (Harvard University Press, 1964); Giorgio Basevi, "The United States Tariff Structure: Estimates of Effective Rates of Protection of United States Industries and Industrial Labor," *Review of Economics and Statistics,* vol. 48 (May 1966), pp. 147–60; David Stafford Ball, "United States Effective Tariffs and Labor's Share," *Journal of Political Economy,* vol. 75 (April 1967), pp. 183–87; and John H. Cheh, "A Note on Tariffs, Nontariff Barriers, and Labor Protection in United States Manufacturing Industries," *Journal of Political Economy,* vol. 84 (April 1976), pp. 389–94.

2. John H. Cheh, "United States Concessions in the Kennedy Round and Short-Run Labor Adjustment Costs," *Journal of International Economics,* vol. 4 (November 1974), pp. 323–40; and J. J. Pincus, "Pressure Groups and the Pattern of Tariffs," *Journal of Political Economy,* vol. 83 (August 1975), pp. 757–78.

3. Mancur Olson, *The Logic of Collective Action: Public Goods and the Theory of Groups,* Harvard Economic Studies, vol. 124 (Harvard University Press, 1965).

smaller fraction of output, he expects lobbying effort and protection to vary inversely with their income share. To account for legislative response, Pincus expects protection to be related to the number of states in which the industry is present.

Pincus's statistical results are the strongest for the variables representing industrial concentration, proprietorial income, and geographic dispersion. However, the decline of the owner-entrepreneur and improved communications in the last 150 years would seem to make the last two variables of limited relevance for modern protectionism. The results confirm the predictions for the role of tariffs on inputs. Surprisingly, the variable for industry size is not significant statistically.

Cheh analyzed U.S. tariff cuts in the Kennedy Round of Trade Negotiations to determine the cause of exceptions from its general 50 percent tariff cut formula (the final average cut was 35 percent). He justifies analysis of tariff cut changes instead of actual levels of protection on the grounds that the modern tariff structure is the legacy of many past negotiations and contemporary political pressure will be more accurately revealed by current tariff changes than by the existing tariff level. Cheh's hypothesis is that the government seeks to minimize labor adjustment problems resulting from tariff cuts and therefore that these cuts will vary across industries in relation to the difficulty of labor adjustment.

For the dependent variable Cheh uses the percentage change in tariffs between 1964 and 1972. Although he tests both effective and nominal protection, he argues persuasively that for analyzing the political economy of protection the nominal tariff is more relevant. The concept of effective protection was unfamiliar to policymakers in the Kennedy Round. More fundamentally, industries seeking protection cannot pursue it as easily by demanding lower tariffs on their intermediate imports as by pressing for tariff protection on their own output, because the first alternative would provoke counterpressure from supplier industries. Cheh also incorporates changes in the tariff equivalent of nontariff barriers, although his data set derived from Baldwin is suspect because, by Baldwin's own account, it proved impossible to estimate tariff equivalents for several of the more important NTBs.[4]

Cheh's first explanatory variable is the absolute size of the labor force in the industry, as an indicator of the political pressure for exception

---

4. Robert E. Baldwin, *Nontariff Distortions of International Trade* (Brookings Institution, 1970).

from the standard tariff cut. He is sensitive to the dependence of this variable on the level of aggregation chosen (approximately fifty input-output categories), but he notes that protection efforts are typically at a fairly broad industry level, much broader than detailed tariff line categories (and, as indicated in chapter 2, in the important case of textiles and apparel the relevant political grouping is even broader than typical industry classifications). His other variables with their expected signs on percentage tariff cuts include labor intensity measured by the ratio of labor to the value of domestic shipments (−), percentage of workers classified as unskilled (−), percentage of workers over age forty-five (−), and annual growth rate of output (+). These variables all reflect the severity of labor adjustment for a given decline in protection. He also adds the level of previous tariffs (−), arguing that because the 50 percent formula's absolute cut for the tariff rises with the size of the tariff, resistance to formula cuts would be larger for higher tariffs. In his full model only the size of labor force and level of past tariff are statistically significant, although separate tests indicate that the other variables (except for labor intensity) correlate closely with tariff cut when the collinearity problem is addressed by including only one adjustment-severity variable at a time. The best results are for nominal tariffs combined with NTBs; the results for effective protection lack statistical significance, supporting the view that nominal, not effective, tariff rates are what matter for the policy process. Cheh's interpretation of his results is somewhat surprising. He emphasizes that the study shows that tariff cuts are explained primarily by "variables that proxy labor adjustment costs,"[5] whereas in fact his econometric results are strongest for the variables that indicate outright political pressure regardless of adjustment cost: absolute number of workers and level of prior tariff, which capture the size of the potential loss and therefore indicate how worthwhile it is for industries to lobby.

James Riedel has applied Cheh's analysis to German tariff cuts in the Kennedy Round.[6] His best results are for cuts in tariffs and nontariff protection, encompassing taxes and subsidies. For this test, Riedel confirms the importance of the size of industry employment. Although labor intensity is not significant, the variables for human-capital intensity

5. Cheh, "United States Concessions," p. 323.
6. James Riedel, "Tariff Concessions in the Kennedy Round and the Structure of Protection in West Germany: An Econometric Assessment," *Journal of International Economics*, vol. 7 (May 1977), pp. 133–43.

and sectoral growth are significant with the right sign. The past tariff level is significant with the wrong sign, however, and Riedel concludes that the tariff-harmonization objectives of the European Community overshadowed the influence of resistance to higher absolute cuts, leading to more-than-proportional cuts for higher tariffs, a sharp contrast to the U.S. case. The results for tariffs alone were poorer and showed no influence of labor size, suggesting (although Riedel does not state it in these terms) that domestic political elements are somewhat thwarted by the Community's determination of tariff policy but manage to secure their protection at the national level through subsidies and other NTBs. Like Cheh, Riedel finds the results for effective protection inferior to those for nominal tariffs with NTBs.

Richard Caves has provided one of the richer studies in the quantitative literature on protection.[7] He examined the structure of Canadian tariffs as of 1963, acknowledging that to do so when the structure has been evolving for nearly a century is "cavalier" (although he later justified the procedure on the ground that the underlying independent variables have been stable for a long time). Caves begins by noting that, although under perfect competition and no specific factors no permanent gains from protection accrue to factor incomes in an industry, consideration of time lags, barriers to entry, and the presence of specific factors leads to permanent gains. He then proposes two principal alternative models: an "adding machine" (AM) model whereby government acts to maximize reelection, adding up votes; and an interest group (IG) model, reflecting the intensity of interest group efforts at protectionist lobbying. In addition, a third "national policy" model is considered. Reflecting national preference for an industrial capability in all sectors, this model suggests such variables as the ratio of value added per worker in the United States to that in Canada (that is, higher domestic inefficiency leads to higher tariff). The nationalistic model would seem more relevant to developing countries than to industrial countries.

Caves's main explanatory variables are value added per worker, industrial concentration, number of plants of minimum efficiency scale (Canadian market divided by average U.S. plant size), transportation cost, location away from Quebec and Ontario, buyer concentration, growth rate, and specialization ratio. Under the AM model, higher labor

7. Richard E. Caves, "Economic Models of Political Choice: Canada's Tariff Structure," *Canadian Journal of Economics,* vol. 9 (May 1976), pp. 278–300.

intensity (lower value added per worker) means higher protection because "labor has the votes," and lower value added per worker means that more workers are covered by a tariff on a given amount of value added.

Despite the importance of labor votes, Caves does not test the obvious variable of absolute employment (found important by Cheh) or industry output size (suggested by Pincus) because there is the problem of arbitrary category width in matching tariff line averages with industry statistics and because industry size is also correlated with consumer awareness of and reaction to protection. The AM model predicts lower tariffs with higher industry concentration because geographic dispersion (and the number of votes) declines as concentration rises. The same consideration of dispersion means that higher transport costs, the absence of economies of scale (larger number of efficient-size plants per market), and location away from the two main urban centers should all be associated with more votes and protection.

The IG model begins with attention to the free-rider problem, or the difficulties of getting all the beneficiaries of protection to pay their fair share of lobbying costs. Because of the free-rider problem, the IG model may predict more protection (more successful marshaling of lobbying efforts) for higher industry concentration and lower number of minimum-efficient plants. However, Caves also argues that the sign on industry concentration is ambiguous because "*if* an unconcentrated industry's many entrepreneurs do manage to coordinate their efforts, they may be a much more effective force than a few oligopolists."[8] The IG model attaches the same (negative) sign as the AM model to value added per worker, under the argument that both the public and the authorities are more likely to be receptive to protectionist petitions from workers deemed to be suffering in relative terms (industries with low wages and low output per worker). This same consideration of sympathy means that the IG model adds two other variables: the industry growth rate and the degree of product diversification. Higher growth and less specialization mean better capacity to withstand tariff cuts, less public sympathy, and lower tariffs. The IG model also adds a variable for buyer concentration, the share of sales accounted for by purchasing industries that provide more than 5 percent of the sector's sales. Higher buyer concen-

8. Ibid., p. 287.

tration indicates the presence of an effective countervailing interest group offsetting the industry's pressure for protection.

In contrast to Cheh, Caves uses effective rates of protection as the dependent variable. He argues that they are clearly superior to nominal rates insofar as the tariff's pull on resources and impact on factor payments are concerned, and he maintains that historical discussions of tariff policy in Canada have long shown attention to tariffs on both inputs and outputs. Because available evidence on NTBs is only impressionistic, Caves omits them from his tests. This omission was more justified when 1963 data were used (Caves's data set) than it would be today, because of the large extent to which nontariff barriers have replaced tariffs as the primary form of protection in the last two decades.

The empirical results are mixed. Collinearity exists between value added per worker and industry concentration. Significance levels are frequently low, and signs are frequently wrong. Caves concludes that the interest group model receives the most support. When industrial concentration is included, it is consistently significant and negative, which supports either the alternative formulation of the argument in the IG model or the AM model. The growth rate has the correct (negative) sign, although its significance level is not high. As a whole, the Caves study is perhaps more useful for the heuristic exercise it provides in setting forth the various political influences on protection than for its specific empirical results, which tend to be ambiguous.

In a subsequent study of Canadian protection, G. K. Helleiner proposes an alternative interest group model of protection.[9] Helleiner argues that the wage rate is a better variable than value added per worker to measure an industry's equity claims for protection and that the wage rate has the advantage of being a better predictor of developing countries' comparative advantage and of not being collinear with concentration (a problem in the Caves analysis). Helleiner also proposes that, once the free-rider problem is captured by concentration, an economies-of-scale variable should be negatively related to protection (rather than positively as Caves suggested) because high protection tends to be against developing-country exports and these tend to be in sectors without returns to scale. Helleiner's statistical tests for tariffs in 1961 and 1970 find better

9. G. K. Helleiner, "The Political Economy of Canada's Tariff Structure: An Alternative Model," *Canadian Journal of Economics,* vol. 10 (May 1977), pp. 318–26.

explanation for nominal than for effective rates. The tests strongly confirm the average wage rate—an inverse indicator of the intensity of unskilled labor use—to be the most important variable determining protection (with negative sign), and he finds weak support for his hypothesis that economies of scale are negatively related to protection once the free-rider influence is removed by industry concentration. However, results for individual variables change significance or even sign when different dependent variables are used (nominal versus effective protection, 1961 versus 1970, level versus change between two years), and the average R^2 (fraction of variation explained statistically) for several tests is only 0.21, compared with an average of 0.51 in the Caves study.

Norman S. Fieleke analyzes the structure of U.S. tariffs as of 1972.[10] Dispensing with more formal exposition of the theory of protectionist pressure and response, he cites traditional influences believed to be taken into account by the policymakers (or even so enjoined by legislation): the degree of import competition, importance to national security, and economic health (profit rate, wage rate, unemployment rate, output growth rate). Without addressing the problem that today's tariffs stem from historical evolution, he regresses 1972 tariff levels on imports minus exports relative to apparent consumption (net import penetration, for foreign competition), the change in this measure from 1962 to 1965, growth over this period, the blue-collar wage rate, the share of defense-oriented sales in output, the industry's employment relative to that of the smallest sector (for political influence), the share of production workers in employment, and the four-firm concentration ratio. Contrary to Caves, Fieleke applies nominal tariffs, arguing that the political process has focused on them rather than on effective tariffs. In alternative equations, the significant variables are net import penetration, wage rate, and the share of production workers in employment. If only sectors showing imports in excess of exports are considered, the growth rate, wage rate, defense involvement, and concentration ratio are significant. Broadly, however, low explanation is achieved. Fieleke concludes that protection is not closely related to the traditionally expected influences. Despite their significant coefficients in various equations, Fieleke concludes that import competition, industry health, and defense involve-

10. Norman S. Fieleke, "The Tariff Structure for Manufacturing Industries in the United States: A Test of Some Traditional Explanations," *Columbia Journal of World Business,* vol. 11 (Winter 1976), pp. 98–104.

ment bear "little or no relationship" to protection (although the results could have been cited to support just the opposite conclusion had the author been so inclined) and that only the wage rate consistently performs well in explaining tariffs. Aside from Fieleke's seeming disinclination to recognize the influence of some of his own statistically significant variables (such as net-import penetration), the study appears to suffer from its specification in terms of tariff level (although equations for tariff change from 1965 to 1972 do even worse) and the omission of nontariff barriers. In view of results obtained by other researchers, Fieleke's conclusion that the traditional determinants of protection have little influence must stand in doubt.

Several recent statistical studies of protectionism have been carried out under the auspices of the World Bank. Frequently their focus is on protection against developing countries. In their study of U.K. protection, Vincent Cable and Ivonia Rebelo work with 1970s data for eighty-seven nonfood manufacturing sectors.[11] First they examine the pattern of U.K. trade with developing countries, finding that human capital is the principal base for U.K. comparative advantage relative to developing countries (whereas the capital–labor ratio has a negative sign for net exports, confirming the Leontief paradox). The study then examines protectionist actions, noting that in the second half of the 1970s the United Kingdom shifted from being one of the most liberal countries in Europe to being one of the most protective. They propose two alternative models: one in which the government seeks to minimize labor adjustment cost and a second in which protection is the result of lobbying by labor and capital. The authors argue that under the first model, indicators of adjustment severity such as the rate of change of import penetration and employment should dominate; under the second model the level of import penetration, not its change, should dominate. They also argue, somewhat opaquely, that under the political lobbying model for a given level of import penetration (imports relative to apparent consumption) protection should be higher for high-wage industries and industries where capital assets are large relative to the number of workers. The opposite could more plausibly be argued, however: given the import-penetration ratio, policymakers and the public are more likely to be receptive to petitions in low-wage industries on grounds of equity.

11. Vincent Cable and Ivonia Rebelo, "Britain's Pattern of Specialization in Manufactured Goods with Developing Countries and Trade Protection," World Bank Staff Working Paper 425 (Washington, D.C.: World Bank, 1980).

An important novelty in the Cable-Rebelo study is that the authors quite rightly consider tariffs to be of little relevance in an analysis of protection against developing countries. Instead, they construct discrete dependent variables with a value of one for presence of protection and zero in its absence, with alternative definitions of protection—quantitative restriction, sensitive tariff status or exclusion from the generalized system of preferences, and semisensitive. A sector is classified as protected if 50 percent or more of the value of imports from developing countries is covered by the protective barrier.

In their test of protection, Cable and Rebelo include the following variables, with the expected sign in parentheses. (1) The model of labor adjustment minimization includes rate of change of import penetration (+); ratio of exports to apparent consumption (−); labor intensity (+); share of manual workers in the labor force (+); share of women in the labor force, under the argument that women are less mobile than men (+); wage rate, under the argument that lower-wage workers have less incentive to move rather than accept unemployment compensation (−); location of the industry in an area that has high unemployment (+); firm size as an indication of access to credit for adjustment (−); output growth (−); and value added per worker (−). (2) The political lobbying model includes labor intensity—following Caves, higher labor intensity means more votes (+); regional concentration of production facilitating political mobilization (+); size of the industry in employment (+); size of the total capital in the industry (+); industry concentration to represent the ease of organization (+); and level of import penetration to reflect the degree of competitive pressure (+).

In their statistical tests Cable and Rebelo apply discriminant analysis, although for the reasons set forth in chapter 2 of this book, an alternative method such as logit or probit analysis that is continuous in its pressure from independent variables, rather than bipolar, would seem more appropriate.[12] The authors achieve up to 90 percent correct classification of industries by protection versus nonprotection. The dominant variables are share of women in the labor force, average wage, regional bias, and share of manual workers in employment. All these are correlated with

12. Discriminant analysis chooses weights on independent variables so that a maximum difference is achieved for their weighted sum between the members of one discrete group and the members of the other (in this case protected and unprotected industries).

comparative advantage of developing countries, and when they are dropped and replaced simply by the level of import penetration, relatively little explanatory power is lost, which makes import penetration "substantially the most important factor."

The authors find that while the level of import penetration is important, the change in import penetration is not. They infer that the notion of government action designed to reduce adjustment difficulty is largely spurious because the change in import penetration (for example, the "sudden rushes" of imports frequently invoked to justify protection) is not statistically important in explaining protection. The authors also find that the size of industry employment, industry concentration, and firm size are not important.[13] Broadly, the authors conclude that protection against developing countries has little to do with minimization of adjustment cost and instead is the consequence of outright resistance to underlying comparative advantage of developing countries.

The Cable-Rebelo study makes a significant advance in that it applies a discrete quantitative method to analyze nontariff barriers, which are far more important than tariffs in protection against imports from developing countries. There are two major shortcomings to the study, however. First, by considering only that set of protective actions of relevance to developing countries' products, the study omits an important range of protective behavior. Thus the major protection in steel and automobiles escapes their group of protected industries. Given the employment size of these industries, this exclusion probably contributes to the failure to find a significant coefficient for the industry-employment-size variable. Second, the study treats the various textile categories as independent sectors, while (as the authors themselves point out) for this analysis they should be aggregated as a single lobbying force. Again the effect is to understate the importance of the industry-employment-size variable, given the massive employment of all textile sectors considered jointly.

Another World Bank study by Glismann and Weiss examines protection in Germany.[14] Citing Downs, Buchanan and Tullock, Krueger, and

13. However, the authors do not classify the criteria for importance. They do not report *t*-statistics, which have little meaning in discriminant analysis in any event. Coefficient size could vary with the units chosen in data specifications.

14. H. H. Glismann and F. D. Weiss, "On the Political Economy of Protection in Germany," World Bank Staff Working Paper 427 (World Bank, 1980).

others the authors place their study in the context of the quest for rents by factors of production and the decisions of politicians to grant rents.[15] Demand for protection is a function of the firms' opportunity cost in eliciting it and the returns to securing it; supply of protection depends on government opportunity cost and the returns to politicians of granting it. Their analysis begins with a time series investigation of German protection since 1880. They maintain that faster economic growth means greater opportunities for factors of production to pursue increased welfare through the market and that slow economic growth with unemployment reduces opportunity costs of lobbying. Although the business cycle has frequently been invoked as a determinant of protective behavior, the authors' formulation of the argument leaves open the question of why profit and income maximization would not lead to rent-seeking even in good times; it also evokes an implausible image of lobbyists as low-opportunity-cost unemployed whereas lawyers in three-piece suits are usually the lobbying agents. Their empirical test regresses the logarithm of average tariffs on time (to remove trend) and the logarithm of net national product. After testing various time periods, they conclude that a political economy of protection was operating (the income variable was significant), at least after the more authoritarian epoch of 1880–1913. The analysis is commendable as one of the few existing tests of the common hypothesis that protection is related to the business cycle; nevertheless, it is clearly only a modest beginning toward a much needed analysis of protectionist trends over time.

Turning to cross-sectional analysis, Glismann and Weiss examine German protection across twenty-six manufacturing industries in 1974. In the German context subsidies are often more important than tariffs, and their effective rate of assistance includes both effective tariff protection and the effective rate of domestic subsidy. Domestic subsidies of 24 percent for aircraft, compared with an effective rate of protection of −0.9 percent, are a case in point. The authors expect protection to be related to lobbying efforts as influenced by a smaller number of firms, smaller number of employees, and greater regional concentration (all because of lower communication costs). They expect the opportunity

15. Anthony Downs, *An Economic Theory of Democracy* (Harper and Row, 1957); James M. Buchanan and Gordon Tullock, *The Calculus of Consent: Logical Foundations of Constitutional Democracy* (Ann Arbor: University of Michigan Press, 1962); Anne O. Krueger, "The Political Economy of the Rent-Seeking Society," *American Economic Review*, vol. 64 (June 1974), pp. 291–303.

cost of protection-seeking to be lower in a declining industry (although the logic here is not clear). For the government supply of protection, they expect decline in employment or low wages to raise protectionist responses (from public sympathy); they anticipate higher protection for industries with larger employment because of the correspondingly larger votes (and the German institution of centralized unions that keeps larger employment from raising communication costs). For a competitiveness variable the authors use Balassa's revealed comparative advantage (exports divided by imports, normalized by the average ratio for all industry), arguing that a measure that incorporates exports is preferable to import penetration alone in an open economy such as Germany's with high two-way trade. Recognizing the problem of simultaneity, whereby comparative advantage causes protection but protection also causes observed comparative advantage, they appeal to different time lags between the two (from comparative advantage to protection takes longer because of the slow political process) as a resolution.

Glismann and Weiss find that domestic subsidies are explained by lower competitiveness, a smaller number of firms, and lower protection by the common external European Community tariff. The number of employees is not significant for total domestic subsidies, but it does emerge as significant when only nonregional subsidies are examined (the regional subsidies have a political behavior of their own). A separate test on Community tariffs finds them higher for more concentrated industries and for industries with lower human-capital intensity and higher intensity of unskilled labor. The authors conclude that protection does respond to the voting power of interest groups and excludability (concerning the free-rider problem) and that domestic subsidies and Community tariffs are substitutes. While the study has important strengths, including an attempt at historical time series analysis and inclusion of domestic subsidies, it has a major weakness in its exclusion of quantitative NTBs, such as those on textiles and apparel, steel, and (recently) automobiles. The absence of these NTBs in large sectors may account for the ambiguous results on the key variable, size of employment in the industry.

A study by P. K. M. Tharakan, also for the World Bank, investigates Belgian protection in 1970.[16] The author considers both nominal and

16. P. K. M. Tharakan, "The Political Economy of Protection in Belgium," World Bank Staff Working Paper 431 (World Bank, 1980).

188   *Exports of Manufactures from Developing Countries*

effective protection and includes NTBs from a GATT compilation (although for that, the method used—dummy dependent variables in a standard regression equation—appears questionable). Regressions for tariffs find the expected negative coefficient on average wage rates but the wrong signs for value added per worker (positive) and geographic concentration (negative) and lack of significance for industrial concentration. The dichotomous regressions for NTBs show poor results, and Spearman rank coefficients relating economic variables to government assistance are insignificant. For Belgium much more than for Germany or the United Kingdom, statistical analysis of protection appears to falter because the European Community largely determines tariff structure.

One of the best empirical studies of U.S. protection is by Robert Baldwin.[17] Baldwin's study (also part of the World Bank series) develops more fully than most previous studies the theoretical basis for the analysis of the political economy of protection, working in a framework that considers the interaction between an industry's demand for protection and the government's supply of it. Baldwin's empirical analysis includes three sets of tests. The first uses probit analysis to explain congressional votes on two important pieces of legislation leading to the Trade Act of 1974. He finds that the votes are significantly related to the percentage of home-district labor in industries opposing the legislation (classified by testimony of their trade organizations). A second set of tests examines the import-relief decisions of the International Trade Commission (ITC), which Baldwin describes as increasingly under the control of Congress as opposed to the president. In a regression explaining the percentage of ITC commissioners voting in favor of an injury determination (in thirty-seven cases from 1974 to 1979), Baldwin uses variables for the recent changes in profits and in employment, the recent ratio of imports to apparent consumption, and a dummy variable that tells whether the investigation was requested by the industry alone or by either Congress or the president. Despite Charles Pearson's previous analysis indicating no rational pattern to ITC decisions on injury,[18]

17. Robert E. Baldwin, "The Political Economy of U.S. Import Policy" (University of Wisconsin, 1981).

18. Charles Pearson, "Adjusting to Imports of Manufactures from Developing Countries," in Joint Economic Committee, *Special Study on Economic Change,* vol. 9: *The International Economy: U.S. Role in a World Market,* 96 Cong. 2 sess. (Government Printing Office, 1980), pp. 427–58.

Baldwin achieves significant results that show the consistent influence of changes in profits and in employment. In various tests he finds, to his surprise, no influence of industry size (employment or output), or origin from Japan or developing countries. Nor does the change in import-penetration ratio matter (despite legislative instructions implying its importance); instead, the commissioners seem to consider the level of import penetration. The absence of an influence of industry size may indicate that protection of truly large industries has been dealt with outside the ITC process: by the Multi-fiber Arrangement for textiles, a voluntary export restraint on Japan for automobiles, and the trigger-price mechanism followed by voluntary quotas for steel. The apparent contrast between Baldwin's results and Pearson's less formal tests perhaps occurs because Baldwin's method would capture submajority variation in ITC commissioner votes, whereas examination of outcomes on a two-class (injury versus no injury) basis (as in Pearson) would not do so. Whether Baldwin's results would be achieved if actual injury determination were examined instead of percentage of commissioner votes is unclear.

The third set of statistical tests by Baldwin examines tariff cuts in the Tokyo Round of Trade Negotiations. Many of his variables refer to influences discussed above in connection with Pincus, Cheh, and Caves. Baldwin usefully groups variables into (1) demand for protection: ability and willingness of labor and capital to finance lobbying efforts, and magnitude of losses to be avoided through successful lobbying; and (2) willingness of the president and voters to grant exceptions from the standard tariff cutting framework. In addition to the standard variables, Baldwin adds several more novel variables. One is the ratio of value added to gross output, under the argument that the smaller this ratio, the larger the percentage gain in factor incomes to be obtained from protection. Another is the share of labor in value added, on grounds that if labor supply is more elastic than that of capital, a larger labor–value added ratio will mean a greater increase in incomes of both labor and capital for a given rise in output price. Baldwin also includes the elasticity of foreign supply and domestic demand, citing Ray (whose analysis is discussed below).

Using 16 independent variables and 292 industry observations, Baldwin finds that the percentage tariff cut in the Tokyo Round is best explained by the number of employees in the industry (representing political strength, with the offsetting influence of greater consumer resistance to highly visible protection swamped by the poor organization of consumers relative to producers), the level of import penetration, average wage (negative sign, serving as a proxy for human capital), the relative importance of unskilled labor, and changes in employment in recent years. Baldwin broadly classifies most of these influences as ones reflecting the degree of public and presidential sympathy to the industry in question, but it might equally well be concluded that (aside from absolute size and change of employment) they are direct or indirect measures of comparative advantage and that essentially protection is being maintained for sectors with comparative disadvantage. Although the large number of observations offers a good chance to detect significance of several variables, many do not perform well. These include variables for difficulty of circumventing the free-rider problem (industrial concentration, number of firms, geographic concentration), variables for relative change in a group's income from tariff cuts (value added relative to gross output, labor share in value added), and variables for the magnitude of an industry's benefits from protection (share of earnings from foreign investment, ratio of exports to shipments, and extent of specialization).

Cognizant of the simultaneity issue of two-way causation between the import-penetration ratio and protection, Baldwin conducts a two-stage least-squares experiment that finds that both supply and demand for protection played a role in tariff cuts. Though skeptical of analysis of current protection levels because of the problem of historical legacy, he concludes with tests on the level of tariffs and an (unexplained) index of NTBs and identifies as major explanatory influences the wage level, skill level, size of industry in either employment or capital stock, import penetration, number of firms, specialization, and value added share in output.

Baldwin's massive analysis is meticulously thorough, but in the end one wonders whether once again most of the data examined have not been chosen because of empirical convenience rather than policy importance. Congressional votes, ITC rulings, and Tokyo Round tariff cuts all lend themselves to analysis because of data availability. But none of these three areas examined by Baldwin addresses the most important areas of protection in the United States today, which include textiles and apparel, steel, and automobiles. Nor is it likely that the brief, concluding examination of tariffs-with-NTBs does so adequately. Discrete analysis (such as logit) with careful attention to proper aggregation according to lobbying blocs seems more likely to explain major contemporary protection than will a regression analysis on hundreds of industry categories that uses tariffs and inevitably arbitrary indexes of NTBs.

At least two other authors warrant inclusion in this selective survey: Edward John Ray and J. M. Finger. Both have struck out in somewhat unconventional directions. Ray examines U.S. protection as of 1970.[19] He adds such new considerations to the standard list of influences as the role that NTBs play in replacing tariffs (as tariffs have fallen in the postwar period), the severity of loss in consumer welfare to be expected from protection, and the effect of price elasticities of domestic demand and foreign supply on the profitability of protection to an individual firm. The prospective profitability of protection, and therefore the industry's lobbying effort, will be higher the lower the domestic price elasticity (preventing consumers from shifting out of the good as protection makes it expensive) and the higher the foreign elasticity of supply (facilitating a reduction in foreign competition as the tariff wedge makes the market less attractive to them). Reinforcing this influence, deadweight welfare loss from protection and the consequent governmental resistance to it will be lower the lower the price elasticity of demand for the product and the lower the domestic elasticity of supply.[20]

Among 225 industries in 1970, Ray finds that the U.S. Tariff Commission's index of NTBs (an arbitrary index that seeks to capture the severity of NTBs) is positively related to nominal tariffs. He concludes, sensibly, that industries with the political influence to secure one type of protection also obtained the other. Yet Ray does not seem to recognize that the positive coefficient tends to contradict his assertion that tariffs and NTBs are substitutes and that NTBs have replaced tariffs in recent years. For that interpretation, the results of Glismann and Weiss are more appropriate: domestic German subsidies were negatively related to European Community tariffs because the former were less necessary when the latter were available.

Ray obtains significant results in the expected direction for the

19. Edward John Ray, "The Determinants of Tariff and Nontariff Trade Restrictions in the United States," *Journal of Political Economy*, vol. 89 (February 1981), pp. 105–21.

20. The traditional measure of static welfare loss from protection is the deadweight loss of the excess of value to consumers over what they actually pay (consumer loss in welfare) net of the gain in the excess of producer revenue over opportunity cost of production (gain in producer welfare).

domestic elasticity of supply in explaining NTBs. These results are obtained despite the use of rather indirect proxies for the two elasticities (economies of scale for supply elasticity and an index of product differentiation for demand elasticity). However, Ray's economies-of-scale variable may not be capturing elasticity of supply but instead may simply reflect the lower protection on sectors with scale economies because of their greater comparative advantage relative to developing-country suppliers (as emphasized by Helleiner). In addition, on the basis of more standard results for other commonly used variables such as skill ratio, Ray concludes (like other authors) that U.S. protection in 1970 was against products in which the United States had a comparative disadvantage.

Finger has examined U.S countervailing duties and antidumping measures—less-than-fair-value policies.[21] His concern was to determine whether these instruments have been used in a way that harasses trade and serves as a nontariff barrier. For 230 cases from 1974 through 1979, Finger found that less-than-fair-value complaints were significantly related to the degree of import penetration and the size of the industry, both standard variables for pressure of industry lobbying. But when examining the government decisions, Finger found no significant explanation of "affirmative" (restrictive) actions from the standard comparative-advantage variables such as labor intensity, physical or human capital intensity, and status of product cycle. He then constructed a two-stage statistical analysis whereby complaints are a function of standard variables, affirmative findings are a function of complaints (instrumental variable) and normal variables (such as import penetration, industry size), and import growth is a function of complaints, affirmative actions (both instrumental), demand growth, and comparative-advantage indicators. He found that, although a simple least-squares regression shows the influence of the incidence of complaints on affirmative findings, the more appropriate two-stage least-squares analysis finds that less-than-fair-value decisions are more objective because the intensity of complaints does not cause affirmative findings. Nor does industry concentration or developing-country origin appear to affect these decisions significantly. The broad thrust of the study is that less-than-fair-value

21. J. M. Finger, "The Industry-Country Incidence of 'Less Than Fair Value' Cases in U.S. Import Trade," *Quarterly Review of Economics and Business*, vol. 21 (Summer 1981), pp. 259–79.

proceedings are not politically dominated, in contrast to tariffs and more blatant nontariff barriers.

In a related study Finger, Hall, and Nelson emphasize the differing politics of protection between trade administration on a "technical track" and protection on a more "political track."[22] Broadly, they argue that as long as a sector's complaints can be confined to treatment in a technical track, complicated procedures and obfuscation can be used to make what is unavoidably a decision favoring one group (consumers or producers) at the expense of the other. Because technical proceedings provide an ideal smoke screen for political decision, decisions in the technical track will favor, somewhat, industry demands for protection. A positive-sum game can be played thereby because as long as the case is relegated to a low-profile technical track, consumers will not be sensitized to it, political credits from satisfying producer demands can be achieved, and producer gains can be obtained.

The authors argue that the less-than-fair-value procedures (countervailing duties, antidumping) are a classic technical track, while the U.S "escape clause" mechanism is in the political track. Truly large cases tend to escalate in public attention and to end up in the political track. Their statistical tests neatly show that, though technical influences such as indicators of comparative advantage dominate the more technical part of less-than-fair-value deliberations—decision on whether imports are priced unfairly—the more political influences (industry concentration, size of industry employment) dominate the more flexible part of such deliberations—decision on whether injury exists, warranting action. These tests suggest the hypothesis that under the semblance of purely technical proceedings, old-fashioned political protectionism is quietly going on. The authors have no comparable tests for escape clause cases, but they present data showing that the average import coverage of a case in the escape clause channel is three times as large as one in the less-than-fair-value channel, which supports the hypothesis that large cases escalate beyond the point where protection can be meted out quietly on a technical track and into the sphere where the public is watching closely. At that point presidential decisions become zero sum: favor gained by industries awarded escape clause protection will cost a loss of consumer favor. The study is clearly a provocative departure

22. J. M. Finger, H. Keith Hall, and Douglas R. Nelson, "The Political Economy of Administered Protection" (World Bank, 1982).

from the mainstream of statistical explanation of protection. There is, however, a certain inconsistency between Finger's earlier conclusion that less-than-fair-value is relatively objective and the Finger-Hall-Nelson result that it is a convenient way for producers to obtain protection if they are obscure enough.

In the literature reviewed here as a whole, some stylized facts of protection begin to emerge.

—Protection results from the interaction between industry demand for protection and government supply of it.

—Trade barriers protect industries that have comparative disadvantage.

—Important explanatory variables (and their signs) usually include the size of industry employment (+) as an indicator of political clout; the degree of import penetration (+), wage rate (−), and unskilled labor (+) as indicators either of comparative disadvantage or of public sympathy; and industry concentration (+) to account for circumvention of the free-rider problem.

—The level of import penetration, not its recent changes, is the relevant influence on protection. Correspondingly, and in view of the limited significance of other variables for adjustment cost, it is a simple protection of industries with comparative disadvantage—not government minimization of labor adjustment cost—that dominates protection (Cable-Rebelo, Baldwin).

—Nontariff barriers are becoming substitutes for tariff protection (Glismann-Weiss, Ray).

Much has been accomplished in a brief span of time in this literature. It has evolved toward more refined recognition of the joint determination of protection on both the supply and the demand sides. It has brought to light variables that were not obvious in the earliest investigations (for example, the role of product supply and demand elasticities). It has evolved from simple regression toward more appropriate discrete techniques capable of handling NTBs that are not continuously specified. But there are major areas for improvement. More attention should be paid to the large obstructions to trade (usually NTBs), and less work should be done with data sets (such as those on tariffs) whose principal commendation is their availability and ease of quantification. In particular, there is a need to develop significant data sets on tariff equivalents of nontariff barriers, especially the major ones, so that they can more credibly be analyzed jointly with tariffs.

A nagging problem in the literature, and one that may be impossible to overcome, is the multiple interpretations that may be placed on particular results. If protection is negatively related to the wage rate, is it because of public sympathy for low-paid workers (availability of protection from the side of policy supply) or because of comparative disadvantage (demand for protection)? If an economies-of-scale variable is negatively related to protection, is it because the United States has comparative advantage in such sectors (demand side) or because a high supply elasticity is present, making the deadweight welfare loss higher and the government more reluctant to protect (supply side)? Caves's study is one of the more precise in this regard because it frequently gives different signs depending on which interpretive model is being suggested, but even his analysis predicts the same sign for some variables under competing models.

Another open question is the policy significance of the growing literature. It would appear that, frustrated by the new protectionism of the 1970s despite economists' well-known injunctions against protection, trade economists have turned to analyzing the sources of protectionism in the vague expectation that knowing the history of the problem will help solve it. It is unclear, however, how the implicit subsequent step—tempering protectionism after having understood it—is to come about. At least one role these studies can play, however, is that of exposure. Empirical studies that reveal blatant political gains by special interest groups as the cause of protection, rather than a more optimal process of rational welfare maximization, can bring clearly into public view the nature of protectionism.

Can the East Asian Export Model of Development Be Generalized?

EXPORT-ORIENTED growth is the fashion today among development analysts. Exhaustive cross-country studies have documented the inefficiencies of the inward-looking strategies popular in the 1950s and 1960s.[1] Recognizing that new converts among policymakers may err in the direction of excessive stimulus to exports, Bhagwati and Krueger have nevertheless argued that resulting distortions would be less severe (and more favorable to growth) than those that arise under regimes of import substitution.[2]

Events of the last two decades have tended to vindicate export optimists, as several developing countries have achieved rapid export growth. Economy-wide growth appears to have been closely related to export performance in part because of the efficiency-stimulating influence of international competition.[3] Experience has cast doubt on the

For their helpful comments I would like to thank, but in no way implicate, Colin Bradford, Norman Hicks, Helen Hughes, Donald Keesing, Jean Waelbroeck, Larry Westphal, and Martin Wolf. This appendix was originally published in *World Development,* vol. 10, no. 2 (1982), pp. 81–90.

1. I. Little, T. Scitovsky, and M. Scott, *Industry and Trade in Some Developing Countries: A Comparative Study* (Paris: Organization for Economic Cooperation and Development, 1970); and Anne O. Krueger, *Foreign Trade Regimes and Economic Development: Liberalization Attempts and Consequences* (Ballinger, 1978).

2. Jagdish Bhagwati and Anne O. Krueger, "Exchange Control, Liberalization, and Economic Development," *American Economic Review,* vol. 63 (May 1973).

3. Bela Balassa, "Exports and Economic Growth: Further Evidence," *Journal of Development Economics,* vol. 5 (June 1978), pp. 181–89.

export pessimism that was dominant earlier and led to the model of import-substituting industrialization in the first place.[4] There is, however, a current running counter to the new emphasis on exports among academics and policymakers. That current is the phenomenon of neoprotectionism in industrial countries. The 1970s saw the tightening or new imposition of trade barriers affecting developing-country exports of manufactures such as textiles, clothing, footwear, television sets, and shipbuilding. A major shortcoming of the Tokyo Round of Trade Negotiations completed in 1979 was its failure to reach agreement on a "safeguards" code limiting the enactment of quotas or voluntary export restrictions on imports causing domestic dislocation.

Without invoking a new specter of export pessimism, it may reasonably be asked whether the recent emphasis on export-oriented growth has sufficiently taken account of the constraints on international market demand. Most studies have concentrated instead on the side of export supply, and specifically on the impact of developing-country policy regimes on that supply.

This appendix examines whether one version of export-oriented growth, the East Asian model, could be generalized among developing countries without violating plausible constraints on the absorptive capacity of industrial country markets. This analysis is of course an acid test. The East Asian "Gang of Four" (G-4)—Hong Kong, South Korea, Singapore, and Taiwan—have pursued strategies relying heavily on exports. Nevertheless, the test is not unfair, considering the regularity with which policymakers and academics extol the virtues of the G-4 model and at least implicitly urge its emulation.[5] Indeed, some analysts have cited the merits of the East Asian export model not only for growth but also for the achievement of equitable income distribution through

4. Ragner Nurkse, *Problems of Capital Formation in Underdeveloped Countries* (New York: Oxford University Press, 1953); and Raul Prebisch, "Commercial Policy in the Underdeveloped Countries," *American Economic Review*, vol. 49 (May 1959), pp. 251–73.

5. *World Bank Development Report, 1979* (Washington, D.C.: World Bank, 1979); Helen Hughes, "Achievement and Objectives of Industrialization," in J. Cody, H. Hughes, and D. Wall, eds., *Policies for Industrial Progress in Developing Countries* (New York: Oxford University Press, 1980), pp. 11–37; and despite their caveats, Ranadev Banerji and James Riedel, "Indusrial Employment Expansion under Alternative Trade Strategies: Case of India and Taiwan, 1950–1970," *Journal of Development Economics*, vol. 7 (December 1980), pp. 567–77.

emphasis on labor-intensive exports.[6] The issue at stake, however, is whether advice to follow the G-4 model involves a fallacy of composition, in that while individual developing countries might thrive by doing so, in the aggregate they would encounter sharp protective resistance to the resulting flood of exports.

Method

The method of this study is one of comparative statics. Using a 1976 base, the analysis calculates the levels of manufactured exports from developing countries that would have occurred in that year if all developing countries had experienced the same intensity of exports in their economies as was experienced by Hong Kong, South Korea, Singapore, and Taiwan, after adjustment for normal intercountry differences associated with size and level of development. These hypothetical levels of developing-country exports are then compared with industrial country apparent consumption, at the sectoral level, to determine how high the resulting import penetration rates would have been. Using an arbitrary threshold ratio of imports (from developing countries) to apparent consumption in the industrial country, one can then calculate the portion of developing-country exports that would be presumptively infeasible because of a likely protective response.

The hypothetical levels of trade under a uniform G-4 regime among developing countries are calculated as

(D-1) $$X_{ijk}^a = \beta_j X_{ijk},$$

where X_{ijk} is the 1976 value of exports of manufactured good k from developing country j to industrial country i, X_{ijk}^a is the same concept but at its hypothetical G-4 level, and β_j is an expansion factor relating the hypothetical level of exports to the actual level.

The expansion factor β_j is calculated on the basis of cross-country patterns of the level of manufactured exports in relation to gross domestic

6. John C. H. Fei, Gustav Ranis, and Shirley W. Y. Kuo, *Growth with Equity: The Taiwan Case* (New York: Oxford University Press, 1979).

product,[7] as estimated in Chenery and Syrquin for the period 1950–70.[8] Their estimates relate the share of manufactured exports in gross domestic product to the logarithms of per capita income and country population, and to the squares of these variables. With λ_j defined as the ratio of a country's actual GDP share of manufactured exports to the level predicted by the Chenery-Syrquin pattern, the expansion factor β_j is calculated as

(D-2) $$\beta_j = \frac{\lambda^{G4}}{\lambda_j},$$

where λ^{G4} is the average of λ for Hong Kong, South Korea, Singapore, and Taiwan. The term λ^{G4} shows how much the manufactured export propensity under the G-4 regime exceeds the standard international propensity for countries of the size and per capita income of the G-4 countries. Equation D-2 states that if a country's manufactured exports are at the level that would be expected given its per capita income and size (λ_j = 1.0), the country's expansion factor to reach a hypothetical G-4 level is merely the ratio of actual exports in the East Asian countries to the exports they would be expected to have according to international norms. If the country itself has atypically high (low) exports, with $\lambda_j >$ (<) 1.0, the country's expansion factor is lower (higher).

The estimate represented in equation D-1 assumes that the product composition and industrial country market composition remain unchanged for a particular developing country as it expands its exports to the G-4 level. But because manufactured exports of developing countries tend to be concentrated already in certain sensitive sectors such as textiles and clothing, it is likely that the scope for market accommodation of export expansion at the margin would be greater if the extra exports had a product composition that was more diversified. Therefore, as an alternative set of estimates, the hypothetical G-4 exports are also calculated as

7. Other criteria could be used instead, such as the percentage of labor force employed in the production of manufactured exports. However, the criterion relating manufactured exports to GDP has the advantage that the Chenery-Syrquin cross-country patterns can be used for normalization to remove the influences of developmental level and country size.

8. H. Chenery and M. Syrquin, *Patterns of Development, 1950–1970* (London: Oxford University Press, 1975).

(D-3) $$X^b_{ijk} = X_{ijk} + (\beta_j - 1)X_{ij}\phi_{ik},$$

where X_{ij} is the total base value of manufactured exports from developing country j to industrial country i, and ϕ_{ik} is the base period share of sector k in the total manufactured imports of country i from all sources.[9] Thus variant b assumes that at the margin the product composition of the developing countries' exports is homogeneous with the general composition of imports into the market in question. This variant implies a sacrifice of some of the gains from comparative advantage in return for greater likelihood of continued market access.[10]

It is worth noting that neither variant applies the product composition of the exports of the G-4 countries themselves. Their exports are heavily concentrated in products that already face stiff protection, such as textiles, clothing, footwear, and television sets. Thus the analysis assumes a generalized move to the level, but not the product composition, of East Asian manufactured exports.

Given estimates of sectoral import-penetration ratios into the industrial country markets, $Z^L_{ik} = M^L_{ik}/C_{ik}$, where Z^L_{ik} is the import-penetration ratio for imports from all developing countries into industrial country i in sector k, M^L_{ik} is the corresponding total of imports from all developing countries in the country and sector, and C_{ik} is the corresponding value of domestic apparent consumption (output minus exports plus imports), the levels of developing-country import penetration under a G-4 regime are calculated as

(D-4) $$Z^a_{ik} = Z^L_{ik}\frac{X^a_{ik}}{X_{ik}}; \qquad Z^b_{ik} = Z^L_{ik}\frac{X^b_{ik}}{X_{ik}},$$

where X_{ik}, X^a_{ik}, and X^b_{ik} are the original, variant a, and variant b levels of total manufactured imports from developing countries into country i in sector k (for example, $X_{ik} = \Sigma_j X_{ijk}$).

The estimates of import penetration from developing countries under a G-4 regime provide the basis for inferences about the market feasibility of generalizing the East Asian export model of development. Using a threshold of 15 percent penetration, the analysis later examines the

9. The first two elements of the final right-hand term give the total increment of exports from the country, and the final element distributes the increment across sectors.

10. If there were reason to believe that some industrial countries would be more receptive than others to an expansion in manufactured exports from developing countries, the market country composition could also be varied from the base year profile.

product sectors in which developing countries would be likely to overburden the political-economic absorptive capacity in major industrial country markets by exceeding this threshold. The frequency of such sectors and, more meaningfully, their combined weight in the total of developing countries' manufactured exports cast light on whether the G-4 regime is infeasible.

The analysis is solely focused on market prospects and does not treat additional factors such as a possible worsening in the terms of trade of developing countries if they all tried to pursue the East Asian export strategy. Even on the issue of market access there is no pretense that the analysis involves a rigorous investigation of the causes of protection as in Caves and in Fieleke.[11] Nevertheless, simple rules of thumb such as the 15 percent penetration ratio do provide a useful point of departure for a general evaluation of market access. Although no unique level of the penetration ratio can be identified as the critical level where protection occurs, the penetration ratio is generally regarded as one of the most important indicators of potential protectionist response.[12]

It might be that the total import-penetration ratio from all sources instead of only developing countries would be more relevant as a criterion for protective response.[13] Because developing countries have little free importation of their own that they can impede in retaliatory moves, and perhaps because of their small size and bargaining strength relative to major industrial countries, it seems reasonable to consider a given degree of import penetration more likely to trigger protection if the suppliers are from developing countries than if they are from developed countries. In any event, even a total penetration ratio (for all suppliers) of 15 percent is sufficiently high to suggest jeopardy to market access. Thus

---

11. Richard E. Caves, "Economic Models of Political Choice: Canada's Tariff Structure," *Canadian Journal of Economics,* vol. 9 (May 1976), pp. 278–300; and Norman S. Fieleke, "The Tariff Structures for Manufacturing Industries in the United States: A Test of Some Traditional Explanations," *Columbia Journal of World Business,* vol. 11 (Winter 1976), pp. 98–104.

12. In their empirical study of British protection, Cable and Rebelo found the import penetration rates to be the single most important explanatory variable. Vincent Cable and Ivonia Rebelo, "Britain's Patterns of Specialization in Manufactured Goods with Developing Countries and Trade Protection," World Bank Staff Working Paper 425 (World Bank, October 1980).

13. For purposes of comparison, the discussion later examines the sensitivity of the results for the United States if instead of the 15 percent threshold for imports from developing countries, the analysis uses a threshold of 25 percent import penetration from all sources.

the use of import penetration from developing countries alone probably tends to understate the incidence of sectors in which problems of protective response would be likely to be encountered under the G-4 regime.

Another issue concerns the offsetting role of industrial country exports. High imports from developing countries would induce high respending by those countries on exports from the North. It is unlikely, however, that this extra source of employment in the industrial countries would offset the protectionist pressures arising from higher import penetration. Because extra imports would tend to be in different sectors from extra exports, the implications for labor dislocation are more appropriately drawn from the gross import changes rather than net trade changes. To be sure, the more the developing countries consciously diversified their new exports into sectors in which industrial countries would also gain exports, moving toward a pattern of intra-industry trade similar to that among industrial countries, the more weight the derived expansion of industrial country exports would have in stemming protectionism.

Data

The trade data used in the calculations are from the United Nations commodity trade data tapes for each of the importing industrial countries examined (Canada, France, Germany, Italy, Japan, United Kingdom, United States). These data, at the five-digit level of the standard international trade classification, are converted to four-digit categories of the international standard industrial classification (ISIC).[14] Eighty manufacturing categories are included (ISIC 3111–3909 excluding 3530, petroleum refineries). Developing countries in the analysis include all countries in Africa except South Africa, Asia excluding Japan, Oceania except Australia and New Zealand, and Latin America and the Caribbean. Import-penetration ratios in the base period are derived from the estimates of import data at the four-digit ISIC level, combined with estimates of the corresponding domestic production and trade in the industrial country markets examined.[15] The developing countries' pen-

14. See appendix A.
15. Ibid.

Table D-1. *Manufactured Export Shares in Gross Domestic Product and Expansion Factors for Developing Countries, 1976* ·

Developing country	Actual (1)	GDP share (percent)		Expansion factor to G-4 base[a] (4)
		Cross-country norm (2)	Ratio of col. 1 to col. 2 (3)	
Hong Kong	60.8	12.0	5.07	...
Singapore	48.6	12.6	3.86	...
South Korea	28.1	6.2	4.53	...
Taiwan	37.4	8.8	4.25	...
G-4	...	...	4.43	...
Argentina	2.4	10.5	0.23	18.80
Brazil	2.0	6.8	0.29	14.92
Colombia	2.5	6.3	0.40	11.02
Mexico	1.5	7.6	0.20	22.53
India	3.0	<0.0[b]	...	0.00[b]
Indonesia	0.4	0.6	0.70	6.27
Israel	13.3	15.7	0.85	5.19
Malaysia	7.5	7.8	0.96	4.58
Pakistan	5.2	1.2	4.44	0.99
Other	...	...	0.47[c]	9.42

Sources: Based on H. Chenery and M. Syrquin, *Patterns of Development, 1950–1970* (London: Oxford University Press, 1975), p. 39; data for 1976 from World Bank, *World Bank Development Report, 1978*, and *1979*.

a. From equation D-2, the expansion factor equals 4.4 divided by column 3 for all except G-4 countries (Hong Kong, Singapore, South Korea, and Taiwan). Exports of G-4 countries remain unchanged in the calculations.

b. The cross-country equation predicts negative value (because of a negative coefficient on the square of the logarithm of population, applied to India's large population). Hypothetical exports are set equal to zero.

c. Based on the export-weighted ratio of actual to predicted manufactured exports for sixty-six other developing countries.

etration ratios refer to imports from developing countries divided by apparent consumption (domestic production plus total imports minus total exports in the sector). For estimates of expected shares of manufactured exports in GDP based on the Chenery-Syrquin patterns, the calculations apply World Bank data on per capita income, population, and manufactured exports, and the U.S. wholesale price deflators.[16]

Export Expansion

Tables D-1 and D-2 report the estimates of the extent to which developing-country exports of manufactures would expand if the export

16. *World Bank Development Report, 1977*, and *1978* (World Bank, 1977, 1978); and International Monetary Fund, *Direction of Trade Statistics Yearbook, 1978* (IMF, 1978).

Table D-2. *Exports of Manufactures from Developing Countries to Seven Industrial Countries, Actual and Hypothetical, 1976*[a]

Industrial country	Actual (billions of dollars) (1)	Percent of manufactured imports (2)	Hypothetical G-4 basis (billions of dollars) (3)	Percent of manufactured imports (4)	Ratio of col. 3 to col. 1 (5)
Canada	1.81	5.8	11.15	27.4	6.15
France	4.20	9.2	37.09	47.7	8.83
West Germany	7.29	12.0	55.54	51.0	7.62
Italy	2.84	10.7	26.13	52.4	9.19
Japan	8.17	35.5	48.84	76.7	5.98
United Kingdom	5.60	13.9	37.43	51.9	6.68
United States	21.30	27.0	166.54	74.4	7.82
Total	51.23	16.7	382.72	60.6	7.47

Source: Author's calculations.
a. ISIC 3111–3909, excluding 3530, petroleum refineries.

strategies of all such countries had resembled those of the East Asian G-4 in the base year 1976. Table D-1 shows that on average the G-4 had manufactured exports 4.4 times as high as would have been expected based on cross-country norms, whereas major Latin American countries had as low as one-fifth the expected levels and a broad grouping of sixty-six developing countries (excluding the thirteen listed individually) exported less than half the amount expected based on these norms. The final column of the table shows the multiple by which a developing country's manufactured exports would have to expand in order to resemble the G-4 pattern. These multiples are high, indicating approximately a twentyfold increase for some Latin American countries and nearly a tenfold increase for the broad grouping of "other" developing countries. The exception is India, whose large population causes a predicted negative value of manufactured exports according to the cross-country regression norm (although the estimates force India's hypothetical exports to zero).

Table D-2 shows the hypothetical expansion of developing-country exports by industrial country market. Overall, generalization of the East Asian export model would multiply developing-country manufactured exports sevenfold. This expansion would imply a rise in the developing countries' share of the market for manufactured imports from 16.7 to 60.6 percent for all seven industrial countries and from 27.0 to 74.4 percent in the United States. These estimates alone are sufficient to cast doubt on the feasibility of a generalized move to the G-4 export strategy.

The nonoil developing countries have only approximately 16 percent of the combined GDP of industrial and nonoil developing countries, and it is highly implausible that they could capture 60 percent of the industrial countries' markets for imports without provoking serious protective responses.

Import Penetration

The impression of difficulty of market access is strengthened by the estimates of import-penetration ratios that would result from a mass shift by developing countries to the East Asian model of export-led growth. Table D-3 shows the estimated ratios of developing-country import penetration into four industrial country markets, for those sectors in which developing-country penetration would exceed 15 percent of the market (excluding a number of sectors with penetration over 15 percent but of only minor importance, sectors having a share of less than 1 percent in both total and developing country–supplied manufactured imports in 1976). As shown in the table, a large number of important product sectors would have developing-country penetration rates above the threshold of 15 percent under the G-4 scenario. Moreover, in several sectors the developing-country import penetration ratios reach improbably or impossibly high levels. Thus, under variant a, in which the product composition is held the same as in the base period, several food sectors show imports from developing countries in excess of the entire domestic market. And approximately half the sectors shown indicate developing-country penetration ratios above 30 percent, so that the pattern is one of frequent incidence of very high penetration rather than one of only modest excess above the 15 percent threshold chosen.

Diversification of product composition eliminates most cases of penetration ratios over 100 percent, but still leaves a high frequency of high-penetration sectors, causing higher penetration in nontraditional sectors. Thus, in variant b, in which the increment in exports from developing countries would be distributed across sectors in proportion to base period imports from all sources (instead of base period developing-country supply), penetration rates decline for traditional sectors such as foods but rise for nontraditional sectors such as chemicals and office machinery.

Out of eighty four-digit ISIC categories, under the G-4 scenario (with base period product composition) developing-country penetration ratios exceed the threshold of 15 percent in 43 sectors in the United States, 41 in West Germany, 44 in the United Kingdom, and 33 in Japan. After taking account of the relative importance of these high-penetration sectors in overall imports, the conclusion is even stronger that the bulk of the market would be vulnerable to closure of access because of high import penetration. Table D-4 shows the percentage of total manufactured imports included in sectors with developing-country penetration exceeding 15 percent for four industrial countries. These figures show the great bulk of these markets being oversaturated with developing-country supplies under the East Asian export model. Approximately 80 percent of the prospective value of the developing countries' export market in these industrial countries would be in products with developing-country penetration exceeding the 15 percent threshold, and therefore of dubious feasibility in terms of market access.

This finding is remarkably uniform across the four industrial countries. Moreover, the results remain unchanged by use of the product diversification strategy (variant b), indicating that the level of exports from developing countries is so high under the G-4 scenario that even diversification cannot avoid high incidence of high import penetration.

Table D-4 reports in parentheses alternative figures for a more restricted case in which only a limited group of newly industrializing developing countries expand their manufactured exports to G-4 dimensions (Argentina, Brazil, Colombia, Mexico, Indonesia, Israel, Malaysia). The alternative calculations apply equations D-1 through D-3 only to these seven developing countries, leaving the manufactured exports of all others unchanged at their 1976 levels. This variant addresses the possible critique that the basic analysis is highly unrealistic because the great bulk of developing countries, especially those at low income levels, are unlikely to follow the East Asian export model. Without necessarily accepting this critique, the alternative analysis indicates the dimensions of the problem if that model is followed by seven newly industrialized countries, most of them countries that have already adopted aggressive policies favoring manufactured exports. In this more limited scenario, developing-country exports of manufactures multiply by a factor of 4.2, instead of 7.5 in the basic model. As the numbers in the parentheses show, even in this more restricted case, the fraction of manufactured exports from developing countries to industrial countries that exceed the 15 percent penetration threshold remains quite high. In variant a, this measure of potential protection difficulty is relatively close to the

Table D-3. Product Sectors with Developing-Country Import Penetration of 15 Percent or More under the East Asian Export Model, Base Period, 1976[a]

Percent

ISIC number	Sector	United States			West Germany			United Kingdom			Japan		
		Actual	Case a	Case b	Actual	Case a	Case b	Actual	Case a	Case b	Actual	Case a	Case b
3111	Meat	*	*	*	3.4	42.2	25.2	6.5	82.8	60.2	5.0	39.6	110.1
3112	Dairy	*	*	*	*	*	*	0.1	0.4	18.0	*	*	*
3113	Preserved fruits and vegetables	1.7	15.0	9.0	11.3	87.0	49.1	4.7	35.0	22.7	6.7	25.4	43.0
3114	Canned fish	17.4	199.0	117.9	3.5	30.0	24.6	2.0	16.1	17.5	15.6	74.3	74.2
3115	Agricultural oils	3.9	30.8	14.9	19.9	206.7	53.9	13.5	92.2	33.0	4.8	37.1	25.0
3116	Grain products	10.7	126.0	37.5	26.7	304.8	58.2	4.5	41.8	17.8	7.6	76.3	40.0
3118	Sugar	13.7	131.0	54.1	*	*	*	27.4	264.7	59.6	16.3	139.6	120.1
3119	Confectionery	12.9	135.5	49.4	17.8	171.4	48.6	10.9	98.6	27.5	5.0	47.1	24.5
3121	Foods not elsewhere classified	16.3	185.5	58.3	26.1	271.7	65.0	22.9	189.5	47.8	5.3	50.2	29.0
3140	Tobacco	3.7	37.4	17.6	2.4	26.2	9.4	8.9	55.2	25.6	1.1	9.8	17.0
3211	Textiles, spinning and weaving	3.5	19.0	19.5	10.1	90.6	49.3	8.8	48.7	34.1	6.8	49.0	40.0
3214	Carpets and rugs	*	*	*	21.1	156.1	56.6	4.6	29.7	16.8	*	*	*
3220	Apparel	9.5	31.6	38.1	13.3	40.4	49.0	16.3	29.5	42.7	8.2	15.5	39.1
3231	Tanneries and leather finishing	18.2	225.3	87.0	8.8	77.4	47.9	22.2	119.9	44.9	7.8	16.4	33.5
3240	Footwear	9.7	55.9	61.2	2.4	7.1	32.2	3.7	14.0	18.4	3.8	6.1	19.9
3311	Sawmills	2.2	10.9	25.3	*	*	*	5.3	34.1	34.4	1.4	5.5	21.2
3320	Furniture	1.5	11.1	17.0	*	*	*	*	*	*	*	*	*
3411	Pulp and paper	0.1	0.9	32.3	0.3	2.9	29.7	0.4	4.0	47.8	0.1	0.8	20.0
3511	Industrial chemicals	1.0	11.7	26.1	0.5	5.0	17.8	1.5	14.0	21.0	1.3	10.5	36.8
3522	Drugs	*	*	*	*	*	*	*	*	*	1.3	4.5	26.8

Code	Industry												
3529	Chemical products not elsewhere classified	1.1	10.4	15.6	*	*	*	2.3	20.2	32.9	1.5	9.4	36.6
3551	Tires	0.9	2.6	26.9	0.5	0.7	21.6	*	*	*	*	*	*
3559	Rubber products not elsewhere classified	4.0	15.5	23.9	1.4	4.0	23.1	2.5	6.9	17.3	*	*	*
3560	Plastics not elsewhere classified	3.6	16.8	22.4	1.2	3.9	28.8	2.3	5.5	33.4	*	*	*
3710	Iron and steel	0.6	5.8	16.5	0.4	3.8	16.0	*	*	*	*	*	*
3720	Nonferrous metals	3.4	34.0	30.5	7.4	64.2	39.5	7.5	54.5	35.2	5.4	46.3	41.0
3819	Metal products not elsewhere classified	*	*	*	0.5	1.6	16.9	*	*	*	*	*	*
3823	Metal- and woodworking machinery	*	*	*	3.0	13.7	352.0	0.2	0.8	23.9	3.6	3.9	332.2
3824	Industrial machinery	0.2	2.4	19.4	0.3	2.4	23.6	0.2	1.9	23.2	*	*	*
3825	Office and computing machinery	1.9	14.4	29.1	1.7	3.7	29.6	1.4	10.5	48.8	0.9	10.0	29.6
3832	Radio, television, and communication equipment	6.1	36.5	43.1	2.7	6.6	24.1	2.2	5.5	21.9	2.0	4.0	17.4
3841	Shipbuilding	*	*	*	*	*	*	0.4	3.9	19.6	*	*	*
3843	Motor vehicles	0.2	4.3	37.4	1.0	15.1	60.3	0.2	1.5	22.3	*	*	*
3845	Aircraft	*	*	*	0.4	3.3	36.2	3.2	27.1	27.7	0.0	0.1	70.5
3851	Scientific equipment	*	*	*	1.4	10.2	44.6	2.7	20.9	47.6	1.1	2.0	70.5
3852	Photographic equipment	0.8	2.2	17.2	7.0	13.0	87.6	1.1	3.4	28.7	1.5	3.6	42.2
3853	Watches and clocks	11.8	39.7	77.1	8.2	16.5	52.2	10.3	22.3	62.6	2.7	3.3	30.2
3901	Jewelry	11.8	63.0	88.2	28.3	170.6	139.3	24.7	201.4	239.4	28.2	165.0	171.2
3909	Manufactures not elsewhere classified	5.2	23.9	32.3	17.0	74.7	83.1	5.8	17.2	28.9	*	*	*

Source: Author's calculations.

* Penetration rates less than 15 percent.

a. Excludes those sectors with less than a 1 percent share in both developing-country and total supply to the market. Under case a, product composition is the same as in the base period; under case b, incremental developing-country exports have the same product composition as total nonoil imports into the market in the base period.

Table D-4. *Percentage of Total Developed-Country Market for Manufactured Imports from Developing Countries Represented by Sectors with Developing-Country Import-Penetration Ratios above 15 Percent*

Market	1976 actual	East Asian export model[a]	
		Variant a (developing-country product composition)[b]	Variant b (homogeneous marginal product composition)[c]
United States	16	80 (71)	85 (63)
West Germany	32	81 (72)	79 (48)
United Kingdom	37	85 (68)	82 (37)
Japan	26	75 (65)	81 (36)

Source: Author's calculations.

a. The numbers in parentheses are G-4 expansion applied to Argentina, Brazil, Colombia, Mexico, Indonesia, Israel, Malaysia, only.

b. Equals $\Sigma_{i\epsilon*} \phi_i^f$, where i is sector i, * is the set of sectors with developing-country penetration above 15 percent, and ϕ_i^f is the share of sector i in base period imports from developing countries.

c. Equals $(1/\beta) \Sigma_{i\epsilon*} \phi_i^f + (1 - 1/\beta) \Sigma_{i\epsilon*} \phi_i^T$, where β is the ratio of expanded to base imports from developing countries, ϕ_i^T, is the share sector i in base period imports from all sources, and other notation is as in note b.

figure in unrestricted generalization of the G-4 model across all developing countries. In variant b, the numbers in parentheses show that potential market resistance would be much lower if only seven newly industrialized countries followed the G-4 model and did so using product diversification. Even in this case, however, penetration into the U.S. market would exceed 15 percent for a relatively high fraction of imported manufactures from developing countries (63 percent). In short, even if only a limited number of newly industrialized countries were to follow the G-4 model, there could be substantial risk of protectionist response.

Another alternative to the basic analysis would be to apply a penetration threshold for imports from all sources rather than from developing countries alone. Limited sensitivity analysis suggests that this approach would not significantly alter the basic estimates.[17]

Qualifications

Several qualifications of these results warrant discussion, although none should fundamentally change the conclusions of the analysis. The

17. If a threshold of 25 percent penetration by imports from all sources is used, the percentage of hypothetical (G-4) U.S. manufactured imports from developing countries in sectors exceeding the threshold falls from 80 percent (table D-4) to 71 percent (with base period product composition).

cross-country norms do not include a variable for natural resource endowment, and it is possible that export differences between the East Asian economies, especially the city-state, island economies of Hong Kong and Singapore, and much more resource-abundant economies, such as those in Latin America, could be explained by such a variable. In that case, the estimated expansion of manufactured exports under the G-4 model would be smaller, because the East Asian countries would not lie so far above the cross-country patterns, nor the resource-abundant countries so far below it.

A dynamic analysis might reach different conclusions from this comparative static analysis. For example, if the protection rule were that serious risk of protection would arise only if the annual increase in imports exceeded some rate considered likely to provoke excessively abrupt adjustment, it might be that even the high penetration ratios associated with generalization of the East Asian model could be accommodated by industrial countries if two to three decades were allowed for the adjustment process. However, Cable and Rebelo have found the level of the import-penetration ratio to be more important in explaining protection than the rate of change in penetration.[18] More broadly, it seems unlikely that dynamic formulations of the problem would reach different conclusions from those found here. For example, the fact that the market in industrial countries would grow along with income would not reduce the estimated import-penetration ratios even with a time dimension in the analysis, because GDP levels in developing countries (and therefore the base for their manufactured exports) would also be growing over time, probably more rapidly than income and markets in industrial countries. Moreover, the experience of the Multi-fiber Arrangement gives little cause for optimism that adjustment will be accepted if it is phased in over a long time period.

Industrial country exports would rise as developing countries earned more foreign exchange by moving toward G-4 export intensities, and the analysis here makes no allowance for possible alleviation of protectionist pressure through the opening of new export jobs. However, if North-South trade continued to be mainly inter-industry (along Heckscher-Ohlin lines) as contrasted with intra-industry (as is more frequent in North-North trade, explained in part by greater dominance of product differentiation and less influence of differing relative factor endow-

18. Cable and Rebelo, "Britain's Patterns of Specialization."

ments), the new export jobs would tend to be in sectors different from those losing jobs to imports, and the resulting reduction of protectionist pressure would be limited.

Market price effects of developing-country export expansion would tend to moderate this expansion long before the higher export propensities of the East Asian countries became generalized. The outward shift in supply would cause relative prices for the exports to decline, causing a new equilibrium with a smaller increase in the quantity supplied than expected at constant prices. However, this qualification reinforces the policy conclusion: the developing countries en masse cannot expect to imitate the G-4 export results.

South-South trade might take up much of the increase in developing-country exports, reducing the pressure on markets in the North. The strategy of South-South linkage has received increasing attention as growth in the industrial countries has slowed.[19] However, it could be even more unrealistic for a typical developing country to wager that the markets of Brazil and India would be open to manufactured imports from the South than to place the same bet with respect to U.S. and European markets. Moreover, past trade propensities suggest that the bulk of the new trade would be North-South.[20]

19. W. Arthur Lewis, "The Slowing Down of the Engine of Growth," *American Economic Review*, vol. 70 (September 1980), pp. 555–64.

20. Nevertheless, there may be some bias in the calculations here toward overstating the portion of increased developing-country exports that would be directed toward markets in the North as opposed to the South. Proportionate expansion of exports to all destinations (equations D-1 and D-3) has the implicit consequence of causing a larger proportionate rise in the developing countries' share of import supply in markets in the North than in this share for markets in the South. The reason is that additional export earnings would cause imports into the South to rise proportionately more than imports into the North, and with equal proportionate rises in the developing country–supplied imports for both North and South, the developing countries' share of manufactured imports would rise proportionately more in the North than in the South. (The greater proportionate rise of total manufactured imports in the South may be seen as follows. Table D-2 implies that manufactured imports into the North would rise by 108 percent in the G-4 scenario. In contrast, the hypothesized 647 percent rise in developing-country exports of manufactures would, when spent on imports, cause a rise of about 160 percent in their manufactured imports, given the current 4 to 1 ratio of developing-country imports to exports in manufactures, and abstracting from nonmanufactured trade.)

An alternative approach would be to assume that the proportionate rise in the developing countries' supply shares in imports is identical in markets of both the North and South. If GATT data on manufactured trade are used, referring to a narrower range of goods than considered here, the consequence would be that the share of developing

Conclusion and Policy Implications

The simulation exercise presented here indicates that generalization of the East Asian model of export-led development across all developing countries would result in untenable market penetration into industrial countries. Generalization of the G-4 export strategy would require developing-country exports of manufactures to rise sevenfold, implying a surge in their share of industrial country manufactured imports from about one-sixth to about three-fifths. If a developing-country import-penetration ratio of 15 percent is used as a threshold beyond which protective response would be expected, fully four-fifths of the industrial country markets for manufactured exports from developing countries would be vulnerable to probable protective action in the face of the flood of such exports caused by a general adoption of the East Asian export model.

These findings suggest that it would be inadvisable for authorities in developing countries to rely in their long-term plans on the same kind of export results that have been obtained by the four East Asian countries. To the extent that these countries have distorted incentives in favor of exports—and there is some evidence that at least South Korea has done so[21]—other developing countries would do well not to imitate these export-biased policies. To the extent that the G-4 countries have merely followed open-trade policies and realistic exchange rates (as seems to have been the case especially in Hong Kong with its free-market orientation), other developing countries would be well advised to adopt

countries in import markets would rise from 7.7 to 33.8 percent in the South and from 6.2 to 27.2 percent in the North, compared with a rise to 21.9 percent in the South and 32.9 percent in the North as implied by the calculations in this study. (I am indebted to Jean Waelbroeck for this point.) Nevertheless, even this alternative approach would cause developing-country exports of manufactures to the North to grow 5.7 times larger, and as was shown in the analysis of the more limited, newly industrialized country–based scenario (table D-4), even a fourfold rise in these exports would be likely to cause market absorption problems. Moreover, under current conditions of developing-country protection, it is not necessarily more realistic to assume that the increase in the share of developing counries in the supply of manufactured imports would be identical in the markets of North and South; instead, the larger rise in markets in the North (implicit in the calculations here) could be more meaningful.

21. Charles R. Frank, Jr., Kwang Suk Kim, and Larry E. Westphal, *Foreign Trade Regimes and Economic Development*, vol. 7: *South Korea* (Columbia University Press, 1975).

similar policies (on grounds of general efficiency), but ill advised to expect free-market policies to yield the same results that were achieved by the East Asian economies, which took advantage of the open-economy strategy before the export field became crowded by competition from other developing countries, and did so when the world economy was in a phase of prolonged buoyancy.

These findings should not be interpreted to favor a closed-economy strategy or discouragement of exports. On the contrary, in many developing countries trade liberalization still has far to go. Several Latin American countries in particular could raise their manufactured exports substantially without even reaching cross-country norms, let alone export dimensions of the East Asian variety, and one strongly suspects that in many such cases liberalization of the trading and exchange rate regimes would lead to more rapid export growth.

The analysis here does mean that it is necessary to consider the aggregate market implications of export-oriented growth as an increasingly popular development strategy. It is seriously misleading to hold up the East Asian G-4 as a model for development because that model almost certainly cannot be generalized without provoking protectionist response, ruling out its implementation. Elevator salesmen must attach a warning label that their product is safe only if not overloaded by too many passengers at one time; advocates of the East Asian export model would do well to attach a similar caveat to their prescription. More broadly, development planners adopting the increasingly popular strategy of export-led growth must take into account the probable capacity of the international market to absorb the resulting increases in exports from their own and like-minded developing countries.

Definition of Manufactures

T H E definition of manufactures used in this study is wider than commonly employed. It is based on the international standard industrial classification (ISIC) categories 3111–3909, excluding petroleum refineries (3530). The more usual, narrower definition of manufactures—typically used by the General Agreement on Tariffs and Trade and by the World Bank, for example—is based on the standard international trade classification (SITC), categories 5 (chemicals), 6 (basic manufactures) excluding 68 (copper), 7 (machinery and transport equipment), and 8 (miscellaneous manufactured goods).[1] Broadly, the ISIC basis includes copper and processed foods while that of the SITC excludes them.

It is a moot point whether the one classification or the other is more appropriate for analysis. The narrow definition tends to omit ranges of products that can be important for development of new processed exports by developing countries, such as frozen orange juice and frozen shrimp. The broader definition includes products that are technically the result of a manufacturing process but nonetheless stereotyped as "traditional raw material exports" (sugar, copper).

Table E-1 compares manufactured imports from developing countries into the seven major industrial countries in 1978 under the two alternative definitions. As noted in appendix A, care has been taken to exclude from the basic data set of this study those portions of the ISIC-based manufactures that represent primarily raw coffee, cocoa, and tea (through complete exclusion of SITC 0711, 0721, and 0741 from ISIC 3116, 3119, and 3121).[2] The table also shows oil imports. It is clear from the table

1. General Agreement on Tariffs and Trade, *International Trade 1980/81* (Geneva: GATT, 1981), p. 195.
2. The only exceptions are that an earlier version of the data base including these three SITC categories was used for preparation of table 1-14, for those logit functions in chapter 2 in which processed foods were included, and for the analysis of appendix D.

Table E-1. *Imports of Seven Industrial Countries from Developing Countries, 1978*
Amounts in millions of dollars

Country	Total		Petroleum and products[a]		Manufactures This study		Manufactures Narrow definition[b]		Other This study		Other Narrow definition of manufactures	
	Amount	Percent	Amount	Percent	Amount	Percent	Amount	Percent	Amount	Percent	Amount	Percent
United States	76,716	100.0	37,684	49.1	29,920	39.0	22,349	29.1	9,112	11.9	16,683	21.7
Canada	5,129	100.0	2,683	52.3	1,780	34.7	1,339	26.1	666	13.0	1,107	21.6
West Germany	22,130	100.0	9,410	42.5	8,490	38.4	5,011	22.6	4,230	19.1	7,709	34.8
France	19,484	100.0	11,459	58.8	4,820	24.7	1,908	9.8	3,205	16.4	6,117	31.4
Italy	15,662	100.0	10,574	67.5	3,210	20.5	1,291	8.2	1,878	12.0	3,797	24.2
United Kingdom	14,378	100.0	5,778	40.2	6,920	48.1	3,712	25.8	1,680	11.7	4,888	34.0
Japan	44,565	100.0	25,437	57.1	10,650	23.9	4,382	9.8	8,478	19.0	14,746	33.1
Seven countries	198,064	100.0	103,025	52.0	65,800	33.2	39,992	20.2	29,239	14.8	55,047	27.8

Sources: Author's calculations; and Organization for Economic Cooperation and Development, *Statistics of Foreign Trade*, series B (Paris: OECD, 1978).
a. Standard international trade classification (SITC) 33.
b. SITC 5–8 minus 68.

that under the broad definition used in this study, manufactures dominate nonoil imports from developing countries. This conclusion is unconventional; the more traditional perception is that aside from oil the exports of developing countries are dominated by raw materials such as coffee, cacao, and iron ore. Of the total value of imports from developing countries in 1978, 52.0 percent was in oil, 33.2 percent in broadly defined manufactures, and only 14.8 percent in nonmanufactures, giving a ratio of 2:1 for manufactures relative to nonmanufactures in nonoil trade. Despite explicit elimination of coffee, cocoa, and tea from the ISIC-based data, this treatment tends to overstate the role of manufactures (and understate that of raw materials) in nonoil exports of developing countries. By contrast, the narrow definition of manufactures (SITC categories 5 through 8 less 68) encompasses only 20.2 percent of imports from developing countries while nonmanufactures (excluding oil) account for 27.8 percent, giving a ratio of approximately 3:4 for manufactures to nonmanufactures. Thus, under the broad definition, manufactures substantially exceed raw materials in exports (excluding oil) of developing countries, while under the narrow definition manufactures are somewhat smaller than raw materials in this trade.

Using more detailed data for the United States, table E-2 provides some indication of the extent to which the narrower definition tends to understate manufactured products. The table lists products that clearly involve a manufacturing process but are excluded from manufactures in the narrow (GATT) definition. Prepared fish and meat, sugar, copper, vegetable oils, coffee extracts, cocoa products (but not raw cocoa), and chocolate are the major items. As shown in table E-2, the list of readily identifiable manufactures of this type amounts to approximately one-third of the value of imports classified as nonmanufactures (excluding oil) under the more traditional (GATT) definition: SITC 0 (food and live animals); 1 (beverages and tobacco), 2 (crude materials excluding fuels), 4 (animal and vegetable oils and fats), and 68 (copper). Other less readily identifiable categories that nevertheless involve manufacturing processes are also probably included in nonmanufactures under the traditional definition.

If the U.S. pattern is typical, at least one-third of the value of nonoil, nonmanufactured imports from developing countries according to the GATT definition are more properly seen as manufactures. Applying this ratio to the seven-country summary data in table E-1, an appropriate modification of the conventional (GATT) definition would reduce nonmanufactures (excluding oil) from 27.8 percent to 18.6 percent of total

Table E-2. *U.S. Imports from Developing Countries of Selected Categories of Manufactured Products Excluded from the Narrow Definition of Manufactures, 1978*[a]
Millions of dollars

SITC number	Product	Value
01	Meat and preparations	418
03	Fish and preparations	1,018
048	Cereal preparations	16
056	Preserved, prepared vegetables	160
058	Preserved, prepared fruit	377
06	Sugar and preparations	803
071.2	Coffee extracts	204
072.2	Cocoa powder	160
072.3	Cocoa butter and paste	101
073	Chocolate and products	178
11	Beverages	59
122	Tobacco, manufactured	18
21	Hides, skins, and furs	46
248	Wood shaped, sleepers	133
271	Crude fertilizers	41
274	Sulfur, iron pyrite	63
288.2	Base metal scrap	22
42	Fixed vegetable oils and fats	452
431	Processed animal and vegetable oil	15
68	Copper	479
Total		4,763
Addendum 0, 1, 2, 4, and 68		13,986

Source: United Nations, *Commodity Trade Statistics, 1978*, series D, vol. 28 (UN, 1980).
a. For purposes of this table only, Israel is not included among the developing countries.

industrial country imports from developing countries and raise the share of manufactures from 20.2 percent to 29.4 percent. These adjusted shares would be relatively close to those identified in this study (14.9 percent and 33.2 percent for nonoil nonmanufactures and manufactures, respectively). In sum, both the ISIC-based analysis in this study and a reasonable adjustment of the narrower definition of manufactures commonly used by GATT and other international agencies suggest that manufactures constitute the greater part of exports other than oil of developing countries.

As discussed in chapter 1, the definition chosen affects the measured growth rate of manufactured exports in the 1970s. Because of the slow growth of traditional products such as sugar and copper, under the broad definition the measured growth of manufactured exports from developing countries is considerably lower than under the narrow definition.

In the protection functions estimated in chapter 2 and in the corresponding projections of future protection in chapter 3, the sectors of processed foods, beverages, and tobacco are omitted from the analysis in most cases. As a result, there is little difference between the two alternative definitions of manufactures in this portion of the analysis of this study.

APPENDIX F

Supplementary Tables

Table F-1. *Correlation Coefficient between Closely Correlated Independent Variables, United States*[a]

Variable	X3	X4	X5	X7	X10
X3 Concentration	1.00	...	...	...	...
X4 Value added per worker[b]	0.95	1.00	...	...	...
X5 Physical capital per worker[b]	0.95	0.96	1.00	...	...
X7 Total capital per worker[b]	0.80	0.91	0.81	1.00	...
X10 Wage rate[b]	0.98	0.99	0.96	0.89	1.00

Source: Author's calculations.
a. Principal variables with correlation coefficients of 0.89 or above, the threshold for significance at the 95 percent level. Others include X5 with X12 (growth rate), −0.89, and X9 (share of labor force) with X8 (skill ratio), 0.94. Data are for seventy-five sectors, including processed foods and consolidating textiles and apparel in one sector.
b. Relative to manufacturing average.

221

Table F-2. *Real Imports into Three Western Industrial Countries of Selected Products Subject to Nontariff Barriers, 1971–81*
Millions of 1975 dollars

| Country and year | Footwear | | Television | | | | | |
	South Korea	Taiwan	Japan	South Korea	Taiwan	Textiles[a]	Apparel[a]	Steel[a]
United States								
1971	41.1	101.1	1,259.8	8.9	197.8	2,132.4	2,332.4	4,179.8
1972	64.0	n.a.	1,398.8	20.1	n.a.	2,241.7	2,764.6	4,299.0
1973	79.5	186.8	1,353.5	56.1	508.7	2,051.6	2,814.9	3,918.2
1974	116.9	187.5	1,116.3	88.3	502.5	1,780.0	2,539.1	5,902.4
1975	129.2	206.2	1,004.9	70.7	304.5	1,233.5	2,550.8	4,695.2
1976	272.0	348.1	2,107.5	129.2	464.6	1,580.5	3,454.0	4,314.9
1977	297.3	401.2	1,869.3	170.7	492.2	1,612.4	3,714.4	5,399.3
1978	366.8	542.3	2,097.2	312.8	743.9	1,923.6	5,117.9	6,704.4
1979	300.0	487.8	1,533.1	338.5	661.0	1,701.1	4,719.2	6,099.3
1980	326.8	584.1	1,367.1	268.9	611.1	1,654.2	4,521.9	5,307.8
1981	342.1	527.6	1,818.6	301.8	673.8	1,833.1	4,847.5	7,251.8
Canada								
1971	129.6		...	...	...	...	...	...
1972	141.6		...	...	...	...	...	...
1973	133.5		...	...	...	...	...	...
1974	152.7		...	...	...	...	...	...
1975	154.8		...	...	...	...	...	...
1976	192.6		...	...	...	...	...	...
1977	196.0		...	...	...	...	...	...
1978	186.6		...	...	...	...	...	...
1979	187.8		...	...	...	...	...	...
1980	179.6		...	...	...	...	...	...
1981	191.9		...	...	...	...	...	...
United Kingdom								
1971	0.2	4.1	...	...	...	...	...	...
1972	0.7	5.0	...	...	...	...	...	...
1973	4.8	6.1	...	...	...	...	...	...
1974	7.9	5.0	...	...	...	...	...	...
1975	8.2	5.5	...	...	...	...	...	...
1976	12.3	15.5	...	...	...	...	...	...
1977	15.8	22.4	...	...	...	...	...	...
1978	31.8	13.0	...	...	...	...	...	...
1979	42.0	17.2	...	...	...	...	...	...
1980	29.8	20.8	...	...	...	...	...	...
1981	n.a.	n.a.	...	...	...	...	...	...

Sources: Organization for Economic Cooperation and Development, *Trade by Commodities,* series C; data tapes, as deflated by U.S. wholesale price index in International Monetary Fund, *International Financial Statistics* (IMF, various issues). SITC categories: footwear = 851; television = 724 (includes communication equipment); textiles = 65; apparel = 84; steel = 67.
n.a. Not available.
a. All sources.

Table F-3. *Real Imports into the European Community of Selected Products Subject to Nontariff Barriers, 1971–80*
Millions of 1975 dollars

Country and year	Textiles			Apparel		
	South Korea	Taiwan	Hong Kong	South Korea	Taiwan	Hong Kong
European Community						
1971	25.2	44.8	127.6	23.9	45.6	585.7
1972	33.3	72.7	128.6	58.0	92.2	736.4
1973	44.3	123.6	134.4	137.7	171.7	907.5
1974	66.0	143.4	135.4	236.2	193.0	842.7
1975	76.3	118.8	122.4	330.0	222.6	988.6
1976	101.3	113.9	127.4	394.6	166.8	1,171.0
1977	135.1	111.1	107.5	472.5	190.8	1,011.6
1978	141.0	103.3	118.4	530.9	203.7	1,131.7
1979	140.5	129.3	137.7	607.3	236.8	1,305.4
1980	137.2	124.8	122.3	631.7	249.4	1,340.5

Sources: See table F-2.

Table F-4. *Projected Annual Average Growth of Income and Population for Seven Industrial Countries, 1978–90*
Percent

Country	Income per capita		Population
	High estimate	Low estimate	
United States	2.3	1.5	0.8
Canada	2.3	1.5	0.8
West Germany	3.0	2.1	0.1
France	3.0	2.1	0.5
Italy	3.0	2.1	0.5
United Kingdom	3.0	2.1	0.1
Japan	4.8	4.0	0.8

Source: World Bank, *World Development Report, 1981* (Washington, D.C.: World Bank, 1981), pp. 10, 167; and IMF, *World Economic Outlook* (IMF, 1981), p. 111.

Table F-5. *Sectoral Estimates of Income Elasticity of Demand*

SITC number	Product sector	Elasticity
311–12	Food products	0.73
313	Beverages	1.00
314	Tobacco	0.60
321	Textiles	1.10
322	Apparel	0.99
323	Leather products	1.02
324	Footwear	0.84
331	Wood products	1.03
332	Furniture	1.10
341	Paper products	0.81
342	Printing	0.87
351	Industrial chemicals	1.24
352	Other chemical products	1.39
353	Petroleum refineries	0.50
354	Petroleum and coal products	0.50
355	Rubber products	1.03
356	Plastic products not elsewhere classified	1.00
361	Pottery, china, and earthenware	0.88
362	Glass products	0.91
369	Nonmetallic minerals not elsewhere classified	0.91
371	Iron and steel	1.12
372	Nonferrous metals	1.49
381	Metal products	1.05
382	Machinery	1.34
383	Electrical machinery	1.92
384	Transport equipment	1.33
385	Professional goods	1.20
390	Other industries	1.31

Sources: Bela Balassa, *The Newly Industrializing Countries in the World Economy* (Pergamon Press, 1981), p. 225; Clopper Almon, Jr., and others, *1985: Interindustry Forecasts of the American Economy* (Lexington, Mass.: Lexington Books, 1974), p. 37; H. S. Houthakker and Lester D. Taylor, *Consumer Demand in the United States 1929–1970: Analyses and Projections* (Harvard University Press, 1966), pp. 166–67; and Wharton Economic Forecasting Associates, "The Wharton Annual Model: Post-Meeting Forecasts, June 1981" (Washington, D.C.: WEFA, 1981), vol. 1, pp. 1–21.

Index

Adding machine (AM) quantitative model, 179–80, 181
Almon, Clopper, Jr., 95n
American Textile Manufacturers Institute, 66
Anderson, T. W., 80n
Argentina, 9–10, 21, 145, 207
Asia: export model of development, 128–30, 197–214; protection and trade effects, 63–65; as supplier, 26, 27. *See also names of specific countries*
Auerbach, Stuart, 51n
Australia, 3, 142, 203
Austria, 142

Balassa, Bela, 7n, 60n, 89, 90, 94, 95n, 119n, 122n, 187, 197n
Balassa, Carol, 60n
Baldwin, Robert E., 177, 188–90
Ball, David Stafford, 175–76n
Banerji, Ranadev, 198n
Basevi, Giorgio, 175n
Belgium, 142, 188
Bergsten, C. Fred, 63n, 87n, 115n, 123n
Bhagwati, Jagdish, 197n
Black, Stanley W., 42n
Bradford, Colin, 197n
Brazil, 10, 21, 22, 145, 207, 212
Buchanan, James M., 185–86

Cable, Vincent, 67n, 183–84, 185, 202n, 211
Canada, 1, 3, 142, 157, 203; import market allocation, 91, 92; import penetration, 15, 137, 151; protection function estimates, 59, 73, 74, 82, 83; protection projections, 100, 104, 107, 112, 114, 127; tariff cutoffs, 53; tariff policy, 179, 181; three-country model, 82–83, 125
Caves, Richard E., 46, 179–81, 182, 195, 202

Cheh, John, 176, 177, 178, 179, 180, 181
Chenery, H., 200n
Cline, William R., 1n, 35n, 42n, 51n, 52n, 63n, 64n, 87n, 115n, 120n, 123n
Cody, J., 198n
Colombia, 10, 21, 207
Commonwealth countries, 24, 25, 32
Comparative advantage, 4, 41; and diversification, 128; logit analysis of protection, 46–48; market share and stages of, 26–30
Crandall, Robert, 51n

Demand for protection, 186; logit analysis, 41–51; predictive model, 36–41
Denmark, 142
Developed countries, 3; exports of manufactures to, 2–3; NICs as suppliers to, 26–30; supplier replacement, 30–31, 33. *See also names of specific countries*
Developing countries: debt, 85, 119–21; East Asian export model, 128–30, 197–214; exports of manufactures, 3–10, 128–30; importance of exports, 119, 121, 124; protection and exports, 1–2, 118; substitution, 26–30. *See also names of specific countries*
Development strategy (outward-looking), 34, 85–86
Discriminant analysis, 42–43
Downs, Anthony, 185–86

East Asia. *See* Asia; *names of specific countries*
Economic growth rate. *See* Growth rate (economic)
Employment, 2, 182, 185, 189, 190, 194; government and protection, 41; imports and, 122; logit analysis and adjustment cost, 50; and policy, 130; protection es-

225

World Inflation and the Developing Countries

William R. Cline and Associates

In the 1970s the severe inflation and recession that afflicted the industrial countries had repercussions on developing countries throughout the world. The industrial countries and the oil-importing developing countries alike suffered from higher oil prices. Both the oil shock and inflation in industrial countries accelerated domestic inflation in most developing countries. Wider commodity price fluctuations increased uncertainty for exporters of raw materials, inflation eroded the real value of development assistance, and the ensuing recession reduced export opportunities. But inflation also reduced the real burden of the developing countries' external debt, and some donor nations (especially OPEC members) increased their flows of development assistance.

The authors of this book investigate the effects of the sharp cyclical shocks of the early 1970s on developing economies by econometric tests of both aggregated and national data relating to the extraordinary international inflation of 1973 and 1974 and the following recession. William R. Cline analyzes the real economic effects of international inflation and Surjit S. Bhalla its nominal effects on inflation in developing countries. Supplementing these generalized examinations are studies of Brazil, by Cline; India, by Bhalla; Guatemala and El Salvador, by Gabriel Siri and Luis Raúl Domínguez; and Malaysia, by R. Chander, C. L. Robless, and K. P. Teh. Their discussions focus on the capacity and inclination of the various countries to respond to externally induced economic problems. The case studies are guides to the needs of different kinds of economies — large and small, open and closed. The broad analysis points to the appropriate policy response of developing countries facing international shocks, and to the global responsibilities of industrial countries in determining their own macroeconomic policies.

266 pp./1981/cloth and paper